TOTAL OLYMPICS

TOTAL OLYMPICS

EVERY OBSCURE, HILARIOUS, DRAMATIC AND INSPIRING TALE WORTH KNOWING

JEREMY FUCHS

WORKMAN PUBLISHING • NEW YORK

Published simultaneously in Canada by Thomas Allen & Son Limited.

Library of Congress Cataloging-in-Publication Data is available

ISBN 978-1-5235-0838-9

Art direction: Janet Vicario
Cover design: Becky Terhune
Interior design: Galen Smith
Photo research: Anne Kerman and Sophia Rieth

Cover credits: Can Stock Photo Inc.: sportpoint; ggraphicstudio; weter777; scusi

Workman books are available at special discounts when purchased in bulk for premiums and sales promotions as well as for fund-raising or educational use. Special editions or book excerpts can also be created to specification. For details, contact the Special Sales Director at the address below, or send an email to specialmarkets@workman.com.

Workman Publishing Co., Inc.
225 Varick Street
New York, NY 10014-4381
workman.com

WORKMAN is a registered trademark of Workman Publishing Co., Inc.

Printed in South Korea
First printing April 2020

10 9 8 7 6 5 4 3 2 1

This book is neither affiliated with, nor endorsed by, the United States Olympic Committee or the International Olympic Committee.

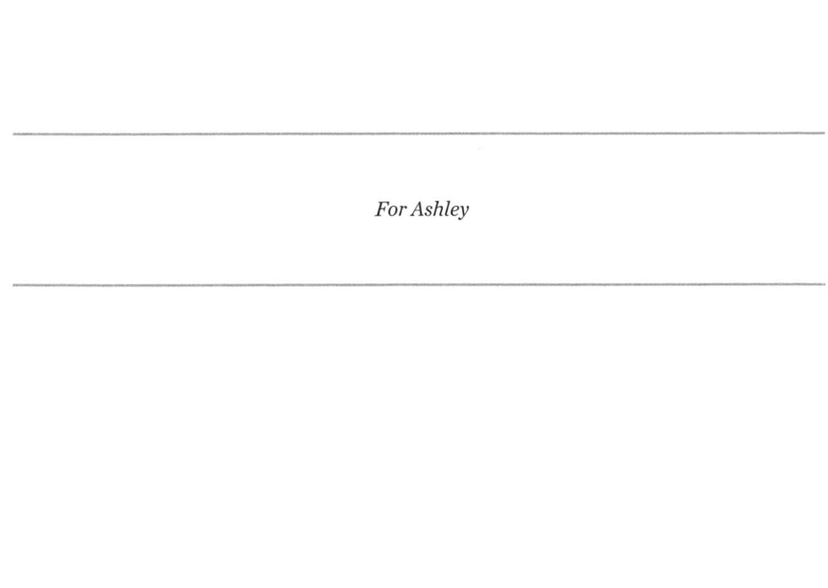

For Ashley

CONTENTS

INTRODUCTION

We all know the story, right? There were the ancient Olympics, those battles of strength and speed, in the center of what was then the known world. And in 1896, they returned to Athens, rejuvenated and modernized, and the Olympics—*Faster! Higher! Stronger!*—became what they are today.

But what if the origin is far more complicated than that? What if the Olympics, as we now know them, really started in a small English town of 2,500 people?

We concede these facts about the ancient Olympics, the forerunner of it all: that in 776 BC, when ancient Greece ruled the world, a cook named Koroibos of Elis won a footrace and a movement was born. That they were, in

The ancient Olympic hoplitodromos was a foot race in which competitors ran with helmets and shields.

large part, a religious ceremony meant to honor Zeus, with cows slaughtered as a sacrifice. That they drew crowds of some 40,000 spectators in Olympia, home to the statue of Zeus, one of the original Seven Wonders of the Ancient World. That they ended in AD 393 when the Roman emperor Theodosius I, banned the Games as being part of pagan cults. That these stories of tremendous athletic achievement survived the fall of the empire and were—and continue to be—passed down through the ages. But the modern revival of the Games wasn't another mythic story about naked runners and godlike feats of strength by godlike figures. The Olympic revival has a lot more to do with the Wenlock Olympian Games than anything else.

Much Wenlock is a small town in the West Midlands of England. It looks permanently stuck in the 1800s, with its charming town square, Victorian architecture, and complete lack of anything cosmopolitan. Today, we're told, you can sit on a bench in the square and "it won't be long before the person sitting next to you is willing to talk of the old times." It was in the old times, 1890 to be precise, that a young Frenchman named Baron Pierre de Coubertin stepped off the train at the town's station, his thick handlebar mustache on display for all to see. It would be here where the modern Olympics were born.

Pierre de Coubertin came from the French aristocracy and grew up in a time of rapid change in his country. He was witness to the establishment of the Third Republic, the Dreyfus Affair, and the defeat in the Franco-Prussian War. Perhaps this time of middle-class revolt, of terror and uncertainty, steered him away from politics; he instead chose a life of the mind, with a focus on educational reform, particularly in regard to his academic studies in physical education. The worldly baron had traveled to this small backwater to meet with someone who shared the same ideals.

William Penny Brookes was Much Wenlock's town doctor. He had studied in London, Italy, and Paris, and also served as town magistrate. He was literate and learned, founding the Agricultural Reading Society, a sort of library for the working class. Like Coubertin, he believed deeply in the melding of a healthy mind and body. He had written to Parliament to petition for educational bills that would promote physical education along with traditional studies. He felt that the mind was only working at its full capabilities if the body was healthy as well. In that spirit, it was his idea to provide a competition to "promote the moral, physical and intellectual improvement of the inhabitants of the town and the neighborhood of Wenlock."

The first such competition, the 1850 Wenlock Olympian Games, featured soccer, cricket, and quoits (a game where you throw rings near or around a peg). Later Games included both a wheelbarrow race and an old women's race, with the prize being a pound of tea. One year, there was a pig chase that ended with the animals cornered in "the cellar of Mr. Blakeway's house." (Suffice it to say that this isn't quite the high-level competition we've come to expect from the Olympics.) Even so, the Wenlock Games became a yearly event, and Brookes had grand ideas. He would go on to establish the National Olympian Association, which held similar events across England.

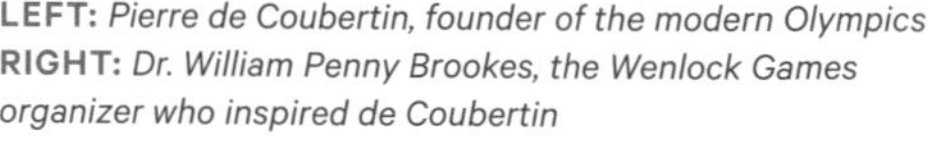

LEFT: *Pierre de Coubertin, founder of the modern Olympics*
RIGHT: *Dr. William Penny Brookes, the Wenlock Games organizer who inspired de Coubertin*

Coubertin, the organizer of the world's first Congress on Physical Education and Scholar Competitions, was keen on improving the state of athletics within schools. He placed a newspaper ad to learn more about the state of physical education, and received a response from Brookes. He traveled to watch the Wenlock Games and saw events like the 120-yard hurdles and tilting of the ring (a form of jousting where a horseback rider attempts to place his sword between tiny rings).

The two hit it off, and letters reveal the plotting of the next Olympic Games. They discussed, as Brookes wrote, that "such gatherings shall be held in rotation in or near capitals of all nations joining the movement." They were both admirers of ancient Greek culture, and of course, their elaborate athletic competitions. Coubertin wrote the idea of the Olympic Society was to make prizes available for the "most outstanding feats of strength and skill."

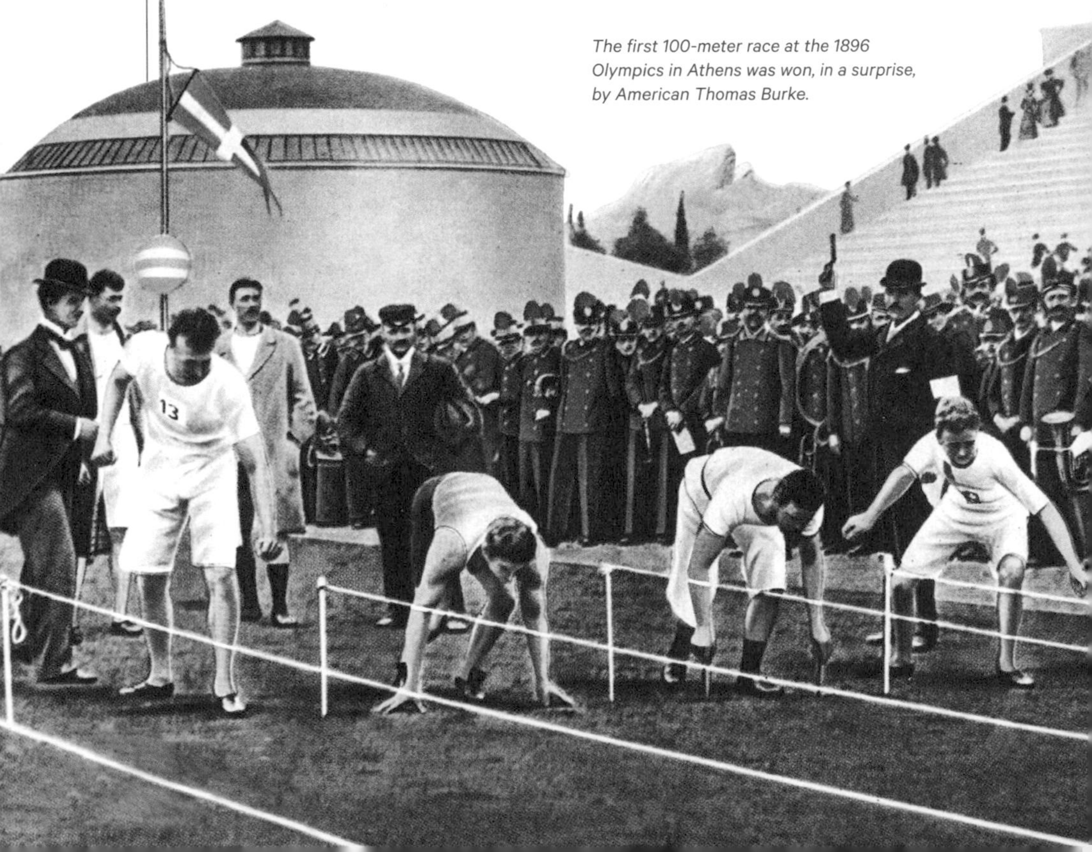

The first 100-meter race at the 1896 Olympics in Athens was won, in a surprise, by American Thomas Burke.

Coubertin would take the ideas generated in Much Wenlock and apply them to the first modern Olympics in Athens in 1896—officially known as the Games of the I Olympiad. Unfortunately, Brookes died just a few months before the Games began. But many of his ideas from the Wenlock Games lived on. There was an opening ceremony, in which the athletes, led by children singing and tossing flower petals, marched around town. The winners were given laurel wreaths. The medals had Nike, the Greek goddess of victory, emblazoned on them, as do many medals today.

The Wenlock Games continue on—today's version is a bit low budget, costing a modest $14,000 to operate. But we remember Wenlock because it is the hidden origin story to a movement that itself has thousands of hidden stories. We watch the Olympics every two years in awe; we learn new names and new faces, and celebrate their incredible achievements. And then we move on, more or less. Sure, some names stick. Most, though, fall to history.

Each Olympics is a mishmash of thousands of little stories, all making up a glorious two-week adventure.

Total Olympics is a book of both familiar and lesser-known tales. The Olympics, by definition, are a wide-ranging, all-encompassing international enterprise. Something is hidden behind every star, every moment, every medal, every nail-biting finish, every heartbreak, every triumph. The Games are a perfect vehicle to look back in time and see what was important—and what, perhaps more tellingly, was not. They give us a window through which to see who we are and what we'll do to win.

Each Olympics is a mishmash of thousands of little stories, all making up a glorious two-week adventure. Multiply those thousands of stories by 51 Olympiads over 122 years, and you get a collection of sports yarns unlike any other. Sure, we all know the major events from Olympics past: Michael Phelps winning everything; Usain Bolt outrunning everyone; Kerri Strug's landing; Michael Johnson's spikes; the Dream Team spreading the gospel of basketball; US Hockey believing in Miracles. But for every story that has been ingrained into the sports fan's consciousness, countless others have slipped through time.

This book recalls those forgotten moments, the rich and controversial history, the untold stories, and the fascinating people who achieved Olympic glory—or, in some cases, Olympic shame. It's about the Japanese marathoner who went missing; the Olympics that Denver lost; the Cuban mailman who took a midrace nap; the first Nazi Games in Garmisch-Partenkirchen. It's about the shooter who was disqualified for drinking two prematch beers; the doves who died; the ducks who lived; the water-filled blood and spylike escapes; and the Games that Shakespeare saw—well, sort of.

The Olympics aren't just about athletes aiming for global glory. They're about people—talented, flawed people who have transformed an ancient pastime into a worldwide spectacle. This book celebrates those people—flaws and all—to illuminate the very best stories that make the Olympics the world's event.

1

FORGOTTEN HISTORY

Though the Olympics are sporting events first and foremost, they are also inexorably linked to historical events of the day. They aren't immune to war, political rivalries, or scandal. The Games are billed as a politically neutral event, but they are often anything but. Geopolitical rivals become foes on the field. Developing countries look to make their marks on the world with winning athletic performances. Some host nations look to announce that they have arrived by the grandeur of their stadiums, the discipline of their opening ceremony dancers, the modernity of their metros. Who could forget all the times broadcasters gushed that the Beijing Games were China's "introduction" to the world?

The Olympics can also be plain odd. They're about bans over coffee commercials, competitions played on the sides of highways, and shin-kicking tournaments. Sure, the Games are a race for global supremacy. But when we look back at its storied history, we are just as liable to shake our heads and ask, "What the—?"

The Great American Gambit

Alex Cushing's Confidence Game Pays Off

How do you persuade the International Olympic Committee (IOC) to hold the Winter Games at a ski resort featuring just one dilapidated chairlift? With some good old-fashioned American chutzpah, that's how.

Alex Cushing wasn't a skier and, apparently, not all that attracted to the Olympics, telling *Time* magazine in 1959 that he had "no more interest in getting the Games than the man in the moon." He was extremely interested, however, in the Games as a ploy to lure customers to his fledgling ski mountain. A lawyer by trade, Cushing had visited the tiny community of Squaw Valley, California, seven miles north of Lake Tahoe while on vacation. He saw tremendous potential there and decided, with financial assistance from the Rockefellers, to develop it into a world-class ski resort in 1949. The bid for the 1960 Olympics was as good a publicity stunt as any.

Cushing was more concerned with ginning up publicity for his new ski resort than the Olympics themselves.

Cushing had the odds stacked against him. After first earning the US Olympic Committee's approval of the site, he met with the unforgiving IOC president Avery Brundage. Upon hearing of the squalid state of the resort, Brundage told Cushing, "This is worse than I thought. If you win the Games, you'll set the Olympics back 25 years."

But a worldwide lobbying tour convinced doubters. Ever crafty, Cushing focused on securing the votes of South American countries, who weren't used to being courted for Winter Games. He built a 3,000-pound model of the site, so big that it didn't fit in the IOC's exhibit hall at its headquarters in Lausanne, Switzerland. Despite the resort already nearing bankruptcy, Squaw Valley won the right to host the 1960 Games. (The more established Innsbruck,

Austria, was the runner-up, with Garmisch-Partenkirchen, Germany, and St. Moritz, Switzerland, also in the running.) That earned Cushing state assistance, which allowed him to renovate the mountain, build more lifts and lodging, and create an ice arena. It did not, however, include funds for a bobsled track, making 1960 the only Games to skip the sport.

Much to Cushing's delight, the 1960 Winter Olympics were the first to be televised. CBS bought broadcasting rights for $50,000, and the network showed 15 hours of competition. (Compare that to 2018, when NBC streamed 1,800 hours. In a sign of things to come, the rights for the 1960 Games in Rome, seven months later, went for $550,000; in 2014, NBC paid $7.75 billion to broadcast all Games through 2032.) The competition was a smash. It fueled American interest in skiing and turned Squaw Valley into a favored destination for the wealthy.

The Squaw Valley Games also marked the first time that computers were used to crunch numbers. There was a glass-walled IBM processor on-site, which was a huge attraction for visitors. The computers had a tangible effect on the events themselves. In previous Games, officials would take up to five hours to post results calculated by hand. Now they were available in less than two minutes.

The brand-new Blyth Arena, site of the opening and closing ceremonies

Though Cushing succeeded in wrangling the IOC to award the Games to Squaw Valley, all that self-assuredness came at a cost. The IOC, fed up with his confidence game, his over-the-top style, his grating ability to persuade, didn't invite him to the opening ceremonies. But Cushing had the last laugh. Today, Squaw Valley is one of the largest and most popular ski resorts in the country. The confidence game paid off.

Like a Spy Novel—Only in a Magazine

Cold War Intrigue at the 1956 Summer Games

Bunked in the Red Star Hotel, on Svabhegy Hill overlooking Budapest, the delegation of Hungarian athletes listened to gunfire. There was a revolution breaking out in their home country, a revolt against the Communist regime propped up by the Soviets. It started with students, marching through Budapest to the Parliament, and continued with the AVO, or state police, firing on the civilians who had torn down the statue of Joseph Stalin in City Park.

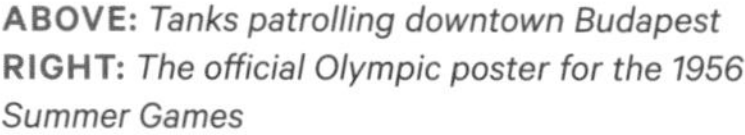
ABOVE: *Tanks patrolling downtown Budapest*
RIGHT: *The official Olympic poster for the 1956 Summer Games*

The athletes—men and women, water polo players and swimmers, divers and fencers, and more—were just weeks away from traveling to Melbourne to compete in the 1956 Summer Olympics. Holed up in the hotel for their protection, they understood the magnitude of what was happening. In an act of solidarity, a few took down the red star that decorated the hotel's facade. But the revolutionary spirit couldn't trump the politics of the day. Upon landing in Australia, the Hungarian delegation found out that

Soviet troops had invaded Hungary and a new puppet government had been installed. Some 2,500 Hungarians were killed, another 20,000 arrested, and more that 200,000 were forced to leave the country.

For the athletes at the Olympics, there wasn't much to be done. The team felt, as long jumper Olga Gyarmati later put it, "a great spiritual depression." Though the Hungarians competed admirably, winning golds in gymnastics, fencing, and water polo, the Games did eventually come to an end, and each team member had to make an enormous decision: Defect or go back home? For 34 Hungarians, leaving was the best option. And in a move out of a spy novel, they called upon *Sports Illustrated* to help them.

2016 REFUGEE OLYMPIANS

In 2016, the Refugee Olympic Team competed for the first time. Consisting of 10 athletes from the Democratic Republic of Congo, Ethiopia, South Sudan, and Syria, these men and women were forced from their homes by war, persecution, and lack of opportunity. They represent the more than 65 million refugees around the world looking for new homes.

Their stories were a triumph of human perseverance. Take Yusra Mardini, of Syria, who got on a boat in Turkey—the motor died in the Aegean Sea, and she and her sister helped push and drag the boat to shore at the Greek island of Lesbos. They walked and rode on trains for 25 days through four countries with the hopes of ending up in Germany. First, though, they had to escape a squalid refugee camp in Hungary. Finally, Mardini found solace in a pool in Berlin.

They all found peace and hope in sport. Competing under one flag before the world, these worthy athletes each played their sport at the highest level. Though none of them scored a medal, one soared: Popole Misenga, a Congolese refugee, became the first from the refugee team to win a match, in judo.

RIGHT: *Congolese refugee Popole Misenga*

The fledgling magazine, using utmost secrecy and code names, became the Hungarians' lifeline. Managing editor Andre Laguerre, who was leading the magazine's Olympics coverage, met privately with the Hungarian delegation several times. Laguerre sent telegrams back to SI offices, and the magazine worked with the State Department to grant asylum for 34 Hungarians.

Though some eventually returned to Hungary, most ultimately defected by staying in the United States. For rower Robert Zimonyi, that meant continuing his sporting career. At the 1964 Games in Tokyo, he won gold on the eights rowing team. Sixteen years after winning his first medal with Hungary, Zimonyi took his place on the podium, this time listening to the "Star-Spangled Banner."

The Golden Girls of Zimbabwe

The Best of the Rest When Boycott Strikes

Sixty-six countries boycotted the 1980 Olympics in Moscow in response to the Soviet invasion of Afghanistan. Although that left a whole lot of medals for the Soviets to win, it also meant that the competition needed some augmenting. Take women's field hockey: Five of the six teams scheduled to play in the competition, including the United States, participated in the boycott, so organizers scrambled for replacements. They were able to call upon Czechoslovakia, India, Australia, and Poland, all countries that had been eliminated in qualifying. But that still left one team. Here's an idea: *How about we call Zimbabwe?*

When the country was known as Rhodesia, it competed in three Olympics. But it was banned from participating in 1972 after other African nations pressured the IOC not to recognize Rhodesia's racist, white-minority government. Independent Zimbabwe came into being in 1980, and it was again eligible for Olympic competition. The Zimbabwean women's field hockey team, however, remained all white. The roster was composed of former members of the Rhodesian national team, which, in keeping with the previous government's policies, had barred any black players.

The Zimbabweans were nowhere near ready to play. They had six weeks to practice and had never trained on artificial turf. The team relied on amateur players. Ann Grant was a bookkeeper. Christine Prinsloo was an insurance underwriter. Their coach, Anthea Stewart, also played. Despite the rush to come together—and flying to Moscow in a plane normally used for shipping meat—the Zimbabweans excelled. They won three games and managed a draw in two others. Pat McKillop was tied for the tournament lead in scoring, with six goals.

At halftime of the final against Austria, the Zimbabwean minister of sport came onto the field. He told the team that if they won, each player would receive an ox. With that extra bit of motivation, they prevailed 4–1 and would take the gold medal, the very first ever for Zimbabwe. "It still feels like a dream standing on that podium," said McKillop. Nicknamed the Golden Girls, they returned to their country as heroes. But they would not get a chance to defend their crown. In 1984, all the traditional field hockey powers were back at the Games, making this golden opportunity a once-in-a-lifetime shot at glory.

The Zimbabwean women's field hockey team found unexpected glory in Moscow.

The Austerity Games

Post-War Belt Tightening at the London Olympics

In order to pull off the 1948 Summer Games in London, some unusual sacrifices had to be made. Female athletes crafted their own uniforms. Gymnastic equipment was borrowed from abroad. Each country's teams brought their own food, and boxers ate just custard and jelly. New Zealanders endured a six-week boat ride to get to the Games.

These weren't minor concessions. The fact that the 1948 Games went off at all was a miracle in itself. London was supposed to host the 1944 Summer Olympics, which were canceled because of the war. And even though the IOC quickly reawarded the Games to London in 1946, the city itself was not in peak condition. Bomb sites littered the streets. Churches had yet to be repaired. Even the House of Commons needed work. Some 700,000 homes had to be built, and only a third of London homes had running water in the bathrooms. Gas and food were heavily rationed as well. No wonder they nicknamed these Olympics the "Austerity Games."

"Our country will not be able to handle the Games," said Frank Butler, the sports editor of the *Daily Express*. "It will take too long to rebuild London. England would be jolly well satisfied never to hold the Games again." But the Olympics were meant to be uplifting, a symbol of international cooperation and rebirth—even if they had to stick to a strict budget. "It was a liberation of spirit to be there in London," said legendary Czech runner Emil Zatopek. "After the dark days of the war, the revival of the Olympics was as if the sun had come out. There were no more frontiers, no more barriers, just the people meeting together."

Things were difficult, but the unique power of the Olympics—that every-four-year occasion of worldwide friendship and peace—made it a bit more tolerable. Male athletes stayed in nearby Royal Air Force camps instead of an Olympic Village while the women lodged in local colleges. (It was better than the original plan, which was to house athletes in prisoner of war camps.) Meals were still rationed, and even though the athletes got increased limits,

OPPOSITE: *Official poster for the 1948 Summer Olympics, which was considered a remarkable success.*

29 JULY 1948 14 AUGUST

LONDON

food wasn't aplenty. Some consumed unrationed whale meat. "It was horrible," said Sylvia Cheeseman, a 200-meter runner, "but I was so intent on getting my protein that I ate it."

Americans had more resources to work with, and passed out steak, bacon, and eggs to their fellow competitors. The French brought wine. Fruit had been so rare during the war that it was a welcome surprise when Australians presented their tins of oranges and peaches. But there just wasn't a ton to go around. The British eights rowing team won silver—and blamed a lack of red meat for not winning gold. And it wasn't just food: The Canadians donated two Douglas firs to make the diving board, and the Finns brought wood for the basketball court.

Despite these challenges, the Games were considered to be quite a success. England won 23 medals, and only three golds, but the spirit of the athletes shone through. More important was regaining a sense of purpose after the war. The sparse conditions didn't detract from the quality of the competition, either. Dutch track-and-field star Fanny Blankers-Koen, a mother of two kids known as the Flying Housewife, won four gold medals, and American Bob Mathias became the youngest person to win a track-and-field gold medal, taking the decathlon as a 17-year-old. Indeed, the Games went on just as they should.

"My contemporaries and I had much more fun and a greater sense of achievement than modern athletes do," said British runner Peter Curry.

Looking back, of course, the 1948 London Olympics look pretty shabby, especially compared with today's high-tech spectacles awash with cash. (Consider the fact that Pyeongchang's $109 million stadium built for the 2018 Winter Olympics was demolished just one month after the Games.) But as bidding prices to host the Olympics continue to rise, it's worth remembering the lesson of the Austerity Games: It really doesn't matter whether Olympians compete in the most expensive stadiums or in dilapidated fields. Boil it down, and the Games are about the unparalleled talent and unflappable spirit of its athletes.

Blood in the Water

The Fight for Gold and Freedom

"The Olympics," wrote Hungarian water polo player Istvan Hevesi, "the whole thing has lost its importance, its beauty, because of what's happening back home."

The team was torn between their sport and their homeland, where a bloodbath had begun. In the autumn of 1956, the Soviet Union was crushing Hungary. A large group of Hungarians had started a revolt in Budapest, hoping to replace the Soviet-led Communist regime with a democratic government, but Soviet forces quickly responded with tear gas and gunfire.

"We were in midair to Melbourne when the pilot told us the news: Soviet tanks had invaded Budapest," remembered Dezso Gyarmati, the water polo team's captain. "We knew they would drown the revolution in blood." More than 200,000 Soviet troops had stormed Hungary's capital. The revolution stood no chance.

The distraught Hungarian delegation walks in the opening ceremony in Melbourne.

Now, with uncertain news about their families back home, the water polo team suited up for Olympic competition. They didn't have much of a choice but to find a way to put the bloodshed aside and compete for their country when they faced off against the Soviet Union in the semifinals. To some at the Games, surely the Olympics could've been just another match. For this group of Hungarians, it was a chance for national pride.

With a spot in the gold medal game on the line, play between these rivals was dirty from the start. They kicked each other under the water and punched each other above it. "We were yelling at them, 'You dirty bastards. You come over and bomb our country,'" Ervin Zador said. "They were calling us traitors."

This wasn't just a semifinal match. This was everything. Gyarmati told his team to fight to their last breath. As the Hungarians led 4–0 with time expiring, it was Zador who bore the brunt of the Soviet aggression that day after calling Soviet player Valentin Prokopov a loser. Zador then looked away for a moment, and Prokopov lifted his entire upper body out of the water, swinging for Zador's head in a sucker punch. A gash spread over the Hungarian's right eye, blood spilling everywhere. "You know," said Lazlo Ujvary, a diver who was in the stands, "a little blood in the water very soon makes a lot."

Officials called the game a minute early and police officers escorted the Soviet team from the arena. The Hungarian fans were hoping to join

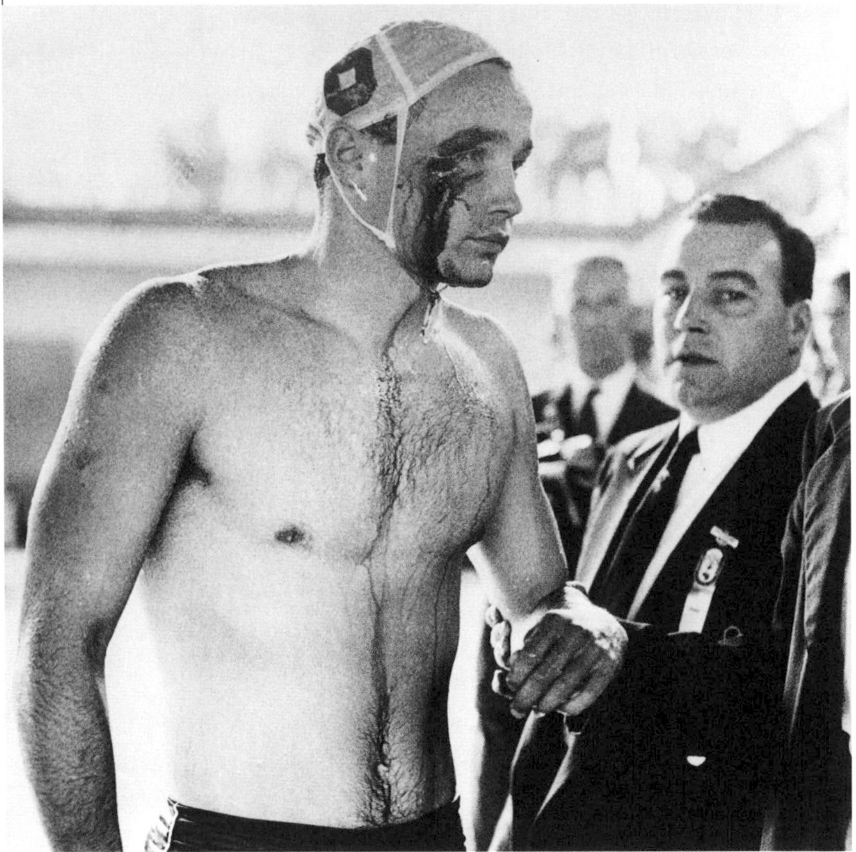

Zador left the pool bloodied, but the Hungarians had the final say with their gold medal.

in on the fight. Zador's cheek was split, so he couldn't play in the final. But Hungary won gold—a huge victory for themselves, an even bigger triumph for their country. After the game Zador sat with his gold medal and cried, knowing that Hungary was in chaos, and that returning home might not be an option.

Zador was one of a large group of Hungarians who emigrated to the United States after the 1956 Games. He settled in California, where he trained Mark Spitz in swimming. Zador's daughter Christine scored the game-winning goal in the 1999 NCAA water polo championship for the University of Southern California. But the photo of blood dripping down his cheek is his legacy. "I deeply regret that picture," he said. "I would have loved to be remembered as one of the best young players in the world, rather than the guy hit by the Russian."

Zador's blood in the water may be the first thing most people will know about him. But if they look beyond the cut, they'll find something else: a group of water polo players who loved their country, who would have done anything to uphold its honor, even as it began to fall.

The Apartheid Boycott

Turmoil at the 1976 Summer Olympics

An international friendly rugby match that wasn't even held in the Olympics threatened to bring down the entire 1976 Games in Montreal. It all started with a trip abroad for the New Zealand rugby team.

The United Nations had implored countries to stop all athletic competitions in South Africa, as part of a growing international boycott to force the end of apartheid. Indeed, the IOC had banned the nation from Olympic participation since 1964—a ban that would last until 1992. Despite this, and the recent uprising in the city of Soweto—in which police killed hundreds of demonstrators only a month earlier—the New Zealand rugby team ignored the boycott and traveled throughout South Africa in the summer of 1976 for games against local teams. It sparked international condemnation, and with the Olympics coming up, African nations responded in unison.

Just days before the opening ceremony in Montreal, 22 African countries announced they would boycott the Games. They would participate only if New Zealand was banned. The IOC, however, found no reason to ban the country, saying that rugby was outside their purview as a non-Olympic sport. "Principles are more precious than medals," said Kenya's foreign minister, James Osogo. Other countries made the trip to Montreal, only to turn around before the Games officially started. "We're leaving as soon as we can make the plane reservations," said Musa Keni Kasonka, the leader of the Zambia delegation.

Only two African nations ended up staying: Senegal and Ivory Coast. None of their athletes made it to the final rounds of their respective disciplines. There were also new strictures in place for the New Zealand delegation. Security was tight, and armed guards kept watch in some of their rooms. The athletes were asked not to talk to the media about the boycott.

The Games would end up losing a million Canadian dollars in cancellations and refunds. But the boycott brought something else: widespread attention to the plight of millions of South Africans under apartheid. It started pressure campaigns across the world, marking a powerful example of sport strongly impacting the political realm.

Amateur Hour

Karl Schranz, the Superstar Scapegoat

Like so many other issues in Avery Brundage's long, controversial tenure as head of the IOC from 1952 to 1972, the issue of amateurism came to a head. In fact, in one of his last acts before retiring, the 84-year-old Brundage was willing to kick out top athletes in downhill skiing—nearly blowing up the sport—just to keep the ideal intact.

From the outset, the Olympics were meant for amateurs only, celebrating a true expression of the love of sports, not the potential for financial gain. Nowadays, of course, that ideal has fallen by the wayside. But both Brundage and Olympic founder Pierre de Coubertin before him were deeply committed to maintaining amateurism and separating the Games

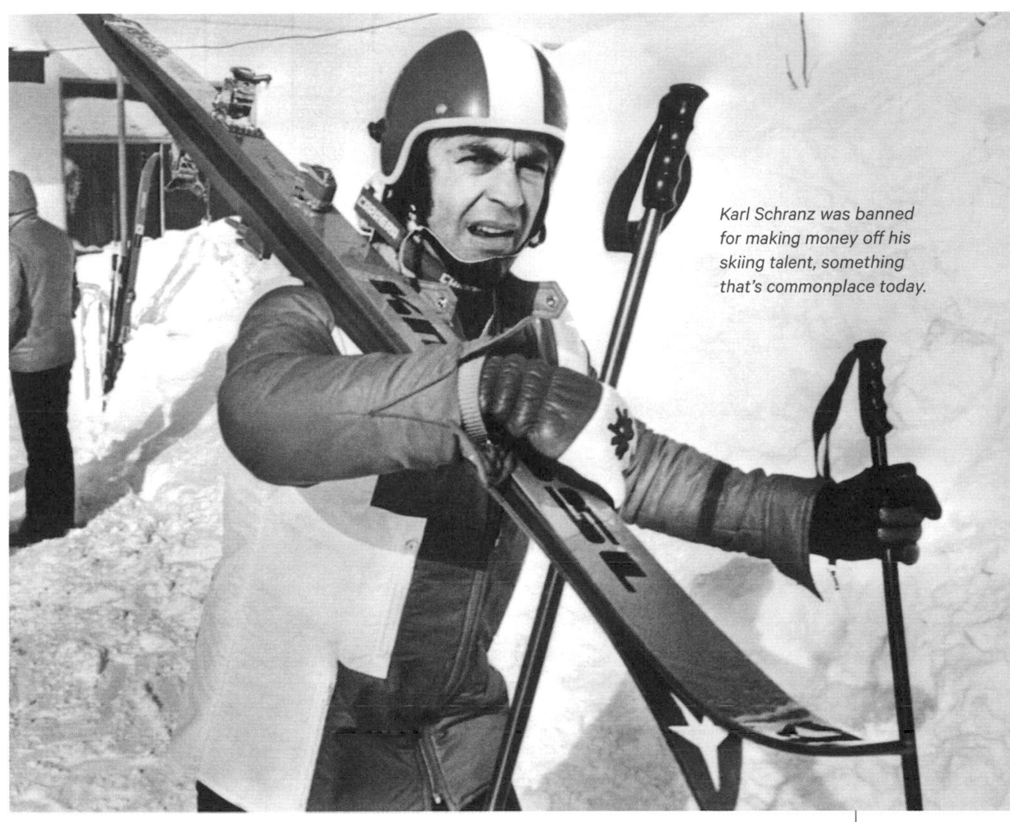
Karl Schranz was banned for making money off his skiing talent, something that's commonplace today.

from the professional realm. For years leading up to the 1972 Winter Games in Sapporo, Brundage had complained about skiers, in particular, receiving endorsements, calling them "trained seals of the merchandisers." He was reported to have a list of up to 40 he wanted to ban. In the end, he chose just one.

Karl Schranz, a 33-year-old Austrian skiing legend, was a favorite to win the downhill. A world champion, he had won every major international skiing honor except an Olympic gold medal. The 1972 Games were his last chance to achieve his dream, but three days before the Olympics started, Schranz was banned for accepting sponsorship offers from a coffee company. He was reportedly making at least $40,000 a year from the sport and endorsements. (That's nearly $250,000 in today's dollars.) Brundage was tight-lipped about his decision, stating publicly only that they had "sufficient evidence."

Schranz became the third athlete in Olympic history, after American decathlete Jim Thorpe and Finnish runner Paavo Nurmi, to be banned for violating amateurism rules. The IOC voted 28–14 in favor of the ban, and Schranz was not invited to make his case before the committee. Other skiers suspected that Brundage was making an example of Schranz as a warning to all Olympic athletes. Schranz was outraged, and an attempt by the Austrian Olympic committee to reverse the ban was unsuccessful. He retired from competitive skiing after the 1972 Games.

"They wanted a head," said French skier Henri Duvillard, "and they chose Karl."

Indeed, the Olympics are not, for most athletes, the cash cow that many believe them to be. There's a reason that every four years we see commercials about how Home Depot graciously allows Olympians to create flexible schedules while they work. It's because Olympic sports, especially the more obscure ones, don't pay much. Schranz, who grew up poor in Austria's Arlberg Mountains, told the press, "If we followed Mr. Brundage's recommendations to their true end, the Olympics would be a competition only for the very rich. No man of ordinary means could ever afford to excel in this sport."

The Austrian people sided with Schranz. Upon returning home, he received a hero's welcome unlike any other seen in Vienna. (Alpine skiing is a huge deal in Austria.) Some 100,000 people lined the streets from the airport to the city. It was a bigger crowd than John F. Kennedy or Queen Elizabeth II received.

In 1988, the IOC deemed Schranz to have behaved in a "fitting manner" since 1972 and agreed to reinstate him. He was given a symbolic medal to mark his participation at the Sapporo Games. But that surely doesn't ease the sting of missing out on a real one.

Seen today, Brundage's view seems absurd. Michael Phelps earned $12 million in endorsements in 2013 alone. Schranz, of course, did what all athletes should be able to do: He used his talents to make money.

BANNED FOR PROFESSIONALISM

In 2014, Americans Ronald and Vivian Joseph won a bronze medal for pairs figure skating at the 1964 Winter Games in Innsbruck, Austria. In case you blinked and missed it, that's a 50-year wait for a medal.

The brother-sister duo had finished fourth in the pairs competition, missing out on a medal by just three-tenths of a point. In 1966, however, the IOC disqualified the 1964 silver medal winners Marika Kilius and Hans-Jurgen Baumler of West Germany when they signed a professional deal to perform in the Christmas show Holiday on Ice. So, the pair had to return their medals and everyone below them was bumped up a spot.

The Josephs received their medals later that year in that most glamorous of Olympic venues: a Sheraton hotel in Chicago. And that was that, until 1987, when the IOC, without much publicity or explanation, gave Kilius and Baumler their medals back. The reasoning? The couple was "rehabilitated."

But no one told the Josephs, and different record books contained different information. It wasn't until someone Vivian Joseph met at a party disputed her claim to a bronze medal that the Josephs began to look into it. In 2014 the IOC officially awarded the bronze to the American siblings, while the Canadian pair shared silver with the West Germans. (The Soviet Union remained the gold medal winners, blissfully unaffected by the whole debacle.)

Marika Kilius (left) and Hans-Jurgen Baumler (right) made a big no-no by signing with Holiday on Ice.

Truckin' (to a Bronze)

Lithuanian Basketball at the 1992 Olympics

Oh, what a long, strange trip it was. On its face, the Lithuanian men's basketball team was a major contender for the 1992 Games in Barcelona—Lithuania's first Olympics as an independent nation since 1928. They had legitimate stars in Arvydas Sabonis, Sarunas Marciulionis, Rimas Kurtinaitis, and Valdemaras Chomicius, and four had played on the gold-medal-winning 1988 Soviet team. They're completely basketball-crazy in Lithuania. But with the country's recent separation from the Soviet Union, money was tight and they still had to qualify. To make their Olympic dreams a reality, they received massive help from . . . the Grateful Dead?

Yes, after reading a story about the Lithuanians' lack of funds in a newspaper, those Friends of the Devil chipped in financially, and provided tie-dye T-shirts and uniforms. Rock on, indeed. "We're always for the underdog,"

These new Deadheads took the support of the legendary band all the way to the medal stand.

said drummer Mickey Hart, "and this wasn't just a basketball team. This was a struggle for life, liberty, and freedom." Subjected to years of bland Soviet style, the Lithuanians agreed that a pop of color and style was a welcome change. Featuring a dunking skeleton and a psychedelic blend of red, yellow, and green—Lithuania's national colors—the shirts were a hit, and fans even offered some players cash for them.

Though the US Dream Team crushed them 127–76, the Lithuanians did manage to capture a bronze medal, beating the remains of the Soviet squad, called the Unified Team, 82–72. "We didn't have any choice," said Marciulionis. "We absolutely had to win at any cost." After the medal ceremony, the Lithuanian locker room was a party. The head of state, Vytautas Landsbergis, visited the team and they sang the national anthem. Alcohol was aplenty, and he ended up soaked in Champagne. So Landsbergis did what any good Lithuanian hooper would do: He suited up in a Grateful Dead tie-dye shirt.

The Not-Quite-Olympics

Unofficial Excellence at the 1906 Intercalated Games

"The Olympic Games of 1906," wrote James Edward Sullivan, the organizer of the 1904 Olympics and one of the founders of the Amateur Athletic Union (AAU), "will go down into athletic history as the most remarkable festival of its kind ever held."

Sure sounds like a blast. So if these Games were so great, why aren't they officially recognized by the IOC? And why have you never heard of them? In many ways, it comes down to politics. King George of Greece wanted the Olympics to remain in his country permanently. The idea makes some sense, given the high costs and logistical challenges of staging the Games in a new location each cycle. But modern Olympic founder Pierre de Coubertin, for his part, wanted it hosted around the world, so it could be a traveling expedition of sport and culture.

As a stopgap measure, the two sides came to a compromise. Every two years an Intercalated Games would be held. (The word *intercalate*, for those without a dictionary handy, means to insert something between existing elements.) It was a smash, and unlike the chaos and disorganization of the early Olympics in Paris and St. Louis, the 1906 version was well-managed and looked very similar to what you see today: Athletes marched in an opening ceremony under their country's flag, the first closing ceremony took place, and medal winners saw their flags rise above them. A total of 826 athletes—only six of them women—from 20 nations competed. Martin Sheridan, an American track-and-field competitor, won five medals and set a world record in the discus. The United States was third in the total medal count, with 24, and the French led with 40, including 15 gold medals.

Though the Intercalated Games were a success, and revived international interest for a flagging Olympic movement, the idea of a Games every two years was not to be. For a number of reasons, including Greece's persistent economic issues and military squabbles with Turkey, a version in 1910 never materialized. By the outbreak of World War I in 1914, the idea had petered out completely. Coubertin had worked to ensure that the Intercalated Games weren't officially recognized—he didn't even attend in

The Panathenaic Stadium in Athens, site of the 1906 Intercalated Games, a one-time Olympics offshoot now considered unofficial

1906. He was apparently peeved that his contributions to the reinstitution of the Olympics hadn't received as much fanfare as he thought it should.

In 1948, at an IOC meeting, one member made a proposal to recognize the 1906 Intercalated Games as official. It was routed to the Brundage Committee, led by future IOC president Avery Brundage, and two other members. Coubertin received letters calling him a "thief," trying to rid Greece of one of its most historic legacies. Despite the public enthusiasm and high level of competition at these not-quite-Olympics, the commission came up with a final ruling: The proposal was rejected, and the Intercalated Games would be lost to time.

The Games would eventually return to Athens 98 years later in 2004. As costs to host an Olympics skyrocket each cycle, many commentators have continued to call for a permanent Olympic site, and many suggest Greece. But even though Olympic bids are expensive, it is still worth exploring new locales. There hasn't been a Games in Africa, nor in the Middle East. We've seen only one in South America (Rio in 2016). We have more places to go, more countries to see, more people to carry the torch.

ZAPPAS OLYMPIC GAMES

The Olympics were reintroduced to the world in Athens in 1896—the first official Games since 200 BC—but there were a handful of important revivals in the interim. Evangelos Zappas, a wealthy Greek businessman, helped fund and arrange a competition in 1859. After he died in 1865, three more were held in 1870, 1875, and 1889. Athletes competed at the Panathenaic Stadium in the capital, and events included racing, pole vault, discus throwing, parallel bars, and wrestling. King Otto of Greece presented the winners with a wreath and prize money.

Though one historian notes that the Zappas games are best considered local competitions, these Games did receive some attention far beyond the confines of Greece. They are thought to have influenced modern Olympic founders William Penny Brookes and Pierre de Coubertin. The pair came together to outline the future of a competition that would become the biggest in the world.

The Cotswold Olimpick Games

A Strange Olympic Precursor

Every year, a rider enters Cotswold, England, on horseback. A cannon is fired. A group of competitors dress up in white coats and stuff their trousers with straw. And then they begin to kick each other in the shins.

No, this is not Fight Club. This is the Cotswold Olimpick Games. Started by lawyer Robert Dover in 1612, these games featured a strange mix of obscure sports and time-honored favorites from the ancient Olympics in Greece. There's King of the Hill—a pentathlon of sorts, featuring static jump, spurning the barre (similar to the Scottish sport of caber toss, which is, essentially, tree throwing), hammer throw, and shot put. Then there is Championship of the Hill (a kind of team version of King of the Hill), tug-of-war, and, of course, the aforementioned shin kicking. Don't forget wrestling, running, and hare hunting, too. Even those lacking athletic skills can dance around the maypole.

The games were held intermittently starting with the English Civil War in 1642 and came to a full close in 1862. They were reinstituted in 1951, but a local outbreak of foot-and-mouth disease delayed any hopes of making them

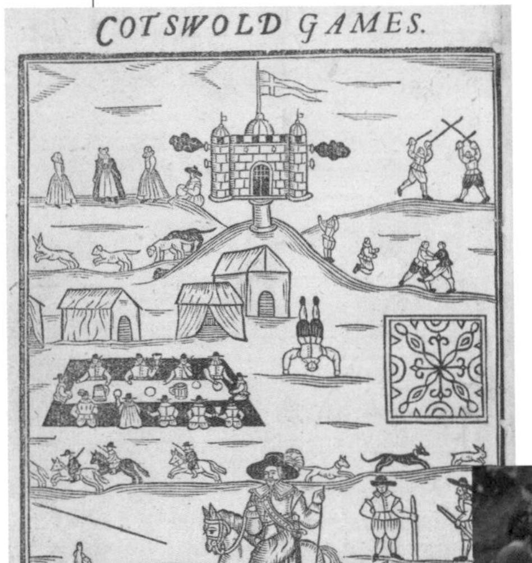

ABOVE: *The frontispiece of the 1636 book* Annalia Dubrensia
RIGHT: *Just a bunch of blokes kicking each other in the shins*

an annual affair. It wasn't until 1964 that the Cotswold Olimpicks became a yearly event, and it takes on the same look today as it did back then.

Though these games aren't quite Olympic in nature, Cotswold has seen some Olympic-size intrigue. There's a possibility that William Shakespeare attended—and that the Olimpick Games found their way into his work. In the comedy *The Merry Wives of Windsor*, one character asks, "How does your fallow greyhound, sir? I heard say he was outrun on Cotsall." (Cotsall is Old English for Cotswold.) Some also contend that the wrestling scene in *As You Like It* was inspired by the event at the games. There is no consensus that the two are related—we will most likely never know. But somehow, the Bard watching a shin-kicking match is a literary twist even he could not have concocted.

The Nordic Games

Winter Sports Found Their International Footing

Before Nordic countries dominated the Winter Games, they had their very own version in which to demolish opponents. The Nordic Games, starting in 1901 and lasting until 1926, were among the earliest international competitions for winter sports. There was ski jumping, ski racing, cross-country skiing (up to 210 kilometers long), and hockey. They also included Summer-type events like fencing and swimming, and then some wacky ones, like ballooning, auto racing, and pulka racing (a type of dogsledding).

In 1909, some 2,000 athletes from Sweden, Norway, and Finland took part. It was, at its heart, deeply political. Viktor Balck, a Swedish general and a charter member of the IOC, thought these games were an important national project, projecting athletic dominance and "honor" to the region. Sweden's years of experience running the Nordic Games left them well set up to organize the 1912 Olympics in Stockholm.

The last Nordic Games were held in 1926, two years after the first Winter Olympics in Chamonix, France. But so much of today's more international winter sports extravaganzas look like yesterday's Nordic Games—right down to the dominance of the Scandinavian countries.

ODD OLYMPIC BIDS

Over the years, most host cities have made sense: Los Angeles for the Summer Games and Calgary for the Winter Games are no-brainers. Increasingly, countries that don't seem like the greatest fits for the Olympics are now hosting them. (Who knew Beijing was a snowy winter destination?) And every cycle, some bids seem like the ultimate long shots.

One repeat bidder for the Summer Games has been Detroit, a city which has tried—and failed—a staggering nine times, the most ever. They aren't the only ones to struggle. Manchester, England, and Havana, Cuba, each made two unsuccessful attempts. San Juan, Puerto Rico, received not a single vote in 2004.

The Winter Games might be odder still. Have you heard of Bear Mountain? Probably not—it's a tiny, 1,283-foot peak north of New York City. That bid failed in 1932, along with both Duluth and Minneapolis. What about Karachi, Pakistan, in 1960? They didn't receive a vote. (The city also never receives snow.) Zakopane, Poland, is home to only 27,000 people, but it put in a bid for 2006. Sion, Switzerland, has made three unsuccessful bids; the same with Jaca, Spain. Borjomi, Georgia, has a population of 17,000—maybe that's why their bid in 2014 didn't go anywhere.

There's a lesson here: If you want the torch, stick to the big cities.

The Liberty Bell Classic

The Games Come Home . . . to the Highway

The United States, along with 64 other countries, boycotted the 1980 Summer Games in Moscow after the Soviet Union's invasion of Afghanistan. But that left a lot of worthy athletes without a chance to show off their athletic prowess to the world. So the United States decided to hold its own competition. It didn't quite go as planned.

The United States State Department considered funding an event in Ivory Coast, whose leader was pro-Western, and looked into organizing a series of multicontinent competitions in Rome, Tokyo, and Beijing, among other cities. Eventually, Congress set aside $10 million for tournaments in a number of sports. The track competition, now known as the Liberty Bell

Classic, was held in Philadelphia, and the International Invitational was a gymnastics event held in Hartford.

Although the Classic wasn't exactly Olympic level—said coach Jimmy Carnes, "We can't call this the alternative Games. There's no alternative"—there were some exciting moments. Renaldo Nehemiah ran the hurdles in 13.31, just .31 off his world record. The American men swept the 100 meters, and Mary Decker, fresh off an 18-hour flight from a track competition in Oslo, won the 1,500 with a US record time.

The public was divided over America's first and only Olympic boycott.

There wasn't quite the same pomp and circumstance of the Olympics, either. One round of the decathlon saw 96-degree heat and traffic piling up on I-76, right in view of the field. But it was certainly cleaner than the Moscow Games, where, as an Australian Senate report noted, "there is hardly a medal winner . . . who is not on one sort of drug or another: usually several kinds. The Moscow Games might well have been called the Chemists' Games." Maybe a slapped-together competition on the side of the highway is better than a drug-fueled Olympics after all.

Standing Next to History

Peter Norman and the 1968 Podium Protest

The 1968 Summer Olympics should have been the highlight of Peter Norman's life. Instead, it was the beginning of his downfall.

The Australian sprinter started the Games by setting an Olympic record in one of the heats of the 200-meter sprint. In the final, he set a personal best—and an Australian record that still stands—with a time of 20.06, earning the silver medal. While Norman may have been content to rejoice on the podium, his fellow medal-winners had other ideas.

Americans John Carlos and Tommie Smith would use this platform to make a powerful statement about racial inequality back home by raising a fist during the national anthem. They wore black socks, black scarves, and they intended to wear black gloves. But when Carlos forgot his pair in the Olympic village, Norman suggested that the two share Smith's gloves. It's why Carlos raised his left hand instead of right, which is different from the typical Black Power salute.

Norman may have been the perfect podium-mate. He had been a vocal critic of the racist White Australia Policy, which had aimed to exclude non-Europeans from entering the country. Along with Carlos and Smith, he wore a badge from the Olympic Project for Human Rights, which advocated against racial segregation in sports. Before the medal ceremony, when the Americans told him that they were planning a protest, Carlos thought Norman would be fearful. Instead, Carlos said, "I saw love." Norman's approval helped the demonstration go on without a hitch.

After the protest, IOC President Avery Brundage immediately expelled Carlos and Smith from the games, and the athletes became persona non grata in the United States. *Time* magazine wrote: "'Faster, Higher, Stronger' is the motto of the Olympic Games. 'Angrier, nastier, uglier' better describes the scene in Mexico City last week." Norman was treated with similar disdain when he returned home to Australia. Though an excellent runner, he was passed over for the next Olympic team. And when the Games came to Sydney in 2000, he wasn't involved in the festivities. "If we were getting beat up," said Carlos, "Peter was facing an entire country and suffering alone."

"If we were getting beat up, Peter was facing an entire country and suffering alone."

He was certainly suffering. In 1985, Norman was diagnosed with gangrene after an Achilles tendon tear, and became addicted to alcohol. When he died in 2006 of a heart attack, both Smith and Carlos gave eulogies and were pallbearers at his funeral. In 2012, the Australian House of Representatives passed an official apology to Norman "for the treatment he received upon his return to Australia, and the failure to fully recognise his inspirational role before his untimely death in 2006."

Norman was thrust into a moment that he perhaps wasn't prepared for. In all likelihood, he would have been happy to bask in the glory of winning a medal. But that was the point of the protest—to upend the typical, to shock the status quo, to change the narrative. That change, of course, has come in fits and starts, if at all. (As Carlos told *Sports Illustrated* on the 50th anniversary of that day: "I've spoken and spoken and spoken, and it ain't gonna make no difference.")

Norman should, of course, be remembered for his impressive racing career. But credit him for not flinching when Carlos and Smith decided to make the biggest statement on the biggest stage. That's a legacy worthy of honoring.

Norman, Smith, and Carlos just after the powerful podium protest that shocked the world

The Other Protesters

Echoes of Smith and Carlos in 1972

What does an athlete owe his country after winning an Olympic medal? What does he owe the crowds at the stadium, the audience on television? Is he supposed to stand perfectly straight, a single tear rolling down his eye as the anthem blares? Should he be stoic? Should he be animated? Or should he have a big smile on his face?

What if the athlete won the medal for *himself* rather than for his country? What if the whole point of the Olympics, in his mind, was to honor not the uniform, or the flag, or the anthem, but all the hard work that *he* put in?

Brundage ruled the IOC with an iron fist and took a hard line against dissent.

All this was going through Vincent Matthews's mind after he won the gold medal in the 400-meter dash at the 1972 Olympics in Munich. He stood atop the medal stand, a hand on his hips as he played with his facial hair. He spun around his gold medal. The crowd began to boo. IOC president Avery Brundage, who encouraged Americans to give a Nazi salute at the 1936 Games in Berlin, said, "The whole world saw the disgusting display of your two athletes, when they received their gold and silver medals for the 400M event."

Ah yes, there was another athlete. Wayne Collett had won silver. He stood barefoot in protest and chatted with Matthews during "The Star-Spangled Banner." He even gave a Black Power salute as they exited through the tunnel. The two were sent home and barred from future Olympic competition. (As a result, the US team was forced to leave the next day's 4 x 400 relay, an event in which they were the defending gold medalists.) The fallout for Matthews and Collett was the same. Their reasoning was different.

Matthews seemed indifferent that he had helped spark an international firestorm. “I know Vince,” said Kenny Moore, a marathoner. “He’s loose. I know the kind of defiance that comes into these situations. It’s a perfectly natural explosion of ebullience.” But loose or not, the 24-year-old from Queens, New York, felt that his country was getting all the praise and recognition for what *he* had done. He wrote in his book, *My Race Be Won,* “Why did the public feel the necessity for some sort of vicarious identification that forced the injection of nationalism and patriotism?”

It is true that the public felt a need for their athletes to be apolitical. It is as true now as it was then, or for John Carlos and Tommie Smith before them in 1968, or anytime someone kneels or bows their head or looks away or makes anything else more important than the national anthem. Why, Matthews thought, does a competition even have to be a battle between countries? “We consider ourselves athletes,” he wrote in an op-ed in the *New York Times,* “not politicians or marching bands.”

Collett (left) and Matthews (right) were permanently suspended from the Olympics.

A PROTEST WAY BACK

The Olympic code says that "No kind of demonstration or political, religious or racial propaganda is permitted," but that hasn't stopped athletes from protesting or making their feelings known. Political expression has been there since the beginning.

One of the earliest protests was staged at the Intercalated Games in 1906, after Peter O'Connor won gold in the hop, step, and jump (today's triple jump), and silver in the long jump. Though Irish, he competed, without much choice, for Great Britain. That didn't sit well with O'Connor, so after receiving his medals, he climbed up a flagpole, tore down the British Union Jack, and replaced it with an Irish flag that read *Éirinn go Brách*, or "Ireland Forever." Unlike the handful of protesters since then, though, O'Connor wasn't banished from sport. He retired on his own accord and served the Olympics as a judge.

Matthews's act of protest may have been casual, but Collett's Black Power salute was absolutely intentional. For it was Collett who said, "I think this country has a possibility of being great but it isn't great now." And then, "I love America. I just don't think it's lived up to its promise." It is this rhetoric that preceded similar words from Colin Kaepernick 45 years later.

Both Matthews and Collett were barred from competition and fell from the spotlight. Why did their bold actions receive so much less fanfare—both at the time and today—than their contemporaries John Carlos and Tommie Smith, who suffered similar unfair punishment and ostracism in 1968? It's tough to say. Perhaps an unsympathetic public preferred to just forget about it in 1972. Or, like with Kaepernick, there was only enough bandwidth in the public's attention span for one or two main figures, while the media drowned out others making the same protests.

We do know this: For protesting—a right enshrined in their country's constitution—these two athletes were barred for life. Maybe the national anthem is about a minute and a half long. But it took just a minute and a half of protest to mean a lifetime of banishment for two world-class athletes.

The First Nazi Games

Mass Propaganda at the 1936 Winter Olympics

It was supposed to be a test run. The newly elected Nazi government wanted to know just how far they could go and what they could get away with. Sure, they made concessions. If you're going to convince the world that all the negative media attention surrounding your country is wrong—the original "fake news"—then you have to make sure that everything is in tip-top shape. The much larger 1936 Summer Olympics, to be held later that year in Berlin, would be the Nazi regime's debut on the world stage. The Winter Olympics in Garmisch-Partenkirchen, a ski resort on the Austrian border, would be their trial.

So they took down the signs that said "Jews are not wanted here"—despite Hitler's reluctance. *Der Stürmer* a deeply anti-Semitic newspaper, wasn't visible. They even allowed Rudi Ball, a Jewish hockey player, on the German team.

Before the Games, Hitler was paraded through the town and was met with Nazi salutes by athletes and supporters alike.

Not that it was all pleasant, even superficially so. The *New York Times* reported that the two towns of Garmisch and Partenkirchen "have become a forest of flag poles and swastika flags." But wouldn't you know: Everyone bought the subterfuge. Gustavus Kirby, the treasurer of the American Olympic Committee, was, according to the *Times*, "convinced the Olympics will not be misused for Nazi propaganda purposes." He later reported that the Germans even cheered as hard for Rudi Ball as they did for any other player. A headline read, "No signs of racial or political prejudice appear."

DEUTSCHLAND 1936
IV·OLYMPISCHE WINTERSPIELE
GARMISCH-PARTENKIRCHEN
6:16.FEBRUAR 1936
ORGANISATIONS-KOMITEE FÜR DIE IV. OLYMPISCHEN WINTERSPIELE 1936
GARMISCH-PARTENKIRCHEN / BAYERN

Looking back in hindsight, of course, the signals were everywhere. The Hitler Youth lined the stadium at the opening ceremony. Political opponents were being sent to concentration camps. And it had been only five months since the passage of the Nuremberg Laws, which forbade marriages between Jewish and gentile Germans.

There was so much hatred in the town that the head of the Olympic organizing committee, Karl Ritter von Halt, was concerned that a backlash to the soft-pedaling of anti-Semitism would make the Germans look bad internationally. "I am not expressing my concerns in order to help the Jews," he wrote to the interior ministry. But "if the propaganda is continued in this form, the population of Garmisch-Partenkirchen will be so inflamed that it will indiscriminately attack and injure anyone who even looks Jewish."

Hitler himself was incensed that the United States did not salute him at the opening ceremonies. He even came down to the US hockey locker room to shout at the coach and team. Just a few weeks after the Games, Hitler would order 3,000 troops into the Rhineland, a clear violation of the Treaty of Versailles. And yet the *Times* wrote, "Any visitor who expected to behold militarism in full display here has been disappointed."

The Olympics are often a whitewash. In Beijing, officials did their part to temporarily reduce smog and conceal China's history of human rights abuses. Or in Rio, thousands lost their homes when the city demolished favelas near Olympic Park. The Games are meant to show the very best of a country, especially when that country has done plenty wrong. Nazi Germany had the most to hide.

The point was to clean things up just enough to make people look the other way. As the *Times* wrote, in its most clear-eyed analysis of the Games after publishing mostly fawning coverage, "this is really the most efficient propaganda conceivable. There is probably no tourist here who will not go home averring that Germany is the most peace-loving, non militaristic, hospitable and tolerant country in Europe and that all the foreign correspondents stationed here are liars."

OPPOSITE: *Official poster for the 1936 Winter Games. The Nazis used the Olympics to downplay their anti-Semitism and military aggression.*

Love or Country?

Glenn Morris at the 1936 Berlin Olympics

In 1930, Glenn Morris left his family's pinto bean farm in Simla, Colorado, as the third-place finisher in the hurdles at the state meet. He was destined for Colorado A&M and, he hoped, much bigger opportunities for fame and fortune than what waited for him back at the farm. His ambitions would be realized—and then some. But his dreams came with a price.

An All-American in college, Morris had his eyes set on the decathlon at the 1936 Summer Olympics in Berlin. Leading up to those Games, his world record of 7,880 points at the US trials put him on the map. *Newsweek* called him the country's "New Iron Man." His time in Germany, though, is when Morris's ambition might have become blinding. It is undisputed what he did on the track—he broke his own world record with a score of 7,900, earning the gold medal. His athletic prowess, it was said, caught the eye of Adolf Hitler, who not only watched the entire competition from his seat in Olympiastadion, but also offered Morris $50,000 to stay in Germany and make movies. Morris, fortunately, declined.

What he did not decline, however, were the advances of Leni Riefenstahl. The infamous filmmaker, whose sweeping shots of the Berlin Games filled the 1938 documentary propaganda film *Olympia*, was enthralled with Morris. "We looked at one another, we both seemed transfixed," she wrote in her memoir. "It was an incredible moment and I had never experienced anything like it."

Riefenstahl also claimed, falsely it would turn out, that after the medal ceremony, Morris "grabbed me in his arms, tore off my blouse, and kissed my breasts, right in the middle of the stadium, in front of a hundred thousand spectators. A lunatic, I thought." (His biographer, Mike Chapman, disputed that account, writing that Morris participated only in a traditional medal ceremony, receiving a laurel from Eva Braun, Adolf Hitler's mistress.) Morris remained tightlipped about his affair with Hitler's favorite filmmaker, and the details are nearly impossible to pin down. Riefenstahl later claimed to be in love with him, and though they did not marry, Morris once told his brother Jack that he regretted not staying with her in Germany.

It's unclear if he held any Nazi sympathies, or whether he wanted to remain in Germany for love, politics, or some combination of the two. But there's no doubt that his rush of fame after winning the gold medal quickly faded away. Yes, there was a ticker-tape parade in New York City. He portrayed himself in the 1937 short film *Decathlon Champion: The Story of Glenn Morris*. In 1938, he played Tarzan in *Tarzan's Revenge*. (He was, in fact, one of four Olympians to portray Tarzan, including gold medalist swimmers Johnny Weissmuller and Buster Crabbe and silver-medalist shot-putter Herman Brix.) Taking a chance on his athletic talents, the Detroit Lions signed Morris in 1940 as an end, playing in just four games and grabbing an interception before being injured.

It was in his life after the foray into football that he faded fully from the public eye and things went downhill. A stint in the navy during World War II reportedly left him with mental health issues. He worked various menial jobs and struggled with alcoholism. Morris, the athletic marvel, ripped and bronzed as Tarzan, would live out his days in veterans hospitals in California, before dying in 1974. Was the son of a pinto bean farmer out of his depth in the bigger world? Was he a political pawn? It's tough to know. But he left Germany a star, an athletic icon. His return to America left him broken.

Morris and Riefenstahl during the shot put event at the 1936 Summer Olympics in Berlin

Terror in Munich

Security Concerns Ignored

There were 26 potential situations for mass destruction at the 1972 Olympics in Munich. Wary of potential threats given Germany's violent recent history, the organizers of the Games asked Munich's police psychologist Georg Sieber to mock up worst-case scenarios for terror. Sieber envisioned the so-called Situation Number 21 this way: At 5 a.m., a dozen armed Palestinians would scale the Olympic village. They would invade the Israeli delegation, kill a hostage or two, and demand the release of prisoners held in Israeli jails.

Surprised by the scale of Sieber's situations, organizers were reluctant to make significant changes to guard against any of them. It would require upending the entire security apparatus of the Games, the first to return to Germany since Hitler's Berlin Olympics in 1936. Amid the still-fresh horrors of the war, the Munich Games were meant to evoke a carefree and fun West Germany. (Indeed, the motto of the Games was "Die Heiteren Spiele," or "The Happy Games.")

But around 4:10 a.m. on September 5, carefree turned into chaos. It played out just as Sieber predicted, eerily so. The Palestinian terrorist group Black September gained access to the Israelis' ground-floor apartment in Olympic Village; there were demands for prisoner exchange; and two Israelis were killed in the opening salvo of the attack. The hostage takers originally demanded the release of 234 Palestinians jailed in Israel. Reports indicated that the Germans offered an unlimited amount of money for the release of the athletes, but the Palestinians declined.

All competition was suspended later that day. In the interim, police hatched a rescue and ambush plan: Two helicopters would transport the terrorists and hostages to a nearby NATO airbase, where an armed assault would await the terrorists. But miscommunication led to some of the West German police retreating, and eventually the one sniper remaining missed the group leader. A shootout ensued and one policeman died.

As more West German police arrived at the airbase, the kidnappers changed course. At 12:04 a.m. on September 6, one began firing; three athletes were killed on the spot. A terrorist then threw a grenade, and the remaining athletes perished. Eleven members of the Israeli team had been murdered. As ABC broadcaster Jim McKay famously said on the air, "When I was a kid, my father used to say, 'Our great hopes and our worst fears are seldom realized.' Our worst fears have been realized tonight."

After a 34-hour suspension of all events, the first in Olympic history, competition resumed. "The Games must go on," said IOC President Avery Brundage, "and we must continue our efforts to keep them clean, pure, and honest." But a dark cloud hung over the proceedings. Many panicking athletes exited from the Games immediately, including Jewish swimmer Mark Spitz, who had just won his seventh gold medal. All other Jewish athletes were placed under protection, and the Egyptian team left the Games entirely, fearing reprisals.

One legacy of that terrible day has been a drastic paradigm shift in the Olympic security program. Munich spent less than $2 million on security. Athens paid out at least $600 million; Rio brought in a police force of 85,000; Sydney mocked up 800 potential disaster scenarios; Pyeongchang deployed drone-catching drones, sensor systems to detect chemicals, and planes with facial recognition technology.

The Games host, in one place, people from nations from every corner of the world. Sometimes those countries are in conflict. There are always political leaders, dignitaries, and world-famous athletes on hand. Protecting all of those people is a massive undertaking, one that has increased exponentially since Munich. It took a massacre to realize that organizers could no longer afford to ignore the warning signs.

Olympic delegates gather to mourn the victims of the Munich massacre on September 6, 1972.

The Forgotten Miracle

The 1960 US Hockey Team Upsets the Soviets

It took most of us until 1980 to believe in Miracles, but had we been paying closer attention, we would have believed two decades earlier.

The 1960 US hockey team was made up of insurance salesmen, carpenters, and college students. The goalie was given leave from the air force. The captain fought fires. They made $7 per week, and that was mainly to cover laundry. With Canada and the Soviet Union tabbed as heavy favorites, the odds seemed insurmountable. From 1920 to 1959, the US national team was just 2–15–2 against Canada in world championship and Olympic play. From 1955 to 1959, the United States was 0–5 against the Soviets. The USSR won those games by a combined score of 21–5.

"Beating the Canadians in hockey," said team member (and insurance salesman) Bob Cleary, "would be like Canada beating us in baseball." But just like in 1980, in front of an American crowd of 8,500—this time in Squaw Valley, California—a ragtag team of underdogs pulled off the impossible.

The 1980 team pushed the 1960 out of our collective memory. But all the same miraculous elements were there.

The United States first beat Canada 2–1 in the quarterfinals. Goalie Jack McCartan, an Army member who was also on the 1956 University of Minnesota championship-winning baseball team, made 38 saves. The next match, against the Soviets, was broadcast in full, marking one of the first times any hockey game was televised nationally.

It got off to a rocky start for the Americans—after five minutes, the Soviets led 2–1. In the locker room, coach Jack Riley said, "Everyone in the nation is counting on you guys. There are millions watching you on television." It would take a pair of carpenter brothers from a tiny town in Minnesota to finish it off. Bill Christian, whose son was a member of the 1980 team, scored on a pass from his brother Roger in the second period to tie it. In the third, Bill scored another for the miracle win.

The US team had won silver in 1956, falling to the Soviets in the final round. Though they lost 4–0, it was just 1–0 with five minutes remaining, and the game was competitive. For center John Mayasich, who was on both the 1956 and 1960 squads, this was a much-needed win. "I got my revenge," he said.

After beating the Soviets, the United States next had to take on Czechoslovakia to earn a gold. Down 4–3 after two periods, the United States got an unexpected visit from Nik Sologubov, the Soviet captain, who convinced the team to take some hits from an oxygen tank to recover faster. (The helpful gesture wasn't exactly a Cold War detente; the Soviets needed a United States win to have a chance at silver.) The Americans scored six goals in the third to win it all.

The 1960 US Hockey team took down the mighty Soviets, yet their upset was mostly forgotten after similar heroics 20 years later.

The improbable gold medal has been dubbed the "Forgotten Miracle." And yet all the same elements are there as they were in 1980: An unknown group of players led by a demanding coach; a hometown audience to cheer them on; a goalie playing on another level; a victory over the Soviets in the semis followed by a come-from-behind win in the gold medal game. And it was all at the height of the Cold War.

Sadly, the 1980 team all but pushed the 1960 squad out of our collective memory. Part of it, to be sure, is that hockey had simply become more popular in America by then. There were just six NHL teams in 1960, and most of those players were from Canada. By 1980, there were 21 teams, plus the World Hockey Association.

Maybe it was just luck. But the Forgotten Miracle deserves to be remembered and admired. For this team's accomplishments were just as miraculous as the ones 20 years later.

THE BEST HOCKEY PLAYER YOU'VE NEVER HEARD OF

John Mayasich, the leader of the 1960 US hockey team, is one of the great hockey stars lost to history. "If you were to name an all-time American team," said teammate Bob Cleary, "he'd be on it, either as a forward or a defenseman." Mayasich entered the 1960 Games as a 26-year-old father of four, with another on the way. During the week, he worked in sales for a Green Bay television station. In the first game of the tournament, against the Czechs, he scored a hat trick. He then racked up five goals in a 12–1 drubbing of Australia.

"He had a great shot and was a tremendous playmaker and skater," said Herb Brooks, who was one of the last cuts on the 1960 team. "But what set him apart was that he was the smartest hockey player I've been around. He was subtle, like a great chess master, and he made players around him better. It was like he saw the game in slow motion."

Mayasich never made it to the NHL and barely played professionally, preferring to stay with the local Green Bay Bobcats, an amateur squad. Even so, he was inducted into the US Hockey Hall of Fame in 1976.

2

LEGENDS

For all the pageantry, the Olympics are about one thing: winning. What's the point of entering if you're not going to make every effort to finish first? With 18,588 medals awarded across 28 Summer Olympics and 23 Winter Olympics to date, some winners come out of nowhere and are never heard from again. But for an elite group of medalists, winning becomes routine, a quadrennial exercise in athletic domination. Those special athletes make easy and lasting work of their opponents, carving their names in Olympic lore.

Legends are born every four years, and if they keep it up, their names become known forever. The more recent Games have belonged to stars like Simone Biles, Usain Bolt, and Michael Phelps. But continually finishing first isn't a phenomenon exclusive to the twenty-first century. The early Games, for instance, were filled with luminaries covered in medals—they often aren't well known but should be.

Accounts of these athletes aren't made-up stories of yore meant as myth. These record-shattering legends were real.

MICHAEL PHELPS
The Greatest Racer Who Ever Walked the Planet

USA | SWIMMING | 28 MEDALS | 1985–

SYDNEY 2000 • ATHENS 2004 • BEIJING 2008 • LONDON 2012 • RIO 2016

Walking out to the pool deck at the Indiana University Natatorium, a 15-year-old Michael Phelps—with braces on his bottom teeth and DMX blasting through his headphones—made his debut into the world. Already a prodigy, Phelps turned heads by qualifying for the 2000 Games at such a young age. He became the youngest male in 68 years to make the US swim team since 13-year-old Ralph Flanagan, who had competed in the 1,500-meter freestyle semifinals in 1932. With his second-place finish in the 200-meter butterfly at the trials, Phelps made his first move in the ultimate Olympic career.

After defeating defending champion Denis Pankratov of Russia in the first heat, and finishing in fifth place in the final—with a time of 1:56.50 that would've earned silver or gold at every previous Olympics—Phelps proved himself a competitor beyond his years. (Though, it must be said, he was still a 15-year-old kid. While at the Olympic Village, young Michael burned one

Phelps at the 2016 US Olympic trials

of his video games because he didn't know about the electricity conversion in Australia. He also accidentally took his roommate's credentials before the final and showed up to the pool an hour late.)

A few months later, Phelps would become the youngest male to break a world record, the start of the most impressive Olympic career in history. He began with eight medals in Athens, six of which were gold, and then went on to complete the most dominant single-Games performance in history in Beijing. He won eight gold medals that Olympics, breaking Mark Spitz's record of seven in 1972. "Epic," said Spitz after Phelps tied the record. "It goes to show you that not only is this guy the greatest swimmer of all time and the greatest Olympian of all time, he's maybe the greatest athlete of all time. He's the greatest racer who ever walked the planet."

Phelps would retire after the 2016 Games with more Olympic medals than anyone in history—23 golds and 28 medals in all. He would become a modern-day Poseidon (perhaps without the temper), the iconic athletic superstar of the twenty-first century, the man whose body was practically suited for water—pterodactyl-sized arms, seal-like flippers—and had a competitive drive to boot. If the original Greek Olympics were meant to honor godlike figures, then here was God on Earth, who came to us in the form of a wiry kid from Baltimore, bopping along to DMX.

THE GREEK PHELPS: LEONIDAS OF RHODES

When Michael Phelps won his 13th individual gold medal in 2016, he broke a long-standing record. How long? Try more than 2,000 years.

Leonidas of Rhodes was the original dominant Olympian. In four consecutive Olympics from 164 to 152 BC, he won three races in each—the *stade* (about 200 meters long), the *diaulos* (about 400 meters), and the *armor* (a run while wearing, yes, armor). Usain Bolt, of course, completed his triple-triple in 2016: three golds in three races in three Olympics (before one gold was stripped). But Leonidas one-upped him. He was an elite distance runner and sprinter, something unheard of at the time. Not much else is known about the ancient champion, but a statue of him in the town of Rhodes reads, "He had the speed of a god."

SHIRLEY BABASHOFF
Wrongly Vilified

USA | SWIMMING | 9 MEDALS | 1957–

MUNICH 1972 • MONTREAL 1976

When Shirley Babashoff walked during the opening ceremony at the 1976 Games in Montreal, she had every reason to be confident. The 19-year-old California-raised swimmer had already won two gold medals and two silvers at the 1972 Games. Tabbed as the "Female Mark Spitz," Babashoff was even featured on the cover of *Sports Illustrated* before the start of the Olympics.

But all that confidence shattered when she looked across the pool and saw her fearsome competitors from East Germany. "It was just the visual of seeing these women looking like shot-putters and wrestlers," she said. "We didn't really know what was going on."

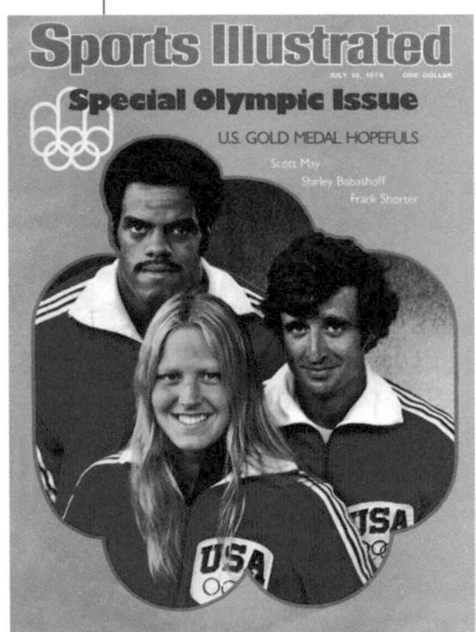

Babashoff was supposed to be one of the Golden Girls of the Games, appearing on the cover of Sports Illustrated.

Here's what was going on: The East Germans, including the female swim team, were part of a systematic, state-sponsored doping campaign. Under "state plan theme 14-25," as many as 10,000 athletes of all sports from 1976 to 1988 were given testosterone in pill form, which had a huge effect on female athletes both in performance and in appearance. Volleyball player Katharina Bullin, who won a silver medal in the 1980 Summer Games, said, "I didn't start to look like a man overnight, it happened gradually. I wasn't really aware of it myself but it was obvious to everyone else."

It was clear to Babashoff, too. She noticed the different physiques in the locker room, and when a reporter asked her about the East Germans, she said, "Well, except for their

"Surly Shirley" became better known for her divisive comments than her Olympic success in the pool.

DOPING: A HISTORY

Performance enhancing—drugs or otherwise—has been around since time immemorial. Norse warriors, known as berserkers, drank a concoction called *butotens* to amp them up before fights. The world of British endurance walking was awash with drugs in the nineteenth century. (Don't laugh, the races were up to 500 miles long!) They took opium or nitroglycerine to stay awake and to improve their breathing.

While ancient Olympian chariot racers were reported to have imbibed herbal infusions before races, awareness of doping wasn't widespread outside the sporting realm until Danish cyclist Knud Enemark Jensen died at the 1960 Games in Rome. Feeling dizzy in the 104-degree heat, Jensen collapsed during a time trial road race and hit his skull on the pavement. He never regained consciousness. An autopsy report showed amphetamine and Roniacol—both administered by the team trainer—in his system. Eight years later, the first drug testing took place at the 1968 Games in Mexico City. Since then, doping (and getting caught for it) has become commonplace.

The biggest doping scandal, however, came after Sochi. A highly coordinated state-sponsored operation saw Russia lab techs swap out tainted urine samples for clean ones. They covered up 643 positive samples over four years, including 139 in track and field and 117 in weightlifting. That led to the Russian Olympic Committee and its athletes being banned from the 2018 Winter Olympics. But it came with a catch: The IOC allowed 169 Russian athletes to compete as neutral "Olympic Athletes from Russia." They won 17 medals.

deep voices and mustaches, I think they'll do fine." Though Babashoff's intuition was right, her candid comments were seen as a major faux pas. She was called "Surly Shirley," and USA Swimming apologized by sending a bouquet of flowers to the East Germans.

The doping program proved extremely successful in the pool. The women's swim team won 11 of 13 events, including four in which Babashoff competed. She won silver in the 200-, 400-, and 800-meter freestyles and in the 4 x 100 medley. Babashoff's performance, along with her comments before the races, led some to label her, as *Time* magazine so harshly put it, a "loser." She did, however, find glory in one race. She was the anchor in the 4 x 100 freestyle relay team, which defeated the East Germans and set a new world record by four seconds.

After the fall of the Berlin Wall, unsealed records from the Stasi, the secret state police, revealed the inner workings of the doping program. Babashoff was vindicated—and bitter. "They took a lot away from me," she said later. "And I can't just let that go." In 2005, she received the Olympic Order, an award given to people who display Olympic ideals through their actions. Babashoff was cheated out of four gold medals, and out of the prestige that comes with being an all-time Olympian. But her obvious swim talent and the strength of her convictions allow her to live on in Olympic lore.

LARISA LATYNINA
Beyond Confident

SOVIET UNION | GYMNASTICS | 18 MEDALS | 1934–

MELBOURNE 1956 • ROME 1960 • TOKYO 1964

She's always been there at the top of the record books, but the most successful female Olympian of all time—and until 2012, the most successful Olympian, period—has long remained a bit of a mystery.

One historian described Larisa Latynina as a "phantom." She reached her apex before television blasted the Games across the world and gymnastics became prime-time, must-see TV. And she was part of a Soviet machine that favored the collective, not the individual. But to Latynina, the whole thing is a bit baffling. How is she not more popular? "If you want to know the greatest of all time," the winningest gymnast ever once said, "the first thing you look at is how many medals they have won."

Confidence aside, Latynina's track record at the Games is unmatched. At her first Olympics in 1956 in Melbourne, the 21-year-old won six medals, including four golds. Four years later, she won six medals in Rome, three of them gold, and repeated as the all-around champion. In Tokyo in 1964, her final Olympics, she again won six medals, this time with two golds.

Latynina finished her career that year with nine gold medals, which means she is tied with Carl Lewis, Paavo Nurmi, and Mark Spitz for the second-most golds of all time. (Michael Phelps has the most, with 23.) She held the record for most total medals (18) for 48 years, until Phelps broke it in 2012. After her career in competition ended, she became the Soviet coach, helping gymnasts to 10 combined gold medals at the Mexico City, Munich, and Montreal Games. "I have trained 10 Olympic medalists," she said. "Let Phelps remember that."

Latynina has mostly stayed out of the spotlight. But get her to talk, and the hits keep coming. What are her thoughts on nine-time medalist Nadia Comaneci? "Comaneci was a great gymnast, make no mistake about it, but she only won one Olympic all-around title while I won [two]. And that's a fact, not fiction." How was her medal mark able to stand for so long? "This was not down to my feats, but was due to the inability of those sportsmen who competed after me," she said. Ouch.

Latynina is famous in Russia, but much of the rest of the world found her

LEFT: *Latynina, the winningest gymnast of all time, might have also been the most arrogant.*

again only in 2012, when Phelps entered the London Games just three medals shy of her record. While she acknowledged that Phelps was deserving of the record, she was also happy to know that another record of hers was still secure: Among women, she will most likely remain number one for a very long time.

Latynina had the perfect mix of skills. She was absurdly talented and insanely successful. She was incredibly brash and outspoken. Had she competed today, she would've been cast in America as the great Russian enemy. Instead, her Games weren't televised, and a generation of Olympic fans has to be asking, "How did we miss out on her?"

MARIT BJØRGEN
The Winter Olympics Queen

NORWAY | CROSS-COUNTRY SKIING | 15 MEDALS | 1980–

SALT LAKE 2002 • TURIN 2006 • VANCOUVER 2010 • SOCHI 2014 • PYEONGCHANG 2018

Here's what it takes to become the most decorated athlete in Winter Olympic history: around 940 hours of exercise per year, a whole lot of squats, intense dedication, and meticulous record keeping.

When researchers examined 17 years of training records from Marit Bjørgen, the cross-country skier who retired after the 2018 Winter Olympics with an astounding 15 medals, they found that longer but less strenuous sessions were the key. Bjørgen shared her workout diaries with scientists at two Norwegian universities, giving them the first-ever detailed look at the exercise habits of a female endurance athlete. Bjørgen's method clearly worked, as measured by not only the races she won, but also by the surprising number of blog posts that honor her bulging biceps.

Bjørgen made her World Cup debut in 1999 and won her first race on the circuit in 2000. Two years later she won a silver in the 4 x 5 km relay at the Salt Lake City Games. In 2006, she took home another silver in Turin, this time as an individual in the 10 km classical, although she was suffering from bronchitis, and was a part of the first 4 x 5 Norwegian team to not medal since 1988.

Already a successful cross-country skier by any reasonable standard, Bjørgen made a major change before the 2010 Vancouver Games that resulted in record-breaking success. She mixed up her training regimen, increasing the number of hours she worked out from 520 to 940 per year (roughly 2.5 per day), and ditched the quick-hit training sessions she had once relied on. She then started winning on a whole other level.

Bjørgen collected three gold medals in Vancouver, as well as a silver and a bronze. In Sochi, she again won three gold medals. She finished her career in Pyeongchang with two more golds, a silver, and two bronzes to bring her

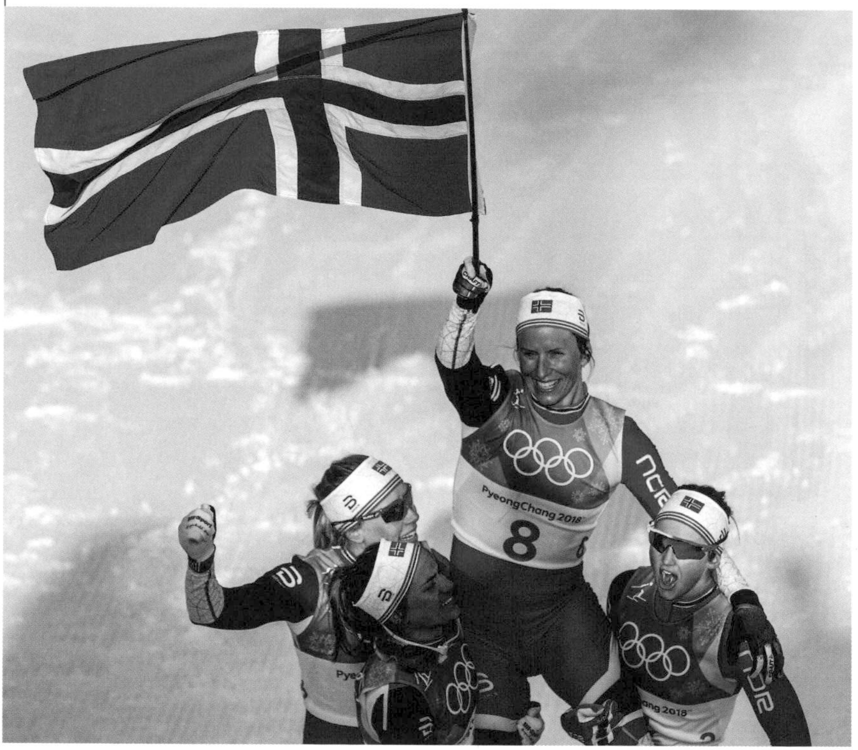

Bjørgen celebrates her final win in the 30 km with her fellow countrywomen.

total medal count to 15. Her last race was in the 30 km, where she won by a comfortable 1:49.5 margin. “It would be difficult to imagine a better ending,” the Norwegian newspaper *Aftenposten* wrote. “This was the perfect finish to the Olympics . . . We have run out of superlatives.”

She passed fellow countryman Ole Einar Bjørndalen for most medals won by a winter athlete, and is tied for third-most medals of all time. Her eight gold medals are also tied for third, and she is the second-most decorated female athlete ever. After stepping away from the sport in 2018, the tributes to Bjørgen poured in across Norway. “She was terribly important to me,” said Therese Johaug, a seven-time world champion. “She was my idol.” Said Jens Stoltenberg, former prime minister and current NATO secretary general, “You have been a source of inspiration and a role model, you made us jump with joy and scream with excitement.”

Now that Bjørgen is retired, surely her workout routine has taken a bit of a backseat. But her reign as most-decorated Winter Olympian will remain front and center.

CROSS-COUNTRY-CRAZED

The US women’s team won their first gold, and only the second medal ever in American history, in cross-country skiing at the 2018 Games. And all things considered, it was a big deal. But there’s a reason that you’re probably scratching your head trying to remember what happened. Cross-country skiing is simply not that popular in America.

In Nordic countries, however, the sport is one of the most watched and talked about. Makes sense, considering it was created in Scandinavia. In Norway, in particular, the sport is king. Johannes Klaebo, who won three gold medals at age 21 in 2018, is a superstar. He was called the Justin Bieber of Norway. He’s on the cover of magazines. A book was written about his relationship with his grandfather, who is also his coach and best friend.

Let’s just say this: As great as their victory was, Kikkan Randall and Jessie Diggins won’t have any books written about their grandparents. Oh, you don’t know those names? That’s right, they are the American women who made history in Pyeongchang. Looks like we’ve got some studying up to do.

RYAN LOCHTE
The Ultimate Bro-lympian

USA | SWIMMING | 12 MEDALS | 1984–

ATHENS 2004 • BEIJING 2008 • LONDON 2012 • RIO 2016

Who is Ryan Lochte? Is he the diamond-grilled, rap-loving bro who attempted to trademark his own catchphrase *jeah*? (Definition: an emphatic "yeah.") Is he the swimmer who was once the world's best, even over Michael Phelps? Is he the twelve-time medalist, the 21-time world champion, the five-time world record holder? Is he the guy with the silver hair, the reality TV flameout, the one who sparked an international crisis over whether he was robbed at gunpoint or defaced a gas station bathroom?

One of the world's greatest swimmers seems better known as a troublemaking bro-incarnate.

He's all those things, which make up the enigma that is Ryan Lochte. Over four Olympics, he became the 22nd-most-decorated Olympian ever, and the sixth-best American. His swimming exploits are legendary. But if he hadn't been born a year before Michael Phelps, Lochte would surely be one of the most famous Olympians of all time. He's won just one out of four head-to-head matchups against the "Baltimore Bullet," and 10 of Lochte's 12 medals came when Phelps was in the same race. He is, it seems, unable to escape Phelps's shadow.

Lochte's legacy is also forever tied up in the infamous early morning events of August 14, 2016, in Rio de Janeiro. He told American media that he and teammates Jimmy Feigen, Jack Conger, and Gunnar Bentz had been held up at gunpoint by robbers posing as police officers while at a gas station. That, at least initially, made him a sympathetic figure. But then, after Lochte had already left the country, Brazilian officials removed Conger and Bentz from a flight back home and seized their passports. The owner of the gas station said that the drunken swimmers had broken a soap dispenser, damaged a door, and urinated all over the property. Lochte insisted that they had committed no vandalism and that his version of the story was true.

Then Lochte changed his tune. Two weeks after the initial claim, he finally admitted to making it all up while still intoxicated. The unsavory affair was called #LochteGate. Members of the US swim team were upset. Maya DiRado, who won four gold medals, said, "We wish that that hadn't taken attention away from our week of swimming because it was a phenomenal week for Team USA and US swimming."

Lochte didn't stay quiet after the incident. Shortly after his admission, he was announced as a member of *Dancing with the Stars*. (Protesters made their way onto the dance floor during his debut.) He would later appear on *Celebrity Big Brother*. To make matters worse, in July 2018, he was suspended for 14 months for receiving a "prohibited intravenous infusion." Though Lochte denied it, in a less-than-genius move he had posted a picture on Instagram of himself receiving an infusion of what he claimed were vitamins.

Ultimately, we'll think of Lochte as the drunk jock who got wasted one night in Rio and then lied to cover it up. The fact that he was one of America's best-ever swimmers, one of the world's greatest, and a legitimate star, seems to fall by the wayside. He will be, it seems, forever cursed by two afflictions, one his own and the other external: that he's bro-personified and that Michael Phelps competed during the same time he did.

Lochte (right) would've been considered one of the best ever if he hadn't had to constantly face Phelps (left).

MARK SPITZ
The Original Golden Boy

USA | SWIMMING | 11 MEDALS | 1950–

MEXICO CITY 1968 • MUNICH 1972

The picture is iconic: the mustache full, the smile wide, the seven gold medals dangling on an Adonis-like body covered only by a skimpy red, white, and blue swimsuit. This is Mark Spitz at the height of his fame and powers, the golden boy, the one who did the impossible. He parlayed those two unforgettable weeks at the Munich Games in 1972 to fame unheard of for any Olympian. He earned endorsements worth $7 million. He appeared with Bob Hope and Sonny and Cher. He hawked for Schick and for the dairy industry. That gloriously kitschy photo became instantly recognizable.

What did that kind of fame cost, though? What did it take from him, both then and now?

The backstory for this all-American hero isn't so tidy. He spent every waking moment of his childhood training for an ideal that seemed almost impossible to attain. At the direction of his hard-to-please father, Arnold, young Mark was swimming for an hour and a half every day by age 10. Swimming itself wasn't even the goal. It was something more than that: a vision, an ideal, a dream of winning at all costs.

"I'm not out to lose," Arnold Spitz once said. "I never said to him, 'You're second, that's great.' I told him I didn't care about winning age-groups, I care for world records." There's a lot of *I* in that statement, as if it were Arnold's body accelerating through the Olympic pool. Or as if it were Arnold who had the hyperextended knee that gave him more power and propulsion in the butterfly, which Mark's coach, Ron Ballatore, called "one of the greatest butterfly strokes of all time."

But it was Mark who dealt with the inhuman expectations of trying to win six gold medals in Mexico City in 1968. The 18-year-old was only human, of course. He won just two, both in relays. He finished last—*dead last*—in the 200-meter butterfly, an event in which he held the world record. His

This 1972 photo of Spitz instantly became one of the most iconic images of the Olympic era.

teammates from his Santa Clara swim club were happy he didn't win. Spitz was the spoiled brat, the cocky kid with the demanding father.

How do you recover when two gold medals—a dream come true for most people—is the ultimate disappointment? You move. Spitz left California and his father's demands, spurning Long Beach State to attend Indiana University. During his freshman year in 1969, he won three events at the NCAA championships and set two American records. He finally, somehow, seemed to enjoy himself. "He fights for the team as much as he does for himself now," said his coach, James Counsilman. "The kids all like him. He's actually learned to smile and laugh."

Maybe that was it. Maybe it was discovering a love for the sport, the joy of being in the pool, and now, the true winning could commence. And what winning it was. Not only did Spitz win all seven events he entered at the infamous 1972 Munich Games (100-meter butterfly, 100-meter freestyle, 200-meter butterfly, 200-meter freestyle, and three relays), but he also set world records in each of them. He simply dominated in a way that hadn't been seen before.

In a dark and tragic turn of events, however, Spitz's accomplishments were overshadowed just hours after winning his final gold medal. The Palestinian terrorist group Black September took 11 members of the Israeli delegation hostage in the Olympic village, later murdering them after a failed rescue attempt by West German police. Spitz, himself a Jewish athlete, was quickly flown out of the country during the hostage negotiations for fear of a kidnapping or another attack. It was a bittersweet two weeks at the Games, and in many ways his Olympic legacy and the Munich massacre are forever intertwined.

Spitz dominated the pool in Munich, even if political terror captured headlines.

After the dust settled, Spitz capitalized on his Olympic fame, turning it into a wildly successful career. He took advantage of the wide variety of media available to him, and in particular, color photos in magazines. "It depends on looks," he said quite candidly. "I mean, I've never seen a magazine of uglies. That's our society. I'm not saying it's right. That's just the facts."

After his initial burst of fame, Spitz mostly stayed out of the limelight. He made an ill-fated attempt at a comeback in 1992 at age 42 and finished a whopping two seconds slower than the qualifying time (though his times were on par with his marks from 1972). He went on to start a successful real estate company in Beverly Hills, California.

Was it worth it? Was the grueling training from an early age, the win-or-die ethos his father instilled in him, worth the medals and the fame? Perhaps. But there must be a part of him—maybe small, but certainly there—that wishes that his Olympic fame after 1972 would fade and he could fulfill his longtime dream: becoming a dentist. (Seriously.) "I wanted to be a dentist from the time I was in high school," he said, "but after the Olympics there were other opportunities."

Spitz never did go back to dental school. But as he said, he did very well for himself, thank you very much. Maybe missing out on dentistry wasn't the worst thing.

DARA TORRES
The Ageless Olympian

USA | SWIMMING | 12 MEDALS | 1967–

LOS ANGELES 1984 • SEOUL 1988 • BARCELONA 1992 • SYDNEY 2000 • BEIJING 2008

The beginning of Dara Torres's career was enough for a lifetime, but the incredible display of athleticism and endurance at the end of her career made it legendary. At the start of her 24-year Olympic journey, Torres won her first gold medal in 1984 in Los Angeles in the 4 x 100 freestyle relay. She was 17. She kept on winning, first in college at Florida, collecting nine national championships. In 1988 in Seoul, Torres won two more medals. She won yet another gold in Barcelona in 1992. And then she retired.

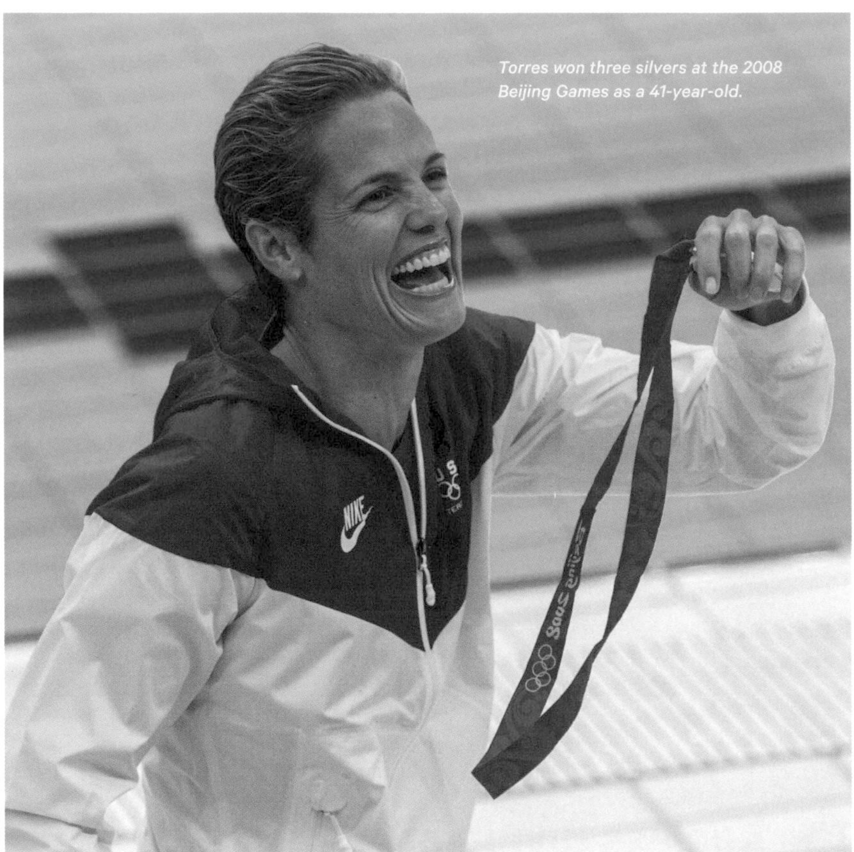
Torres won three silvers at the 2008 Beijing Games as a 41-year-old.

Torres was just 25. She didn't swim competitively for seven years, focusing instead on a burgeoning modeling career. But that itch was still there. "I couldn't get it out of my head," she said. It's a good thing she couldn't—Torres won five more medals in Sydney in 2000, including two relay golds and three individual bronzes. This time, surely, would be enough.

After those Games in Sydney, which were supposed to be her last—for real this time—she cried on the way to the mandatory urine test following her final race, facing the uncertainty of what was next. But then 2008 came around. Maybe it would *never* be enough. And the 41-year-old was feeling that itch again. She won the 100-meter freestyle at the US trials, becoming the first

American swimmer to compete in five Olympics and the oldest female swimmer in Olympics history.

Before the Games, she broke an American record in the 50-meter freestyle and became one of only five women to swim the event in less than 24 seconds. "I can't sit here and lie and say, 'Oh, I'm just glad I'm going'," she said. "I want to win a medal."

To ensure she won that medal, Torres invested a lot of time and money. Her team included a head coach, a sprint coach, a strength coach, and even two stretchers, two masseuses, and a chiropractor. Torres had shed 12 pounds in the years after Sydney and spent time doing weight training and resistance stretching.

"I know the water doesn't know what age we are."

Her elaborate routine worked. She won three medals, including a silver in the 50-meter freestyle, and became the oldest swimmer to win a medal in Olympic history. In that 50 meters, she set an American record, trailing the winner by only .01 seconds. "Age is just a number," she said. "When we're in the water, I know the water doesn't know what age we are."

Torres didn't retire immediately after the Games. She won the 50-meter freestyle at the US Championships, and was set to compete for the 2012 Olympics. But it wasn't to be. At age 45, she finished fourth in the 50 meter at the US trials, .04 seconds shy of qualifying. After 28 years of competing, Dana Torres's Olympic career came to an end. "This," she said, "is really over."

THE OLDEST OLYMPIAN

The oldest-ever Olympian did his best work on the canvas. No, not in the boxing or wrestling ring, but with a paintbrush. At a ripe 73 years old, John Copley won silver in the mixed paintings, graphic arts competition at the 1948 Summer Olympics in London, for a work titled *Polo Players*. Makes sense, given that painting isn't the most demanding athletic activity. That's not to take anything away from all the others who suited up for competition in their golden years. Like Oscar Swahn, a 72-year-old shooter in 1920. Or Arthur Von Pongracz, who finished fourth in equestrian at age 72 in 1936. Go, Gramps!

CARL OSBURN
The Quiet One

USA | SHOOTING | 11 MEDALS | 1884–1966

STOCKHOLM 1912 • ANTWERP 1920 • PARIS 1924

5 4 2

He's the best shooter of all time and one of the most decorated Olympians in history. And yet Carl Osburn's myriad competitive accomplishments and distinguished naval career have all kind of just faded away. Maybe it's because he was quiet himself. After all, a 1907 entry in the Naval Academy yearbook described him thusly: "Once made a speech of ten words, but as his roommate fainted, he hasn't tried it since. . . . Never known to show much excitement over anything."

Even details about Osburn's life were off. He was called "Deadshot Cy, the Jacksonville Wonder"—but he grew up in Jackson*town*, Ohio. So he was a man of few words, but it seemed to work for him. By all accounts a remarkable shooter, Osburn was a captain in the navy and served on ships until 1945, when he retired, living out his days in California. He died in 1966, at age 82.

But here's the rub: Shooting, both then and now, never gets much attention at the Olympics. It's a complicated and technical sport, with 15 events featuring three different types of guns, all at varying distances and angles as competitors

LEFT: *"Deadshot Cy" poses with his rifle in 1920.*

try to hit bull's-eyes or even fake clay pigeons. Most of a spectator's time is spent watching shooters slow their heart rate through breathing and concentration to achieve perfect accuracy. Indeed, their heart rate becomes so slow that they fire between beats.

So while shooting never became all that popular among the viewing public, Osburn certainly should have enjoyed the attention befitting his staggering medal count. Starting in 1912 in Stockholm, he would go on to win 11 medals over three Games. His best performance was in Antwerp in 1920, when he collected four gold medals, a silver, and a bronze. He is still the most successful shooter of all time, and his 11 medals stood as the most won by an American until Mark Spitz tied him in 1972.

Olympic icons from 1912 don't always get their due. But Carl Osburn remains one of America's—and the world's—top Olympians. We may not know much about his life. We should at least know that.

CARL LEWIS
The Polarizing Star

USA | TRACK AND FIELD | 10 MEDALS | 1961–

LOS ANGELES 1984 • SEOUL 1988 • BARCELONA 1992 • ATLANTA 1996

If you're trying to pick the best pure athlete to ever compete in the Olympics, you should probably stop looking when you reach Carl Lewis.

The track and field star won nine Olympic gold medals, and 10 total, across two disciplines in Games stretching from 1984 to 1996. He's held world records in the 100-meter sprint and the long jump. He had 65 consecutive wins in the long jump over 10 years. He is one of only three athletes who has won a gold medal in the same event—long jump—in four consecutive Olympics. (And that might've been five had the United States not boycotted the 1980 Games in Moscow.) Or consider this: At one point he had 16 of the best 30 long jumps in history. He anchored six—*six!*—world-record-setting 4 x 100 relay teams.

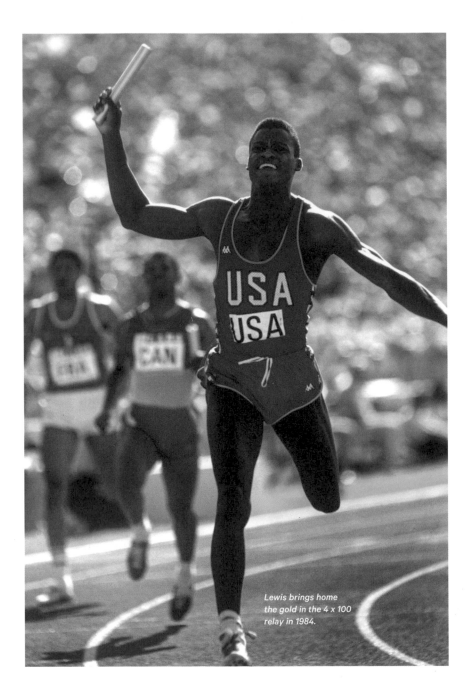

Lewis brings home the gold in the 4 x 100 relay in 1984.

It's no wonder, then, that pro teams from other sports wanted to get in on the action. In 1984, the Chicago Bulls selected Lewis in the 10th round as the 208th pick—they didn't seem to mind that he had never played high school or college basketball. (Give the Bulls some credit, however, for also picking Michael Jordan that year, making their 1984 draft perhaps the most athletically spectacular of all time.) Then the gridiron came calling when the Dallas Cowboys selected Lewis as a wide receiver in the 12th and final round of the NFL draft in 1984. (Fortunately, Lewis stuck to track.)

And maybe it shouldn't surprise us that all of this dazzling athleticism was met with, well, disdain. "He rubs it in too much," said Edwin Moses, a two-time gold medalist in the 400-meter hurdles. "A little humility is in order. That's what Carl lacks." Lewis was described as aloof. He was perceived as above everything, better than you, and never grateful. He was the greatest, the Alpha, the Omega. As one Nike representative put it: "He was arrogant." As Lewis himself admitted, he was good and he knew it. "There are going to be some absolutely unheard-of things coming from me," he predicted in 1992. But in his defense, he did some pretty unheard-of stuff.

Even with his out-of-this-world Olympic success, however, Lewis failed to secure even one major ad campaign in the United States. Coca-Cola, which Lewis initially turned down, rescinded their offer after the 1984 Games. Nike, his original sponsor, openly acknowledged they didn't like his over-the-top, outspoken, flamboyant image. "If you're a male athlete," the Nike rep said, "I think the American public wants you to look macho." But that just wasn't Lewis. He was over-the-top and in your face. He was lightning-quick, not ultra-strong. He wasn't a "man's man." And so, perhaps his arrogance wasn't as palatable because it didn't come in a familiar form for Americans. (He did, however, have significant success as a spokesman in Europe and, especially, Japan. His overseas endorsement money earned him seven figures.)

For many people, the indelible image of Carl Lewis is not of him jumping farther or running faster, but rather his 1993 rendition—or butchering—of the national anthem before an NBA Finals game. One ESPN host couldn't contain his laughter on-air, calling him "Francis Scott Off-Key." Lewis, for his part, is glad it happened. "It's a part of your journey," he said.

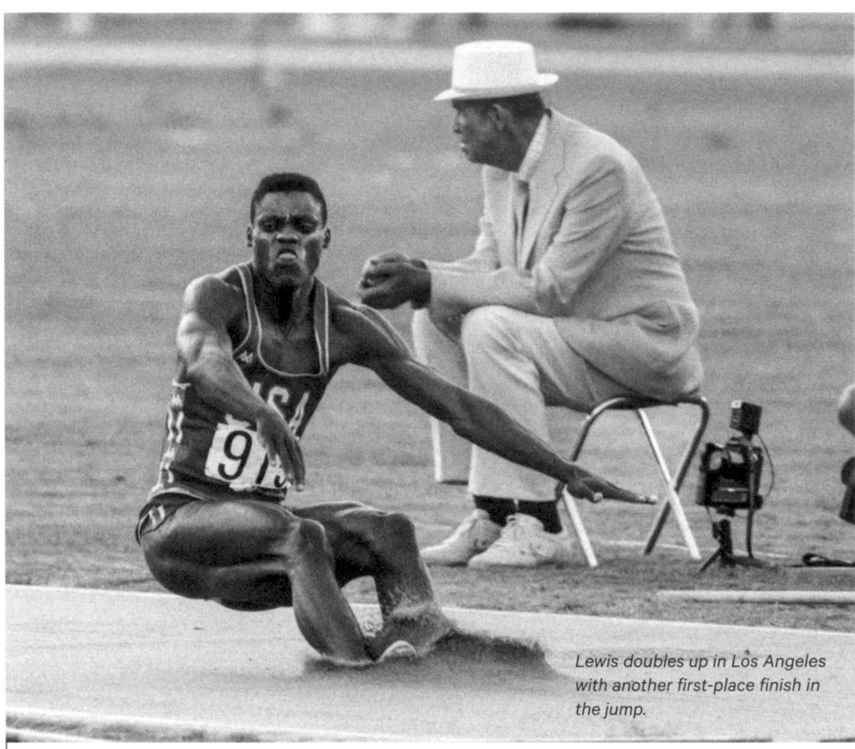
Lewis doubles up in Los Angeles with another first-place finish in the jump.

Lewis tried bringing attention to his running through other means. He appeared in movies and TV, both as himself and as an actor, and ran unsuccessfully for state senate in New Jersey. He now coaches at his alma mater, the University of Houston.

For the man who wasn't accepted, who wasn't loved, who wasn't macho enough, Lewis seemingly tried everything to earn that acceptance. And while many athletes have varied interests, Lewis's activities had a throw-it-against-the-wall-and-see-what-sticks attitude to it. None of it, though, really stuck. It's probably a good thing that Lewis tries to look forward. "I'm not so much moved by winning," he once said, "especially winning things I've won before, as I am by a new challenge." In that regard, Lewis has succeeded—even if he never quite won again.

OLYMPIAN POLITICIANS

Well, **Carl Lewis** didn't quite make it in politics, but the Olympics can be a springboard to higher office. **Bill Bradley** won a gold medal in basketball in 1964, and after a successful NBA career, served nearly 20 years in the Senate. **Tom McMillen** also played Olympic hoops, parlaying a silver medal in 1972 to a three-term stint as a representative from Maryland. Two-time decathlon gold medalist **Bob Mathias** served four congressional terms as a representative from California, and **Ralph Metcalfe,** part of the 4 x 100 gold-medal-winning relay team with Jesse Owens in Berlin, was a representative from Illinois. And it doesn't have to be elective office: two-time medalist **Michelle Kwan** was named as a senior adviser for public diplomacy and public affairs for the US State Department.

Figure skater Michelle Kwan on Capitol Hill

GARY HALL JR.
The Chilled-Out Olympian

USA | SWIMMING | 10 MEDALS | 1974–

ATLANTA 1996 • SYDNEY 2000 • ATHENS 2004

Gary Hall Jr. didn't stare down his opponents before races; he wasn't all-business like many of his teammates. No, Gary Hall Jr. had a chilled-out vibe going on. Before the 1996 Summer Olympics in Atlanta, he bought a bass guitar, hoping to memorize Funkadelic's "Cosmic Slop." He wore tie-dyed shirts, bell-bottoms, and lime-colored suits. The self-described Deadhead said he wanted to "take a year off after Atlanta and just follow the Grateful Dead around the country." He's that offbeat, what's-he-smoking dude in the pool.

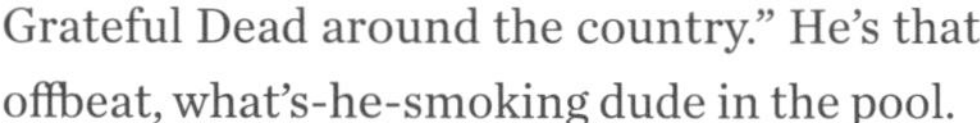

But Hall had quite a legacy to follow. His father, Gary Hall Sr., won three medals over three Olympics—but never gold. "Gary has always had to carry a lot more baggage than the rest of us," said Troy Dalbey, a gold-medal-winning swimmer and Hall's coach. "I mean, Matt Biondi's dad is an insurance salesman. My dad's a chiropractor."

Hall Sr., it should be noted, was one of the golden boys of USA Swimming. He just had the bad fortune to be going at the same time as Mark Spitz. And, by his own admission, he choked in Mexico City in his best race, the 400-meter individual medley. "It was a panic, like an impending death," he said. "By the time I hit 200 meters, I was paralyzed with fear.

LEFT: *Hall's laid-back vibe didn't prevent him from cleaning up in the medal department.*

Hall Jr. also had to follow in the gigantic footsteps of his grandfather, Charles Keating, an NCAA championship swimmer in the 1940s who later made a fortune in real estate. But he's probably best known for his role in the savings and loan scandal in the 1980s that saw five US senators accused of corruption. Growing up outside of Phoenix, Hall Jr. was very close with his grandfather. The two would often race at the 25-yard pool at the family house. When Hall was still a teenager, his grandfather was sent to prison. Keating served four and a half years before his conviction was overturned.

When Hall finally made it to the Olympics in 1996—the Big One, as he called it—he performed well. He swam the fastest 100-meter split in history in the United States' relay win in the 4 x 100, but lost in the 100-meter freestyle by .07 seconds. The intervening years between Atlanta and Sydney were difficult for Hall. In 1998, he was suspended for three months after testing positive for marijuana. He was dropped by his sponsor, Speedo. In 1999, he got a diagnosis of diabetes. He injected himself with insulin up to eight times a day and took blood sugar readings every 30 minutes.

The colorfully dressed Deadhead surpassed his family's legacy and rocked the pool in Sydney.

Though difficult, it may have been a blessing in disguise: He had to learn perseverance. It paid off. Hall won gold in the 50-meter freestyle (in a tie with teammate Anthony Ervin) and won another gold in the 4 x 100 medley. Four years later, in Athens, he won again in the 50-free, despite living up to his free-spirit reputation by dressing in stars-and-stripes-decorated boxing trunks, which earned him a $5,000 fine from USA Swimming. (No word on whether it was a violation for being too patriotic.) "Very few people have been able to defend their Olympic title," he said. "I'm proud to be part of a very small class."

Hall retired in 2008 after just missing a chance at a fourth Olympics, and now works as a diabetes advocate. He's grown up now, no longer the chilled-out guy hanging by the pool, but rather the life-changing adult. And he's got 10 Olympic medals to show for it. Not a bad way to surpass a family legacy.

SIMONE BILES
The Legend in Her Own Time

USA | GYMNASTICS | 5 MEDALS | 1997–

RIO 2016

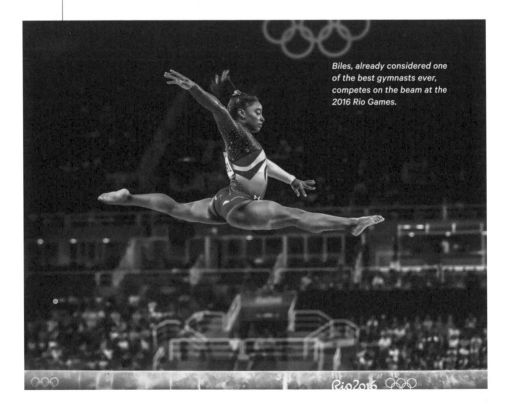

By the 2020 Tokyo Olympics, Simone Biles had already accomplished the following: won four gold medals; collected 14 world championship titles (the most of all time); become one of five gymnasts to win four gold medals at a single Games; become one of six gymnasts to win the all-around title at the World Championships and the Olympics. And, oh yeah, she took off all of 2017.

Biles, already considered one of the best gymnasts ever, competes on the beam at the 2016 Rio Games.

Biles's career story is still being written, but what's been put down on the page thus far is nothing short of extraordinary. She was born in Columbus, Ohio, to a mother who struggled with substance abuse, and Simone and her siblings were placed in foster care. When Biles was three years old, she was adopted by her maternal grandfather, who lived in Houston. She immediately took to the sport after visiting the gym Bannon's Gymnastix on a field trip as a six-year-old. That was a fateful day out—the best gymnast of all time was officially born. "Just when we thought we were at the physical limit of the sport, then here comes Simone Biles," said Mary Lou Retton, who won five medals at the 1984 Games. "She's the best I've ever seen."

It's not just her physical ability—it's that she continually pushes that ability to the limit. At the 2019 national championships, Biles broke out a new move that seemed almost physically impossible. Her triple-double jump—three twists, two flips—had her moving at 14.7 miles per hour and reaching 9.5 feet in the air. This is, according to one physicist who analyzed the jump, at the limit of feasible human performance. Or consider that between 2012 and 2016, the average difficulty rating on each major apparatus was as follows:

BEAMS—5.40 FLOOR—4.97 BARS—5.44 VAULT—4.93

For Biles, the numbers look a little different:

BEAMS—6.36 FLOOR—6.15 BARS—6.02 VAULT—5.56

She is simply obliterating the competition. "If we're talking about domination, nothing like that has ever happened in our sport," said Nadia Comaneci, a nine-time medalist from Romania considered one of the best ever. Biles is extremely talented, yes, but she also uses that talent to establish new norms and new ideas of what's possible.

And here's the best thing: Tokyo doesn't have to be her last Olympics. Larisa Latynina, whose 18 medals are second-most of all time and most among all female Olympians, competed in three Games. Biles has time to catch her yet.

MUHAMMAD ALI
When the Greatest First Reigned

USA | BOXING | 1 MEDAL | 1942–2016

ROME 1960

Before he was the greatest, before impossible became nothing, before he took a stand as a conscientious objector, before he floated like a butterfly and stung like a bee, Cassius Clay was just an 18-year-old hopeful at the Games. And before he could shake up the world and become Muhammad Ali, he had to achieve Olympic glory.

While Ali didn't yet possess the rapid-fire right hook that would make him nearly unbeatable, he came to the 1960 Games in Rome with quick feet and an even quicker wit. Named the unofficial goodwill ambassador for the US team, he was effortlessly charismatic and already being described in heroic terms. One spokesman for the US Olympic Committee said, "In the ring he murders 'em with his fists. Outside the ring he kills them with kindness and his solid Americanism."

Ali first became a worldwide phenomenon at the 1960 Games in Rome.

Ali knew how to answer a question, and he wasn't shy about his opinions. But he still expressed a naïve deference for his country that he would soon shed after becoming a politically active freethinker. Did he like Europe or the United States better? "Europe has many attractions," he said. "But a man loves his own country best. Mine is the USA."

"Mr. Clay, with the intolerance in your country, you must have a lot of problems," one foreign reporter said. "Oh yeah, we've got some problems," Clay replied. "But get this straight—it's still the best country in the world."

Ali posed with 28 Olympic delegations and signed reams of autographs. His personality and force of will were so apparent that even as just an Amateur Athletic Union and Golden Gloves champion, he was already the most popular athlete at the Games. He hadn't even boxed yet! And what about the famous confidence, all that "I'm the greatest" stuff? Yeah, it was there too.

And here's the odd thing: Ali almost didn't make it. Not because he wasn't good enough—he was afraid of flying. The scared teenager begged to travel by boat or train and had to be talked into it. "I convinced him if he wanted to be heavyweight champion of the world, then he had to go to Rome and win the Olympics," his mentor, Joe Martin, told him. Ali even bought a parachute and wore it for the whole flight.

He calmed down once he arrived in Italy. One teammate called him the mayor of the Olympic Village. He breezed through the light heavyweight division tournament, beating defending champ Gennadiy Shatkov of the Soviet Union in the third round in a unanimous decision. In the gold medal final, he "soundly whipped" Polish competitor Ziggy Pietrzykowski, as the *New York Times* put it: "Clay battered the Pole mercilessly in the last round with a flurry of left and right combinations that had his rival groggy. He opened a cut over the Pole's left eye and almost finished him."

Upon his return home, Ali was the toast of the sporting world and he predicted he'd be the heavyweight champion within three years. He was off by just a few months, beating Sonny Liston in February 1964 and shocking the country by changing his name to Muhammad Ali shortly thereafter.

RIGHT: *Ali receives his light heavyweight gold medal in Rome.*

WHO STARTED THE FIRE?

During the ancient Olympics, a sacred fire was kept burning throughout the entirety of the proceedings. The flame burned out for centuries until it was reignited before the 1928 Summer Olympics in Amsterdam. While torches are now lit by an athletic icon from the host country, the Dutch kept things lowkey—an employee from the local electric had the honor.

Today's flame is lit in the months leading up to the Games in Olympia, Greece, at the site of the former temple of the goddess Hera, Zeus's wife. So begins the ceremonial torch relay, in which the flame is transported to the host country and makes stops at multiple cities along the away. Unfortunately, the history behind the relay isn't so benign. The practice was instigated by Carl Diem, the main organizer of the 1936 Berlin Olympics. The torch traveled from Greece across seven countries in 10 days to the Olympiastadion in Berlin, where Adolf Hitler himself declared the Games open as the airship *Hindenburg* flew overhead.

Ali never competed in another Games. He didn't have to. He was on his way to becoming the greatest boxer—and athlete, perhaps—of all time. But Ali made a powerful Olympic coda in 1996, lighting the flame at the opening ceremony. Atlanta's organizing committee had wanted the less controversial hometown champ Evander Holyfield to do it, but NBC Sports president Dick Ebersol managed to convince them otherwise. "Muhammad Ali may be, outside of perhaps the pope, the most beloved figure in the world," he told them.

Ali, then in the throes of Parkinson's disease, struggled to light the Olympic flame, and the torch's flames kept whipping up his forearms. At times, it looked like he might drop the torch. He made no sign of pain, however, and eventually managed to get it lit. Viewers at home saw an edited version that eliminated the fire stopping and starting. But what we remember most is the sheer surprise of our greatest fighter defying the odds.

OPPOSITE: *Ali stood alone as the champion, a position he would find himself in often as a professional.*

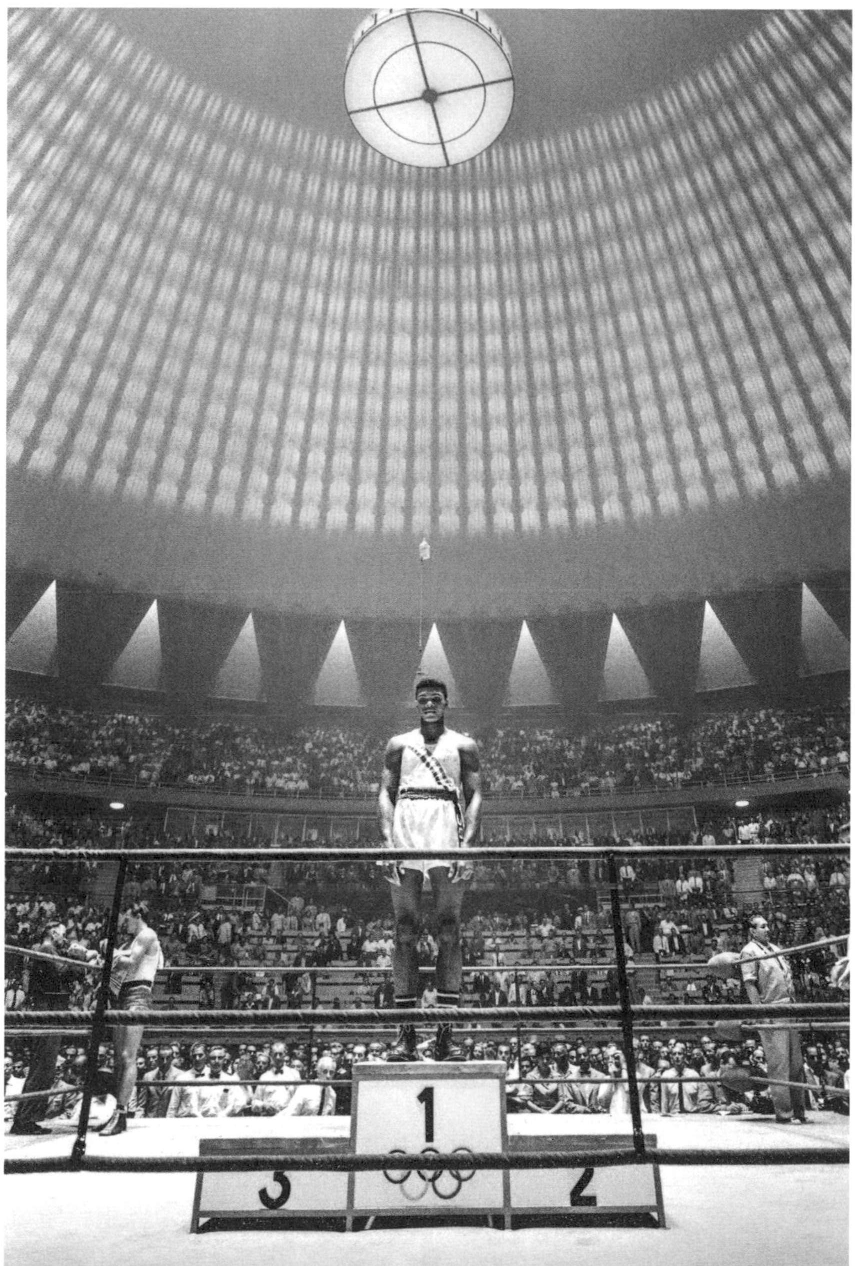
1
3
2

MARY LOU RETTON
The Original Olympic Sweetheart

USA | GYMNASTICS | 5 MEDALS | 1968–

LOS ANGELES 1984

One of the most popular athletes in American history started her legendary career as an alternate. Fifteen-year-old Mary Lou Retton, a virtual unknown, was able to participate in the American Cup in 1983—the top competition in the United States that year—only because Dianne Durham, the 1983 national champion, got hurt.

Though Retton hadn't yet received the attention of the gymnastics world, her athletic lineage suggested that she had talent in spades. Her father, Ron Retton, was co-captain with Jerry West on the 1959 West Virginia basketball team that went to the NCAA Finals, and had played shortstop in the Yankees' minor league system. Her cousin Joe Retton was at one point the winningest college basketball coach of all time, earning victories in 83.6 percent of his games at Fairmont State. Her brother Ronnie Jr. played on West Virginia University's baseball team, and her sister Shari was West Virginia's first female All-American.

"Well, nobody thought it could be done. But you know what? I went and did it."

So that she would go on to win the all-around, the vault, and the floor and tie for first on the bars at the American Cup should not have been such a surprise. Nor that she would win the national championship by scoring 10s on the floor and the vault, and qualify as America's top gymnast for the 1984 Games.

It seems like the United States is incapable of losing at gymnastics nowadays, but it wasn't always that way. Before 1984, the Americans had never won an individual all-around medal, nor on an apparatus. In fact, the US women's team had only one medal, a bronze in the team all-around in 1948. Retton, the gutsy teenager with the West Virginia drawl, would be the one to break the spell.

Going into the individual all-around, Retton held a slim .15 lead over Ecaterina Szabo of Romania. After the first rotation, that lead became a tie. After the second, Retton trailed by .15. "You know, we're both about 4'9"," Retton said. "I've seen her work, and she's terrific. But what she doesn't know about me is that I'm tougher than she is." With the final disciplines left—Szabo on uneven bars, Retton on vault—Retton trailed 69.225 to 69.175.

The West Virginian, though, had a special trick up her sleeve. It's called the Tsukahara, a back somersault with a double twist. She stuck the landing, winning by .05. "Well, nobody thought it could be done. But you know what? I went and did it."

Retton continued her stellar performance, winning silver in the vault, bronze on the uneven bars and in floor exercise, and another silver in the team event. The US team as a whole broke their individual apparatus curse. In addition to Retton, the Americans earned individual medals on bars (Julianne McNamara, gold); beam (Kathy Johnson, bronze); and floor (McNamara, silver).

Retton's improbable win vaulted her into superstar status.

Retton quickly became the face of the US sporting movement, despite being just 16. She personified toughness. Six weeks before the Games, she had arthroscopic surgery on her knee and battled through a rigorous rehab program. She was the American ideal, wrapped up in a four-foot-nine-inch dynamic package from coal country.

Retton would earn endorsements from McDonald's, and was the first-ever female on the front cover of a Wheaties box. By 1993, according to one study, she was, along with figure skater Dorothy Hamill, the most popular athlete in the United States, some eight percentage points ahead of Michael Jordan. Just a year before her triumph in 1984, Retton was a relative unknown. Then she was the most famous person in the country. Maybe the officials at the American Cup should've let her pick her spot, not beg to be on the program.

JIM THORPE
Unduly Dismissed

USA | TRACK AND FIELD | 2 MEDALS | 1887–1953

STOCKHOLM 1912

It was just $2 per semi-pro and minor league baseball game that would disqualify Jim Thorpe—perhaps the greatest athlete in American history—from the record books.

It all came down to the IOC's Rule 26, which forbids an athlete from competing in the Games if he or she has been paid to play a sport. Though you see mostly professional athletes in the Games nowadays, the Olympic credo is centered in amateurism, or the idea that neither athletes nor countries could profit off the Games. Of course, we know now that's far from true, as Olympic stars the world over become advertising gold and countries make bank. (The United States Olympic Committee, for instance, posted a revenue of $336 million in 2016.)

While the ideal of amateurism had begun to wane by the early 20th century, Jim Thorpe playing a little minor league baseball was still a big no-no. After a legendary performance at the 1912 Olympics in Stockholm, in which Thorpe won gold in decathlon and pentathlon—both new events—Olympic officials made an example out of him and stripped his medals. It would take 70 years for the IOC to restore his double-gold—though Thorpe's records still aren't recognized, and he still shares both his medals. (He is also the first Native American to win an Olympic medal.) But this is, on its face, completely absurd. Thorpe's dominance at the Stockholm Games is unprecedented. Consider this:

- In the 100-meter hurdles, he ran 15.6 seconds. That was faster than legendary, gold medal–winning decathlete Bob Mathias's time in 1948.
- Thorpe ran the 1,500 meters in 4:40.1. That would've beaten 1960 gold medalist Rafer Johnson by nine seconds. No one matched it until 1972.
- Thorpe's total score of 8,412.95 would not be beaten for another four Games.

Thorpe's disqualification from the Games seems out of place now, but amateurism was taken seriously in the early Olympics.

All this from someone who, until that year, had never once thrown a javelin or pole-vaulted. When he competed in the Olympic trials in Celtic Park in New York, he didn't know he could use a running start in the javelin.

That he still has to share his gold medals remains one of the greatest farces in Olympic history. Thorpe was so clearly the best at the 1912 Games—the Associated Press even named him "The Greatest Athlete of the First Half of the Century"—that it was downright reasonable when Hugo Wieslander (decathlon) and Ferdinand Bie (pentathlon) refused to receive their gold medals after Thorpe's were stripped.

Thorpe throwing the shot put at the 1912 Olympics in Stockholm

Thorpe would move on from the Olympics by proving himself to be probably the most versatile athlete of all time. He played major league baseball for six seasons, starting in 1913, and finishing as a career .252 hitter. In 1915, he joined the Canton Bulldogs, a professional football team (and future NFL franchise) as player-coach. He helped them win three championships, was first-team All-Pro in 1923, and played pro football until 1928. As if this weren't enough, Thorpe toured with a barnstorming basketball team during his later career. Oh, and one more thing: He even won a ballroom dancing championship, for crying out loud. He was the ultimate do-it-all athlete.

Though the end of Thorpe's life and career would take a sad turn—he worked construction during the Great Depression, and died, suffering from alcoholism, in a trailer park—his legacy as an athlete cannot be ignored. In spite of the IOC's dithering on his medals, it's clear as day that he is one of the best Olympians of all time.

After he won the decathlon, King Gustav V of Sweden handed Thorpe a silver chalice, shaped like a Viking ship and lined with gold and jewels. "Sir," King Gustav said, "you are the greatest athlete in the world."

Thorpe, ever humble, replied only, "Thanks."

GREG LOUGANIS
Not Defined by One Dive

USA | DIVING | 5 MEDALS | 1960–

MONTREAL 1976 • LOS ANGELES 1984 • SEOUL 1988

It's best to start here with Greg Louganis, because everyone's thinking it and we might as well get it out of the way: Yes, he's the guy who hit his head on the diving board.

We can trace it all back to the dive known as 307c, a near-impossible three-and-a-half reverse somersault with a tuck. Louganis, who entered the 1988 Seoul Games as one of the most decorated divers of all time, was one of the few in the world who could pull off the move. He had overcome a tremendously difficult childhood to win silver at age 16 in 1976 and took

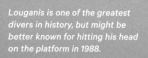

Louganis is one of the greatest divers in history, but might be better known for hitting his head on the platform in 1988.

home gold in the 3m springboard and 10m platform in Los Angeles in 1984. He also had five world championship gold medals to his name.

The 307c became known as the Dive of Death in 1983 when Soviet diver Sergei Chalibashvili hit his head on the concrete platform in the middle of the dive. His skull broke and he fell into a coma. Louganis was there—and up next. "I had a premonition," Louganis once said of the accident. "I knew something terrible had happened when I felt the tower shake." Less than 30 minutes later, Louganis had to attempt the same dive. He did it perfectly.

How could that not be in the back of his mind five years later in Seoul as he prepared to make the dive again, even if he was now the greatest in the world? Wasn't he still the boy with bad asthma, who was dyslexic and stuttered, who, before they nicknamed him Mr. Perfect, was bullied and called "sissy" or "retard"? A troubled kid, he had started smoking at age nine, started drinking soon afterward, and had made three suicide attempts.

After hitting his head on the springboard, Louganis still had to dive again to qualify. He nailed it.

Louganis was a closeted gay man, hiding his HIV-positive status he'd learned about just six months earlier. And so when the "clank," as he called it, happened, when blood spilled from the gash on his head and into the water, he didn't know what to do. Would he reveal his secret? With the world watching, would the quiet, scared Louganis both come out about his sexuality and disclose a disease with still so much stigma?

"I was so stunned," he remembered. "I mean, what was going on in my mind at the time was, 'What's my responsibility?' Do I say something?" Even worse, the doctor wasn't using gloves. (The physician, James Puffer, later tested negative, and experts ruled that no other divers were in danger.) But Louganis still had to jump again the next day. So he did what he always did and sang "Believe in Yourself" from *The Wiz* to himself.

Louganis nailed it. It was the highest-scoring dive in Olympic qualifying history. The crowd rose to its feet and he would go on to win gold. Louganis came out in 1994 and announced his HIV-positive status the following year. The once-shy athlete has since become a powerful and outspoken advocate for numerous LGBTQ causes.

THE 1992 DREAM TEAM
The Best There Ever Was

USA | BASKETBALL | 1 MEDAL

BARCELONA 1992

Simply put, the 1992 United States Olympic basketball team was the most dominant team ever assembled in a country that has long dominated basketball. The entire squad, led by Michael Jordan, Magic Johnson, Charles Barkley, and Larry Bird, is in the Hall of Fame (yes, even Christian Laettner made it in as a member of the team). It was, in some ways, a culmination of more than a half century of American greatness at the sport on the grandest stage. So how did we get here?

First, let's jump back about 56 years, when basketball made its debut at the 1936 Summer Olympics in Berlin. It wasn't a very polished affair. Canada met the United States in the gold medal game on an outdoor court. "Adolf Hitler said it was an outside game," remembered Joe Fortenberry, the team's captain, "and that's where we were going to play it." There was a steady rain that day, and the court turned into mud. Dribbling wasn't really an option, and wind made passing difficult. Backup Frank Lubin said, "It was almost like watching a water-polo match." At halftime, the score was 15–4. The Americans would win gold with a less-than-rousing final score of 19–8.

But that game, which basketball's inventor James Naismith said "did much to increase the interest in basketball over the entire world," was the start of an incredibly successful Olympic run. The Americans won seven straight gold medals, but their streak snapped after the officiating shenanigans at the end of a controversial 1972 gold medal game against the Soviets.

Then there was gold again in 1976, a missed opportunity to repeat with the 1980 boycott, and another gold medal in 1984—but 1988 was not such a romp. The US team, made up of college all-stars like David Robinson and Danny Manning, had entered the tournament as favorites. They lost in the semifinals to a Soviet team composed of professionals, and the United States had to settle for a hugely disappointing bronze medal.

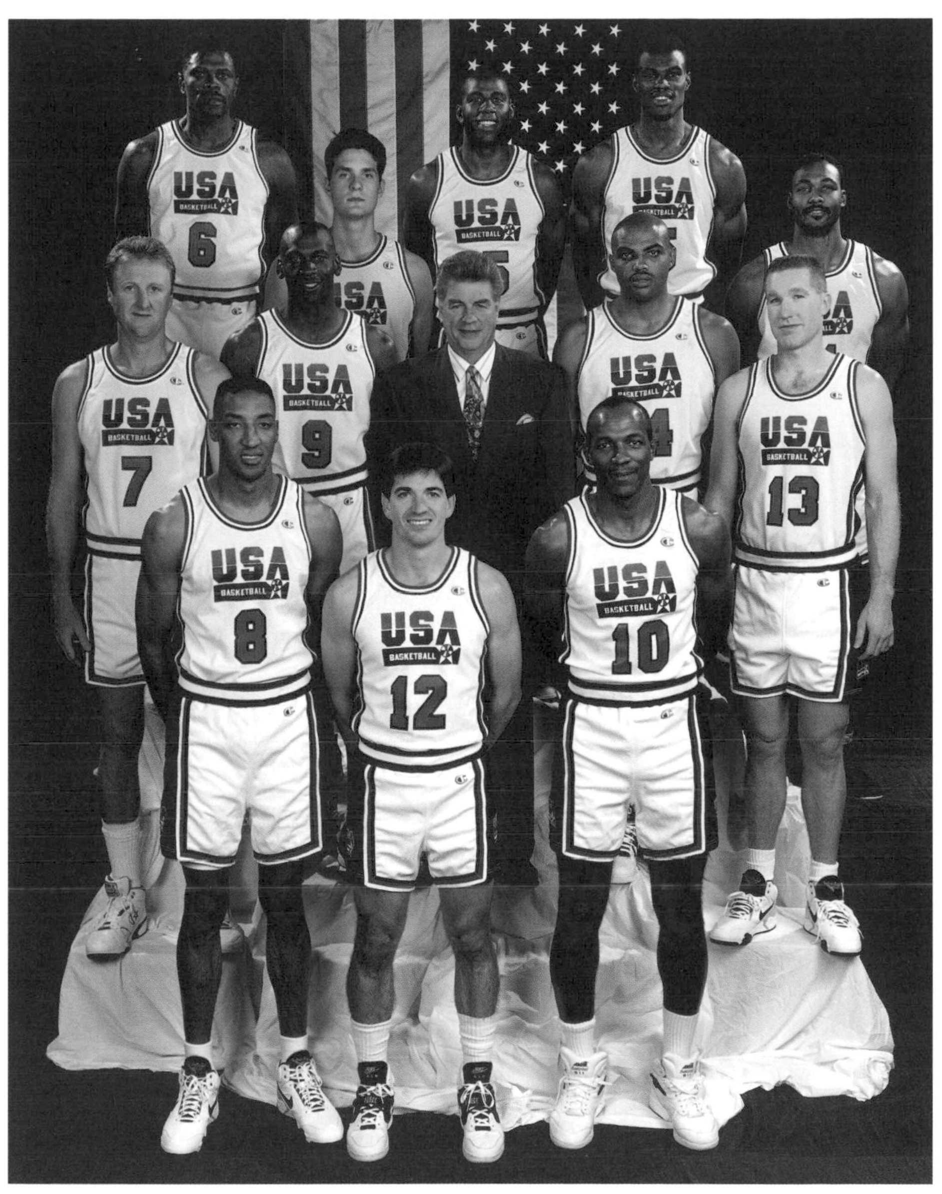

TOP ROW: *Patrick Ewing, Christian Laettner, Magic Johnson, David Robinson, Karl Malone*
MIDDLE ROW: *Larry Bird, Michael Jordan, Chuck Daly, Charles Barkley, Chris Mullin*
BOTTOM ROW: *Scottie Pippen, John Stockton, Clyde Drexler*

DREAM TEAM OLYMPIC RESULTS

GAME	USA POINTS	OPPONENT POINTS	OPPONENT	POINT DIFFERENTIAL
1	116	48	Angola	+68
2	103	70	Croatia	+33
3	111	68	Germany	+43
4	127	83	Brazil	+44
5	122	81	Spain	+41
6	115	77	Puerto Rico	+38
7	127	76	Lithuania	+51
8	117	85	Croatia (final)	+32

How do you respond to a nightmare? You hope for a perfect dream.

The 1992 squad, first dubbed the "Dream Team" by *Sports Illustrated,* had a collection of talent like none other, for the first time selected straight from the NBA. In previous Olympics, FIBA rules dictated that the United States had to send amateur athletes, though many other countries managed to send pros from their own leagues. (Communist countries became experts at flouting amateurism rules, giving their players phony jobs to get past regulations.) After years of lobbying efforts, FIBA relented and allowed the United States to send their professional best. "It was like Elvis and the Beatles put together," said coach Chuck Daly.

Indeed, some of the best players to ever touch a basketball were, for a few weeks in Barcelona, together on the same side. Magic Johnson, who was playing his first team ball since retiring after testing HIV-positive, said, "I look to my right, there's Michael Jordan. I look to my left, there's Charles Barkley or Larry Bird . . . I didn't know who to throw the ball to!"

They were larger-than-life basketball gods. Unlike the rest of the US delegation, they were treated like superstars, surrounded constantly with armed guards and staying in a luxury hotel outside the Olympic Village. Autograph seekers hounded them at every opportunity. Charles Barkley—who would lead the team in scoring with 18.0 points per game—made nightly excursions to Barcelona's Las Ramblas, a pedestrian boulevard, where he had to fend off adoring fans. (Mild-mannered, 6' 1" John Stockton, however, managed to blend into the crowds easily.)

The United States won each game by an average of 43.8 points. They beat poor Angola by 68. In the closest game, the gold medal final against Croatia, the Americans won by 32. It was basketball played at the absolute highest-possible level. As expected, they were a well-oiled machine on offense—one Croatian begged Stockton not to shoot. But they showed the same hustle and intense focus on defense too. In particular, Toni Kukoc of Croatia, a talented forward set to join the Chicago Bulls the following year, faced the unrelenting wrath of ultra-competitive Michael Jordan and Scottie Pippen, who both wanted to assert their status as alphas on the Bulls.

"It was like Elvis and the Beatles put together."

The United States would win again in 1996 and 2000, before a shocking bronze in 2004 as Argentina emerged victorious. ("That was the most disappointed I've been in sports," said team member Dwyane Wade.) The United States returned to glory with another gold in 2008—this time, as the self-styled Redeem Team—and again in 2012 and 2016.

The Dream Team might have made the biggest impact outside the United States. They are widely credited with sparking a global boom in basketball talent. The 1980s and early '90s saw just a few foreign stars in the NBA, like Hakeem Olajuwon and Detlef Schrempf. Today, international players abound. The 2018–19 MVP was Giannis Antetokounmpo of Greece, and Luka Doncic of Slovenia won Rookie of the Year. That season also marked the fifth-straight year in which every team had at least one international player on its roster. The Dream Team was, surely, unbeatable. But it launched a dream for players around the world, turning an American sport into something truly global.

BABE DIDRIKSON ZAHARIAS
An All-Time Phenom

USA | TRACK AND FIELD | 3 MEDALS | 1911–1956

LOS ANGELES 1932

The 1932 Olympics in Los Angeles were a decidedly Hollywood event. If you were a movie star—if you were famous at all—you were at the Games. Look, there's Clark Gable! Say "hi" to Tallulah Bankhead! Give a wave to Cary Grant! But the brightest luminary in this constellation of stars was a 5′7″ multi-sport athletic genius from Beaumont, Texas.

Mildred "Babe" Didrikson was coming off a legendary performance at the 1932 Amateur Athletic Union Championships. She was the only one on her team, won five out of 10 events, and tied for first in a sixth. Her performance single-handedly won the Golden Cyclones the title. In Los Angeles, her big personality fed the hunger of the reporters. Didrikson's comments would have made her a viral superstar today. "I came out to beat everybody in sight and that's just what I'm going to do," she said. "Sure, I can do anything." Or this: "People think it is a little strange that I do not seem to be worried or nervous before I run a race. . . . All I'm doing is running against girls." They called her the Texas Tornado and the Terrific Tomboy.

Didrikson backed up her boasting with results on the field. She won the javelin on her first throw, beating her own world record by 11 feet, despite tearing cartilage in her shoulder on the throw. She won the 80-meter hurdles in record time, and Hollywood could not have drawn it up better. She and teammate Evelyn Hall hit the tape at the same time. Didrikson yelled to Hall, "Well, I won again." And, of course, she did. As Hall put it, "Babe had had so much publicity, it was hard to rule against her."

Although the crowds and the media loved Didrikson, the US track team pretty much despised her. Going into the high jump, her main competitor was teammate Jean Shiley. "We were very high-strung and we put a lot of pressure on Jean to beat this obnoxious girl," Hall said. Once again Didrikson tied her teammate, but Shiley was awarded gold after Didrikson was unfairly

Zaharias (far right) winning the 80-meter hurdles at the 1932 Summer Olympics in Los Angeles

ruled to have done an illegal "Western Roll" jump. (Both were later recognized as the co-holders of the world record.)

In true Didrikson fashion, "Babe was awful about it," as Shiley later said. But it was Didrikson who got all the love. She was given a free flight home to Texas while Shiley exchanged her train ticket for cheaper bus fare to save money, and Hall drove home in a car that was on the verge of being repossessed. Didrikson's life was forever changed—she was now one of the most famous people in America. Legendary sportswriter Grantland Rice called her "without question, the athletic phenomenon of all time, man or woman."

She was brash, she was outspoken, and she *knew* she was the best—not just in track and field. After marrying pro wrestler George Zaharias in 1938 (and taking his last name), she won 10 Ladies' Professional Golf Association majors, including three in 1950. At one point, Zaharias won 17 straight golf tournaments. She pitched a few exhibition innings against major league teams in 1934 and was even a competitive pool player. But she wasn't all bravado. After receiving a diagnosis of colon cancer in 1953, she used her stature to raise money for research, becoming a spokesperson for the American

Cancer Society. Unfortunately, she would succumb to that disease in 1956, at the age of 45.

Yes, on the field she rubbed her teammates the wrong way. But she also proved to a generally skeptical and often sexist public that women were just as athletic, just as powerful, and just as good as their male counterparts. As the first female athletic superstar, Zaharias made it possible for others to follow her. She made the path clearer for Olympians and non-Olympians alike, from Allyson Felix to Serena Williams, from Shirley Babashoff to the current US women's soccer team. Yes, she was brash, but when you're that good—when you're the best in the world—why hold it back?

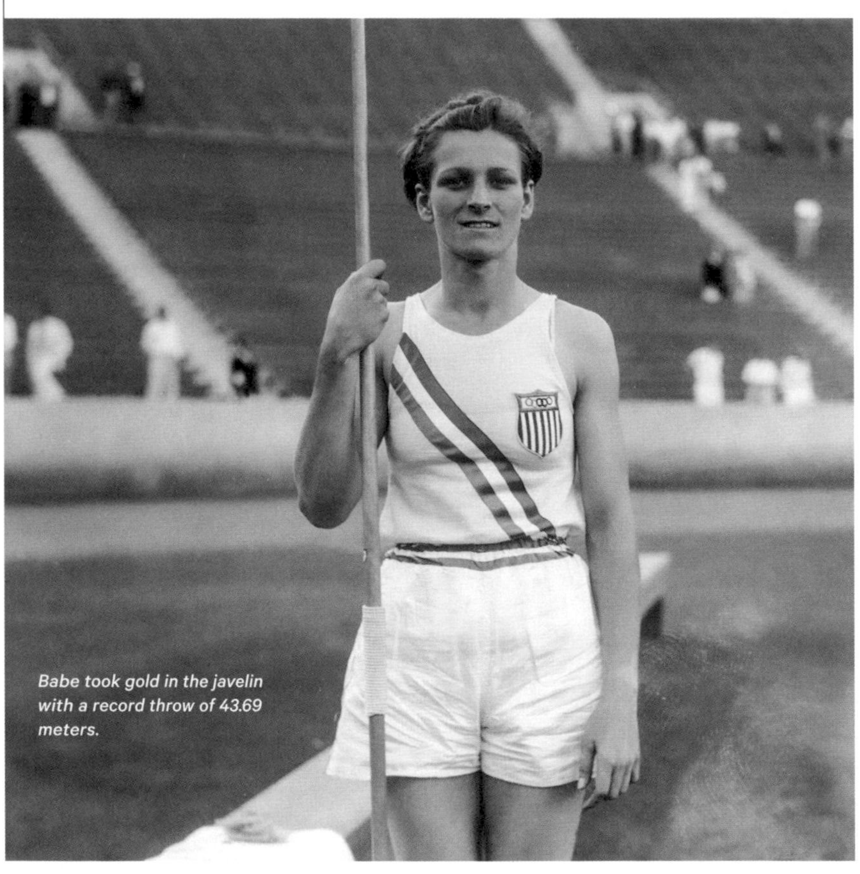

Babe took gold in the javelin with a record throw of 43.69 meters.

CAITLYN JENNER
A Life in the Headlines

USA | TRACK AND FIELD | 1 MEDAL | 1949–

MUNICH 1972 • MONTREAL 1976

In an era in which celebrities are somehow famous for being famous, it's worth remembering what Caitlyn Jenner was actually famous for in the first place: an Olympic gold medal in decathlon.

Though Americans have dominated decathlon since its Olympic debut in 1912—the United States won gold in all but three Olympics from 1932 to 1972—no winner has captured the imagination of the public the way Jenner did. Then known as Bruce, he won with a world record of 8,616 points at the 1976 Montreal Games. And after he was assured victory in the last event, the 1,500 meters, someone gave him a small American flag that he carried around the track. It became an iconic moment, one replicated by sprinters from around the world at each Games. Immediately, newspapers were asking if Hollywood was next.

Jenner's decathlon victory lap became an iconic moment in sports.

Jenner became a megastar. He drove a Porsche and made lucrative speaking engagements. His face was on the front cover of a Wheaties box. Playing days over, Jenner then starred in some made-for-TV movies. He would later appear in seemingly every reality show. And it's because of the fame sparked by the decathlon victory that his transition to Caitlyn Jenner was such enormous news. Jenner talked at length about how, despite being the ultimate symbol of masculinity, she was incredibly uncomfortable in that body and with that gender. "To be able to wake up in the morning, be yourself, get dressed, get ready to go out, and just be, like, a normal person. That's a wonderful feeling to go through life," she said. "I've never been able to do that, it's always been confusion."

But the announcement was met with incredulity and backlash, much of it plainly transphobic. Some criticized Jenner, who documented her transition on yet another reality show—complete with appearances from the Kardashians—for using her new status to become even more famous. Others are uncomfortable with her representing the transgender community yet perhaps still not understanding many of the issues that plague it. In some ways, she bumbled her way into becoming a spokesperson, while not being fully accepted by the community itself. On the other hand, Jenner has undoubtedly brought more attention to transgender issues, and she has donated thousands of dollars to various causes through the Caitlyn Jenner Foundation.

Jenner is a complicated figure, now more famous for her endlessly televised Hollywood family than for being an elite athlete. She is both a superstar who sought out the limelight at every possible moment, hawking seemingly any product, and a powerful advocate for a vulnerable community. Will Jenner be remembered for her Olympic gold? For the association with the Kardashians? For helping to advance the conversation around acceptance for transgender people? All of the above. Perhaps that's how she will—and should—be remembered.

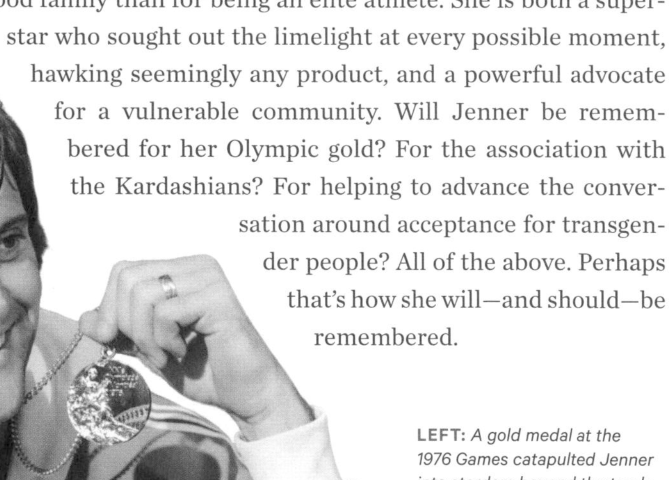

LEFT: *A gold medal at the 1976 Games catapulted Jenner into stardom beyond the track.*

IAN THORPE
The National Hero

AUSTRALIA | SWIMMING | 9 MEDALS | 1982–

SYDNEY 2000 • ATHENS 2004

One of the all-time best swimmers in history grew up allergic to chlorine. Go figure.

Australian swimmer Ian Thorpe had plenty of other sports to pursue besides swimming. He could try cricket, like his father, Ken, who played at a high level. But whenever his dad pitched the ball to him, Ian would swing and miss. He could try soccer, but as a goalkeeper, he often yawned from boredom. So what else do you do? When you have your heart set on swimming, you put on a nose clip and swim with your head out of the water.

Thorpe in action during the 400-meter freestyle at the 2000 Sydney Games

It was a good decision. Thorpe, who would outgrow the allergy, has the perfect body for swimming. His feet are flexible enough that his toes can touch his shin. He uses a unique kicking technique, swimming in a six-beat cycle that allows for less drag and more force. One swimmer described it as "like being in a washing machine." And in a bout of perfect timing, the Sydney native's rise coincided with an Olympics held in his home country in 2000.

When Thorpe was 15, his coach declared him the swimmer of the century. He became the star of the Sydney Games, his face everywhere, with endorsements in place for cars, cereals, banks, airlines, and more before he ever swam a lap. But Thorpe delivered. In the span of an hour, he set a world record in the 400 freestyle, and then, right after the medal ceremony, was the anchor in an upset over the United States in the 4 x 100 relay, an event the Americans had never lost since the event's inception in 1964. In the final leg, as Thorpe caught up to the United States' Gary Hall Jr., the crowd went bonkers—"the loudest noise I've ever heard in an arena," said John Havlicek, an NBA Hall of Famer who was in attendance. "And I've heard some noises."

The hometown star of the Sydney Games delivered an upset win for the host country.

Both teams would beat the world record, but it was Thorpe who touched the wall first to win gold. He would finish the 2000 Games with a total of five medals. "How can you enhance the opinion I've got of him?" his coach, Don Talbot, said. "I don't have the superlatives." Between the end of the Sydney Games and the start of the Athens Games in 2004, he won nine individual and nine relay golds at major events and set multiple records. In Athens, Thorpe repeated his gold in the 400 freestyle, and bettered his 200 freestyle silver in Sydney to gold. He also added a bronze in the 100-meter freestyle.

Though Thorpe, after he retired, would be surpassed in some ways by Michael Phelps, it's important to remember just how big he was. If it weren't for Phelps, it's clear that we would be referring to Thorpe as the best of all time. Meanwhile, the man they called the Thorpedo has spent his post-swim career active in philanthropy. But for eight years, the kid with the way-too-big feet and the allergy to chlorine was, truly, the best swimmer in the world.

USAIN BOLT
The Fastest There Ever Was

JAMAICA | TRACK AND FIELD | 8 MEDALS | 1986–

ATHENS 2004 • BEIJING 2008 • LONDON 2012 • RIO 2016

Usain Bolt's Olympic legacy is unmatched: nine races, nine gold medals. (His ninth, the 4 x 100 relay in Rio, was stripped a year later after a teammate, but not Bolt, tested positive for performance-enhancing drugs.) He is the only sprinter in history to win three consecutive 100- and 200-meter races at the Olympics, and there's no question he is the most successful athlete in track-and-field world championship history. From 2009 to 2015, his only loss was a false start.

But here's the scariest thing: Bolt, whose first sport of choice was cricket, rose to dominance in the 100 meters so quickly that there is simply no precedent. He didn't come quite out of nowhere—he was first a 200-meter star, winning the world junior title at age 15 (the youngest ever) and silver at a world championship in 2007. When Bolt began to switch his focus to the 100 meter, his coach, Glen Mills, initially objected. Bolt wanted to do it, but Mills worried that, at Bolt's six-foot-five-inch height, it would be tough to get to full speed in such a quick race.

In his third-ever 100-meter race in 2008, Bolt ran a 9.76, the second-fastest of all time. Less than a month later, he set a world record at 9.72. "We look like junior high kids out there compared to the man,"

Bolt's longevity in a fleeting sport made his domination even more impressive.

No, it's not a lightning bolt. His trademark "To Di World" celebration copies a famous Jamaican tourism ad.

said Darvis Patton, an American sprinter. "What an impressive athlete. Twenty-one years old, six-foot-five. Sky's the limit, man."

If the legend of the Jamaican superstar was well known in track-and-field circles, the entire world would come to know just how fast Usain Bolt was. At the 100 meters in Beijing, he ran a 9.69, breaking his own world record. He did that despite letting up and pumping his chest in the final 10 meters. Astrophysicists at the University of Oslo calculated that, had he kept running at full speed, his time would have been 9.55 seconds.

Bolt is a natural entertainer. After the race, he played to the crowd, shooting his trademark "To Di World" pose, and pumping his chest and pointing to the "Jamaica" emblem written on his uniform. "The crowd is your friend," former sprinter Donovan Bailey told him.

Bolt also broke a world record in the 200 meters, one that stood for 12 years. It had belonged to legendary American sprinter Michael Johnson, who was in Beijing working for the BBC as an analyst. Bolt also won gold in the 4 x 100 and instantly became one of the world's biggest stars. He was effortlessly comfortable in front of the throngs of media, and the moment before him. "All I did was relax," he said of his pre-race preparation. "I ate my nuggets at McDonald's, I chilled, I focused. That's all it is." (Yes, the fact that one can eat chicken nuggets *and* set a world record in the same day is truly unfair.)

Most mind-boggling is Bolt's ability to repeat unimaginable feats more than once.

Taken alone, Bolt's Beijing bonanza would have stood in Olympic lore. But what makes Bolt—and indeed, so many other Olympic heroes—mind-bogglingly great is the ability to repeat unimaginable feats more than once. In 2012, he set another Olympic record in the 100, then repeated his wins in the 200 and 4 x 100. And then he did it all again in 2016, winning three more gold medals.

After the Games, with the Rio crowd chanting his name as he took an extended victory lap, Bolt summed up his Olympic career with a surprisingly modest statement. "I wanted to set myself apart from everybody else." It's pretty clear, after eight gold medals, that Bolt will forever be in a different stratosphere than all other sprinters.

THE SUPERHERO OF ANCIENT GREECE

He killed a lion with his bare hands on Mount Olympus! He pinned a bull by the hoof until it collapsed! He stopped a fast-paced chariot barreling at him! Polydamas was feted for his strength, and in 408 BC won the *pankration*, a mix of wrestling and boxing without virtually any rules—no biting or gouging out your opponent's eyes, of course. Fitting for a Greek tragedy, however, Polydamas's strength was his downfall. The story goes that he was sitting in a cave that began to crumble. He tried to hold it together with his hands, but alas, the man who had killed a lion and tamed a bull was no match for it. The rocks came crashing down and buried him to death.

APOLO OHNO
From Rebel to Role Model

USA | SPEED SKATING | 8 MEDALS | 1982–

SALT LAKE 2002 • TURIN 2006 • VANCOUVER 2010

At age 13, Apolo Ohno was the youngest-ever skater to be accepted into the US Olympic Training Center program in Lake Placid, New York. A year later, he was a national champion, also the youngest of all time. And yet, the prodigy's career was in danger of falling apart. His interest in training waned, and he often slipped away from exercise periods to head to Pizza Hut. He then dropped out of an honors program in middle school. He would sneak out of his house in Seattle on weekends, staying up all night with friends. "His attitude changed toward me," his father, Yuki, said. "I certainly felt that I no longer knew him."

By the time the US trials for the 1998 Games in Nagano came along, Apolo was out of shape. He finished last and did not qualify. Afterward, Yuki drove his son to a cabin he rented in Iron Springs, a campground site right on the Pacific. Apolo was to train and reflect with no electronics, no way out, and just enough food to survive. "You think it over," Yuki said to his son. "If speed skating is not what you want to do, I want you to know."

Ohno spent the next eight days running on the rocky beaches and on the side of the highway, all under nonstop rain. Eventually, he decided he needed to get serious and commit himself to speed skating. "To be able to come out of that mess as I did is special," he said. Ohno won two medals in Salt Lake, including gold in the 1,500. He continued his run over two more Olympics, with a gold and two bronze in Turin, and a silver and two bronze in Vancouver. Ohno finished his Olympic career with eight medals all told, making him the most decorated American in Winter Olympics history. "I love to compete and I love to train and I love the lifestyle of an Olympic athlete," he said. "I love what it means to call yourself an Olympic athlete."

Ohno's nascent career could easily have fallen apart when he was 15. Instead, quiet contemplation—and a stern push from his father—made him one of the best American Olympians of all time.

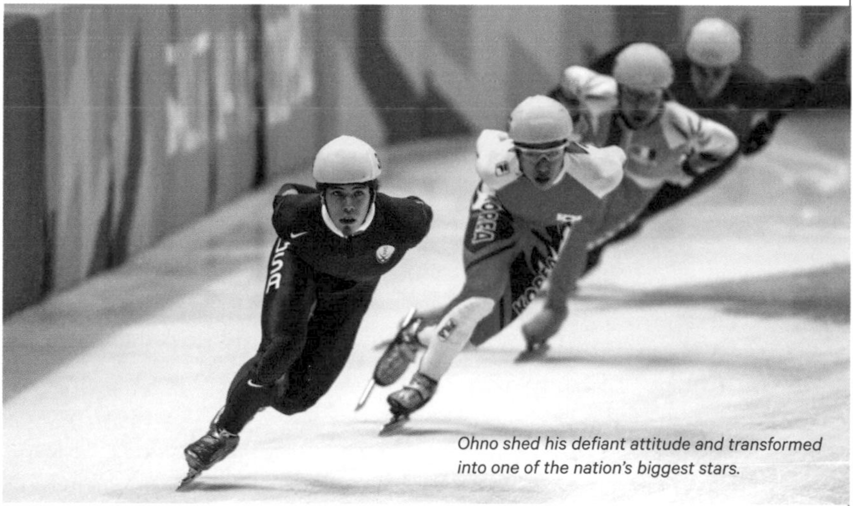

Ohno shed his defiant attitude and transformed into one of the nation's biggest stars.

CHARLES DANIELS
Phelps Before Phelps

USA | SWIMMING | 7 MEDALS | 1885–1973

ST. LOUIS 1904 • LONDON 1908

In the early days of the Olympics, the world's best swimmer was a New Yorker named Charles Daniels. At the 1904 Olympics in St. Louis, the first held in America, Daniels put on a Phelpsian performance. He was the first American to win an Olympic swimming event, earning gold in the 220-yard freestyle, the 440-yard freestyle, and 4 x 50-yard freestyle. He also won silver in the 100 freestyle, and bronze in the 50.

Daniels didn't just dominate at the Olympics. He was the star of the New York Athletic Club, where he also excelled in squash and bridge. Over a four-day period in 1905, he set 14 world records. From 1904 until 1911, he won 31 Amateur Athletic Union championships. In 1910, he set eight new records. At one point in 1911, he held world freestyle records in every distance from 25 yards to one mile. Not too shabby.

Daniels won seven medals, four of them gold, over two Olympics in 1904 and 1908.

It makes perfect sense that Daniels was the world's best freestyler because he was responsible, in some part, for improving upon the stroke itself. The front crawl—or freestyle—has been around since time immemorial but was popularized in competitive swimming by Dick Cavill of Australia, who became the first to use it in a recorded race. Daniels's innovation was to use his legs as two separate appendages scissoring through the water rather that just splashing about.

In 1906, Daniels returned to the Olympics, this time at the Intercalated Games, which at the time was recognized as part of Olympic history, but now is not. Daniels won gold in the 100-meter freestyle. In London in 1908, he won gold again in the 100-meter freestyle and bronze in the 4 x 200 freestyle relay.

After setting his records, Daniels mostly retired from swimming in 1911 and seemed intent on giving up the sport. "Understand, after I retire—if there are life preservers enough to go around, I shall simply crawl into one and float until some kind-hearted soul picks me up," he told the *San Francisco Call*. "No, siree; I won't even swim ashore." That may have been a bit extreme, as Daniels's post-swimming career included an early morning workout, where he swam two miles across Bear Pond and had a butler meet him at the shore with a cup of coffee and the *New York Tribune*.

Daniels finished with seven medals (eight including his gold at the Intercalated Games). That total stood as most by an American in swimming until Mark Spitz broke it in 1972 and Michael Phelps after him. The lineage of American swimming, then, is clear: Though Michael Phelps will likely forever be at the top, the history of great swimmers will always start with the exploits of Charles Daniels.

Daniels nears the finish line at the 220-yard swimming event at the 1904 Games in St. Louis. He held on to win gold.

SHANNON MILLER
The Forgotten Star

USA | GYMNASTICS | 7 MEDALS | 1977–

BARCELONA 1992 • ATLANTA 1996

Shannon Miller isn't usually the first person to come to mind when we think of American gymnastics heroes. We remember Mary Lou on the Wheaties box, Kerri in her coach's arms, Simone wowing the crowds in Rio. But it's worth remembering, before the 2020 Games, that the most-decorated US gymnast of all time was Shannon Miller.

Indeed, Miller's contributions to gymnastics tend to get a bit lost among the parade of stars. It's easier to remember Simone Biles's physics-defying feats, or Laurie Hernandez's thousand-watt smile, or McKayla Maroney's glare. Even in 1992, when Miller won five medals, she wasn't supposed to be the hero. "Other people may not have had high expectations for me in Barcelona," she said. "But I had high expectations for myself."

At just 15 years old, and standing at a slight four feet seven inches and 71 pounds, Miller went in as the clear number-two gymnast behind American Kim Zmeskal, who was the world champion a year before. But while Zmeskal floundered on the big stage, the quiet Miller shone, putting together the best performance by a US gymnast since Mary Lou Retton in 1984. "I don't know if Shannon Miller really wants the attention," her coach, Steve Nunno, said. "But if she gets it, she deserves it."

Miller got overshadowed again four years later in Atlanta. Kerri Strug received the most attention, and deservedly so, after her hobbled vault helped secure gold for the Americans in the team event. But Miller was the team's highest scorer. She also won gold on the balance beam, the only American to win on an individual apparatus that year.

Miller would go on to law school, and in 2011, she was given a diagnosis of ovarian cancer, though she beat it after eight months. Today, she owns and operates a gym in Jacksonville, Florida, helping the other quiet gymnasts stand out from the pack.

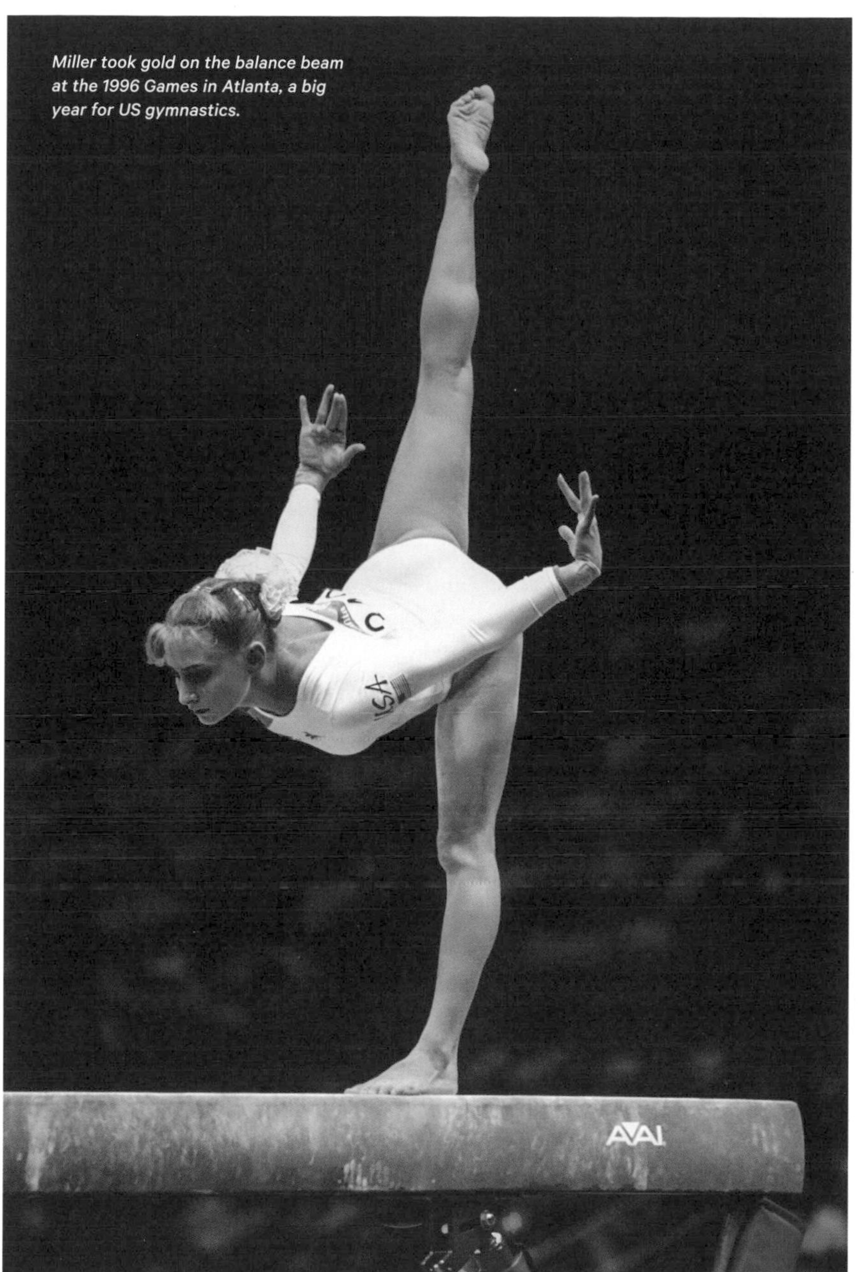

Miller took gold on the balance beam at the 1996 Games in Atlanta, a big year for US gymnastics.

MICHAEL JOHNSON
Doubly Great

USA | TRACK AND FIELD | 4 MEDALS | 1967–

BARCELONA 1992 • ATLANTA 1996 • SYDNEY 2000

More than anything, Michael Johnson wanted the double gold. He had already won a gold medal at the 1992 Barcelona Games in the 4 x 100 relay, but Johnson wanted to make history in 1996. He dreamed of winning both the 200 meters and 400 meters at a single Olympics, something no other man had ever done. (Two women have done it: Valerie Brisco-Hooks of the United States, in 1984, and Marie-José Pérec of France, in 1996.)

Winning the 200-400 double is so difficult because each event requires slightly different skills: The 200 is more of a straight sprint, whereas the 400 requires a bit more strategy and runners use different speeds at different parts of the race. Johnson was so dedicated to completing the feat that it became more important than setting any other record. "I would take being a 200-400 double gold medalist over being the world-record holder in the 400 any day," he said.

Johnson's custom gold shoes were more than just a color—they were a state of mind.

His best opportunity to do so was at the Atlanta Games. He worked with Nike to create golden-colored spikes, and the image of a golden blur became iconic. As Johnson would put it, how could you have silver shoes, when gold is the goal? Whether the spikes had a material effect on Johnson's runs is up for debate, but what he accomplished in Atlanta is crystal clear—it's one of the greatest Olympic performances of all time.

It started in the 400. Johnson ran an effortless 43.49 for gold, and felt relieved. "I had always been afraid," he said, "of ending my career without having won an individual gold medal." But it was the 200 that cemented his

Johnson had reason to celebrate in Atlanta, finally winning his coveted double-double gold in the 200 and 400 meters.

legacy. Pressure? No way. He craved it. With his gold chain bouncing back and forth, his neck muscles visibly straining, Johnson passed by everybody and ran a 19.32, a new world record. He beat the silver medalist by four meters, the largest winning margin in that race since Jesse Owens in 1936.

Johnson had finally earned the double, flashing a golden blur around Centennial Olympic Stadium and etching his name into track history. In 2004, the United States Track and Field Hall of Fame named the 200 race the greatest track-and-field moment of the previous 25 years.

Before the Games, Johnson was pretty certain he was going to pull it off. Famously self-assured, he said, "There are two household names in the history of track and field—Jesse Owens and Carl Lewis. I'm in position to be the third. It'll be the biggest show of the Olympics. I'm going to be the man at these Olympics."

The man he was. But it didn't stop there. Two months later, at the world championships in Sweden, he repeated the double gold again. Johnson was billed as the World's Fastest Man. Four years later in Sydney, he injured himself in the 200-meter final, but he still won a gold in the 400. At age 33, he was the oldest gold medalist at any track event shorter than 5,000 meters. (By comparison, at his final Olympics, Usain Bolt was age 30.) Johnson also became the first man to repeat in the 400. More than anything, "The Man with the Golden Shoes" knew how to double up.

FAMOUS OLYMPIC AD CAMPAIGNS

There are few better opportunities to market your brand globally than the Olympics. The world, literally, is watching.

There are, of course, the recurring sponsors whose ads we come to expect like clockwork. How many Coca-Cola and Visa commercials have you seen? (Answer: a lot.) But some Olympic ads are worth rewatching. Like the tear-jerking Procter & Gamble ads that said, "Thank you, Mom." There was the Dream Team in 1992 hawking McDonald's. (It was the "gold medal meal": a *triple* cheeseburger, with fries and a drink! The perfect meal for Olympic success! If only.) Or, way back in 1998, a prescient IBM ad showing fans checking scores on the internet late at night.

JESSE OWENS
The Defiant One

USA | TRACK AND FIELD | 4 MEDALS | 1913–1980

BERLIN 1936

After capturing the world's attention with four gold medals and stunning Hitler himself on his own turf, Jesse Owens came home as a hero—for a moment. Sure, he returned from the 1936 Summer Olympics in Berlin aboard the luxe *Queen Mary*. His hometown city of Cleveland honored him with a gold stopwatch, and there was a $40,000 offer to appear in Eddie Cantor's act. But the overarching reality of Owens's life—and that of the nation's 12 million other African Americans living under the yoke of racism and segregation—would soon hit him.

In the cruelest of ironies, he was given a ticker-tape parade and a celebration at the Waldorf-Astoria hotel in New York—but could access the hotel only by the freight elevator. President Franklin D. Roosevelt never bothered to congratulate him. "Hitler didn't snub me, it was our president who snubbed me," he said. "The president didn't even send a telegram."

He had trouble finding a job after the initial frenzy, so he worked as a playground janitor, as a gas station attendant, and at a dry cleaner. He raced against horses, trucks, cars, and bikes, and when facing off against local sprinters, he would give them a 20-yard head start. He'd still win. "People say that it was degrading for an Olympic champion to run against a horse," Owens said,

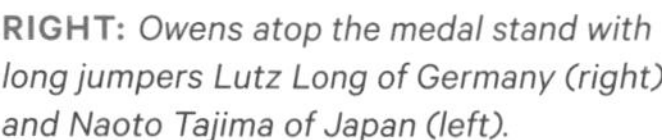

RIGHT: *Owens atop the medal stand with long jumpers Lutz Long of Germany (right) and Naoto Tajima of Japan (left).*

"but what was I supposed to? I had four gold medals, but you can't eat four gold medals." In 1939, he was forced to file for bankruptcy. "Things hadn't changed," said John Woodruff, an African American middle-distance runner who won gold in the 800 meters, upon returning home from the 1936 Games.

But didn't *something* change? Jesse Owens didn't just win four gold medals in a single Olympics, a dazzling performance that went unmatched until Carl Lewis 48 years later. Owens won them while competing before, of all people, Adolf Hitler. Most memorably, in the 100 meters he crushed German star Erich Borchmeyer. It was an essential moment. The Nazi regime built their entire existence on the idea that only Aryan whites were worthy, that they were superior to every other race in both body and mind. Owens, a black man from Ohio, rushed into Berlin and blew away the white competitors, right in front of the racist Nazi dictator himself. How could they claim to be "superior" now, when the whole world was watching? Hitler was reportedly incensed and said that black athletes should be excluded from future Games.

It took Owens 10.3 seconds to win a gold medal and change the course of history.

Owens's performance did more than expose the Nazi ideology as bogus. It also illuminated America's own deep-seated problem of racism. Owens struggled for respect in a country that claimed to represent freedom and democracy but treated him as a second-class citizen. But as the United States has slowly evolved over time, so did its reaction to the runner. Toward the end of his life, Owens began to find business success, traveling the world as a paid motivational speaker for Ford and the United States Olympic Committee. He's now recognized not just for the medals he won, but for transcending the sport itself.

Owens's victory was a moment beyond sports. Its meaning has endured over decades, as powerful today as it was 40 years ago. He helped prove that sports are political—they encapsulate our society. It took Owens 10.3 seconds to win a gold medal in the 100 meters. It may be some of the most important 10.3 seconds in history.

Owens drove a stake into the dark heart of white supremacy before the very eyes of Adolf Hitler himself.

KERRI STRUG
Vaulting to Stardom

USA | GYMNASTICS | 2 MEDALS | 1977–

BARCELONA 1992 • ATLANTA 1996

She hung out with Bruce Willis and Demi Moore. Shaquille O'Neal, Jason Priestley, and Sylvester Stallone all wanted to lift her up in their arms whenever they saw her. She went on *Beverly Hills 90210, The Tonight Show,* and *Saturday Night Live.* She attended Bill Clinton's 50th birthday party, wrote an autobiography, and rang the opening bell at the stock exchange. She earned $24,000 per appearance to do an uneven parallel bars routine that concluded with a glitzy landing into the arms of a few bare-chested men. Random couples invited her to wedding rehearsal dinners, and she received teddy bears with gauze on the ankles.

It was an iconic, powerful moment when the US women's gymnastics coach, Béla Károlyi, carried the injured Kerri Strug to the podium to receive her gold medal. (Needless to say it was endlessly imitated too.) "All this," Strug said, "from one vault." And all this, it must be said, from a vault that was unnecessary.

The performance that launched her into celebrity, did not, contrary to popular belief, secure gold for US women's gymnastics—their first ever—at the 1996 Games in Atlanta. Even without Strug's 9.712 score after tearing the medial and lateral ligaments in her left ankle, the Americans would have beat the Russians in the team all-around by .309. And that gutsy (but ultimately unneeded) second vault prevented her from competing in the individual all-around. Winning that event, more than anything, was Strug's longtime goal. In 1992, she had missed qualifying for the competition by an excruciatingly slight .0012 points.

Strug's vault completely overshadowed the rest of the gold-medal winning squad, which led to some resentment from her team members. While the other gymnasts from the Magnificent Seven—so named for its incredible assemblage of talent, led by three national champions—went on a 34-city

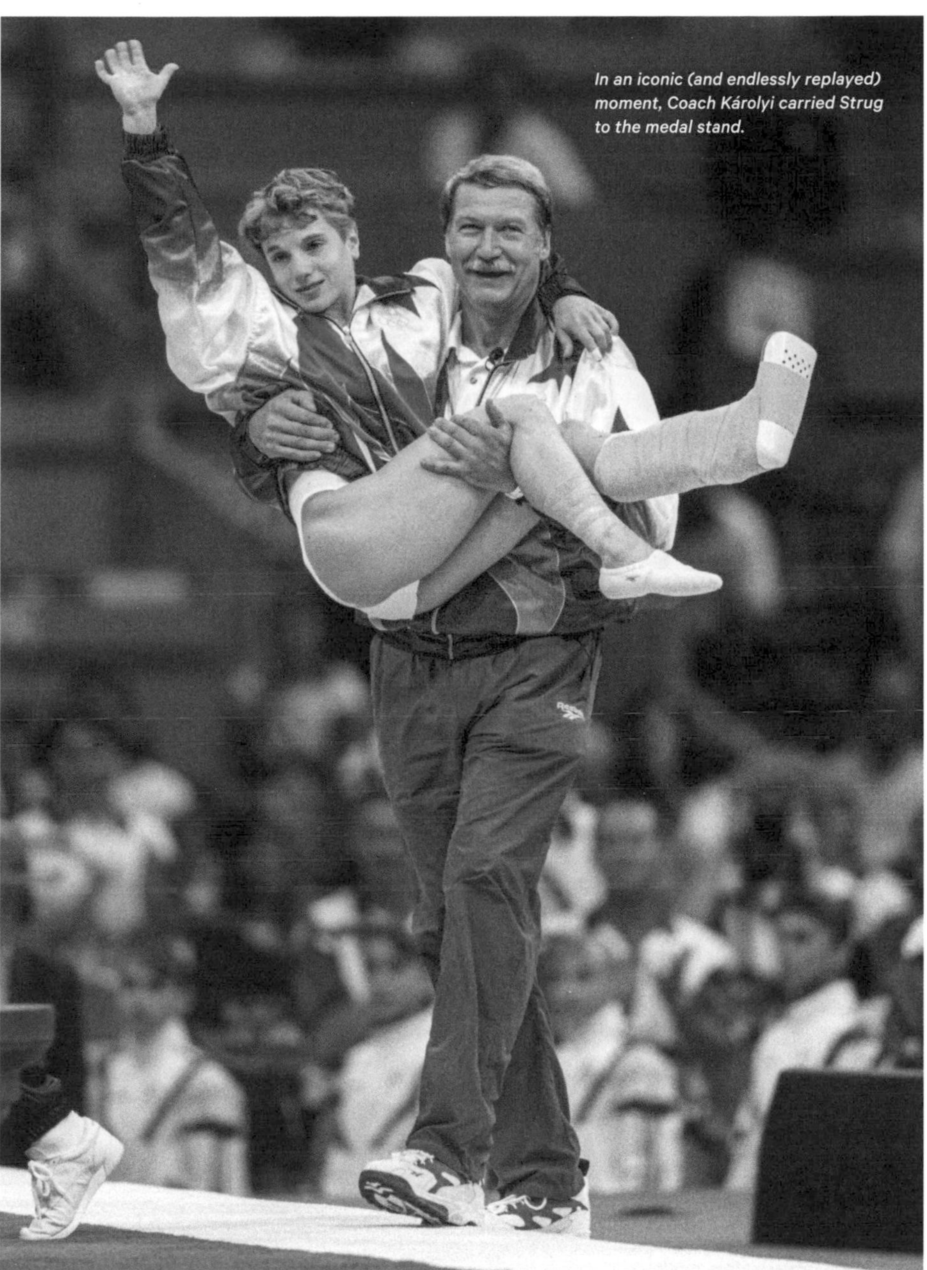

In an iconic (and endlessly replayed) moment, Coach Károlyi carried Strug to the medal stand.

tour, Strug was not there. She was chasing her "one-in-a-million opportunity to be like Mary Lou Retton," as she put it. Still, Strug wrote them all letters, just to say hello. It stung badly when they didn't write back. She was the megastar, and the world seemingly forgot that it was a team medal they had won.

Strug hadn't entered the Games as the most recognizable gymnast, and she eventually wanted to break out of the post-Olympic media frenzy. She studied abroad in 2000, traveling with the Semester at Sea program. In India, she wandered the streets by herself. She bought toys for young kids in Ho Chi Minh City and watched a Fidel Castro speech in Cuba. After living in the fishbowl of Olympic mega-fame, Strug explored the world for herself and became her own person. She next earned a master's degree in sociology from Stanford and ran marathons.

Strug's gutsy vault launched her into worldwide celebrity—at the expense of the Magnificent Seven.

Strug currently works in the Department of Justice, in its office of juvenile justice and delinquency, which helps provide opportunities for at-risk youths. "If you had told me I'd be working as a program manager in the [office] back when I was in Atlanta, I would've laughed," she said.

That vault, in the following year, earned her $1.3 million in endorsements and other opportunities. The video gets replayed in every Olympics. It is now a piece of American lore—the ultimate representation of grit, of winning at all costs, of never, ever surrendering. And it is, at least from the outside, the defining moment of Kerri Strug's life. But after the whirlwind tour, after the strangers asked to carry her just like coach Károlyi carried her to the medal stand, Strug tried to chart out a life that's more than her 30 seconds of glory. Even though one moment in her teens brought her riches and fame, Strug would probably prefer that the remainder of her life—her life's work—be what stands out.

1980 US MEN'S HOCKEY TEAM
Miracle on Ice

USA | ICE HOCKEY | 1 MEDAL

LAKE PLACID 1980

Although there are plenty of team events at the Olympics, most of them are in the form of a relay. A track or cross-country event, for instance, consists of a few people coming together right before a race and then just running it. But one of the truest team sports at the Winter Olympics, perhaps more than any other, is hockey. These teams—each more than 20 members strong—go through qualifying together, then preliminary rounds, and finally, if they're lucky, the medal round.

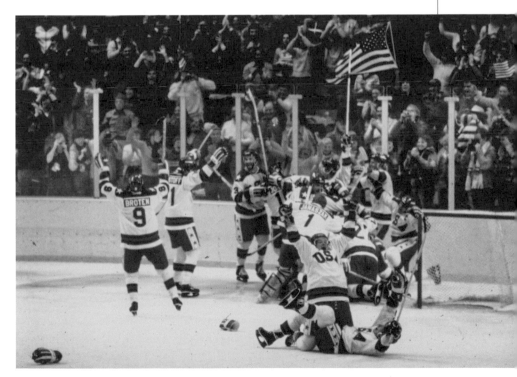

At the final buzzer, the Americans show the true elation—and disbelief—of their shocking upset of the Soviets.

No one expected much out of the US hockey team in 1980. In an exhibition game against the favored Soviets before the Games in Lake Placid, the Americans got trounced 10–3. "I don't mean to sound defeatist," coach Herb Brooks said after that game, "but you've got to combine idealism with pragmatism, and practically speaking, we don't have a chance to beat the Russians."

It was an inauspicious start, to say the least. And making things even harder, this team was composed of disparate parts. Only amateurs were allowed in Olympic Hockey until 1998. The American squad was the youngest in the competition. Of the 20 men on the roster, nine were from the University of Minnesota. The others consisted of collegiate stars from Boston, North Dakota, Wisconsin, and elsewhere. Meanwhile, the Soviets, experts at skirting amateurism rules, packed their team with seasoned professionals experienced in international play.

But what the US team had, unlike so many other teams, was time to learn how to play together. The squad played 61 exhibition games over five months, finishing a brutal schedule with an impressive record of 42–16–3. Still, were they good enough to beat the Soviets? No way. From 1964 to 1976, the USSR had just one Olympic loss. They won gold in every world championship except one from 1963 to 1975. No one was going to beat the four-time defending Olympic gold medalists, who had the best goaltender in the world in Vladislav Tretiak and several players who would go on to become NHL All-Stars. But Coach Brooks saw a vulnerability: fatigue. "The Russians were ready to cut their own throats," he said. "But we had to get to the point to be ready to pick up the knife and hand it to them."

Though the Soviets scored first in this semifinal matchup, the Americans matched five minutes later. The USSR then took a 2–1 lead, and the US scored with one second left in the first period to even it up. That seemed to stun the Soviets, who replaced their legendary goalie with Vladimir Myshkin. This sub was no slouch, but it suggested that they were panicking. When the Americans took a 4–3 lead with 10 minutes left in the third period, the Soviets—who weren't really used to losing—didn't pull their goalie for an extra attacker. The US held on for the world-shaking win. "I still can't believe it," said center Mark Johnson. "We beat the Russians."

OLYMPICS ON FILM

Many Olympic stories seem almost too good to be true. But the best part about the Olympics is that, yes, these storybook endings actually *are* true. It's nothing that Hollywood can't improve on, however. Here's a very subjective list of the best Olympic movies ever:

1. *Miracle*
2. *Munich*
3. *Foxcatcher*
4. *Race*
5. *Chariots of Fire*
6. *Unbroken*
7. *I, Tonya*
8. *Personal Best*
9. *Prefontaine*
10. *Downhill Racer*

The Americans, who would defeat Finland 4–2 in the gold medal game, instantly became the country's most loved and recognized hockey team of all time. And the magic that animated that team would carry over for the rest of their lives. For many Americans they became a powerful symbol for Cold War triumph, that the United States could beat the Soviets in anything, even as dramatic underdogs.

Although some of the Miracle members went on to great hockey success—defenseman Ken Morrow won a Stanley Cup with the New York Islanders later in 1980—others faded. Goalie Jim Craig played just 30 games in the NHL. Mike Eruzione, the captain who scored the game-winning goal, retired immediately after the Games.

But one player summoned up his Olympic past for another big moment. Neal Broten played 17 years at center in the NHL and is the only person to win a collegiate championship, a Stanley Cup, and an Olympic gold medal. In Game 4 of the Stanley Cup against the Detroit Red Wings in 1995, it was Broten who scored the championship-clinching goal for the New Jersey Devils. He did it after Red Wings defenseman—and 1980 Soviet team member—Slava Fetisov fell to the ice.

KERRI WALSH JENNINGS and MISTY MAY-TREANOR
The Ultimate Duo

WALSH JENNINGS | USA | BEACH VOLLEYBALL | 4 MEDALS | 1978–

SYDNEY 2000 • ATHENS 2004 • BEIJING 2008 • LONDON 2012 • RIO 2016

MAY-TREANOR | USA | BEACH VOLLEYBALL | 3 MEDALS | 1977–

SYDNEY 2000 • ATHENS 2004 • BEIJING 2008 • LONDON 2012

Beach volleyball has been around since the early 1900s, but it didn't gain widespread notoriety until the 1960s. Although the sport is relatively young, making its Olympics debut in 1996, it has quickly become one of the most popular on the summer slate. And in that time, one duo has risen far above the rest of the competition.

Individually, Kerri Walsh Jennings and Misty May-Treanor were terrific volleyball players. Walsh Jennings was a four-time All-American at Stanford and the co-national Player of the Year in 1999. May-Treanor captained a Long Beach State team that, in 1998, became the first volleyball team to have an undefeated season. Together, though, they were unstoppable. The pair won three straight beach volleyball gold medals from 2004 to 2012. In both Athens and Beijing, they didn't lose a set. All told, the pair won 112 straight matches and 19 straight titles.

The two made a perfect team. They were quick to transition from offense to defense, and Walsh Jennings's six-foot-two-inch height made her formidable at the net. They played off each other magnificently. Both were excellent indoor players who made a seamless switch to the sand. Walsh Jennings was unstoppable as a blocker; May-Treanor tracked down anything her partner missed. "Misty and I are both relentless," Walsh Jennings said, "but she has this quiet focus and determination when she plays. When she's pissed off, I can see her talking to herself, and I feed off that." Or, as May-Treanor put plainly: "We're a bitch to play against."

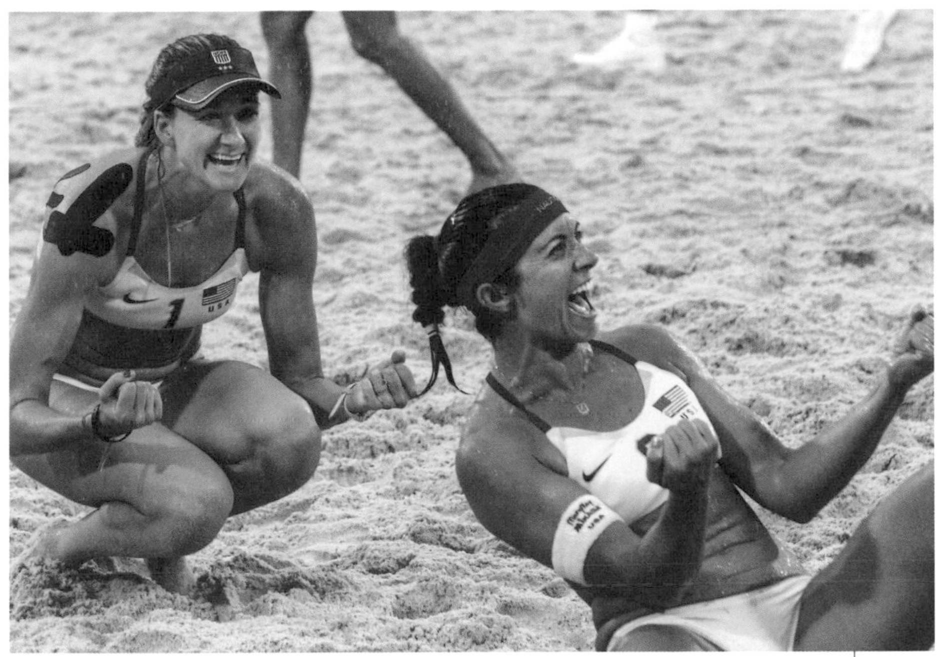

Walsh Jennings (left) and May-Treanor (right) were the best and baddest beach volleyball players ever.

After their gold medal win in 2012, May-Treanor announced her retirement. "I was telling Kerri on the podium, 'This is what we dreamed, and we lived it.'" The pair beat Jennifer Kessy and April Ross, two up-and-coming Americans. But Walsh-Jennings wasn't through—at the end of the game, she went up to Ross and said, "Let's go win gold in Rio."

They wouldn't capture gold—they settled for bronze, losing a close match to Brazil's Ágatha Bednarczuk and Bárbara Seixas in the semifinals. Still, their good run of success left Walsh Jennings as the winningest beach volleyball player of all time after she hung it up in 2018.

Walsh Jennings and May-Treanor have been active with other pursuits in their retirements, but they will share, forever, an unbreakable bond that comes from two of the best in a sport teaming up for unparalleled success. "We both know there's someone out there who will be a friend for life," Walsh Jennings said.

ERIC HEIDEN
Mr. Perfect

USA | SPEED SKATING | 5 MEDALS | 1958–

INNSBRUCK 1976 • LAKE PLACID 1980

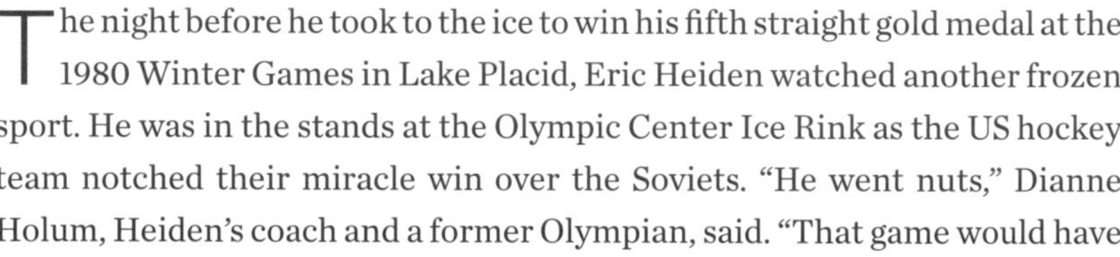

The night before he took to the ice to win his fifth straight gold medal at the 1980 Winter Games in Lake Placid, Eric Heiden watched another frozen sport. He was in the stands at the Olympic Center Ice Rink as the US hockey team notched their miracle win over the Soviets. “He went nuts,” Dianne Holum, Heiden’s coach and a former Olympian, said. “That game would have psyched anyone up. He left there thinking he could conquer the world.”

Heiden may have thought himself a world conqueror, but instead of getting “psyched up,” he may have just tired himself out. He overslept and awoke just two hours before the race, normally around the time when he would enter the rink. Instead of his traditional three bowls of corn flakes, he grabbed three slices of bread from the cafeteria. (At least they were whole grain.)

Fortunately, straying from his careful routine didn’t have a major impact. Heiden dominated the 10,000 meters in a way that has never been matched. He beat defending champion Piet Kleine of the Netherlands by 7.90 seconds, or nearly 100 meters. Heiden shaved 6.20 seconds off the world record. With the crowd chanting his first name, Heiden accomplished what no other winter athlete has ever done: win five individual gold medals at a single Games. (He also won in the 500, 1,000, 1,500, and 5,000 and set Olympic records in all of them.) “I thought I could win one or two,” he said. “You guys said five, but that went in one ear and out the other.”

Consider this: Entering 1980, the most medals that a US winter team had won was 12, six of them gold. In five races, Heiden alone nearly matched that haul. That he would succeed quite like this wasn’t a total surprise, however. After finishing 19th in the 5,000 as a 17-year old at the 1976 Games, he took an unprecedented leap. A year later, he won the world championship, leading from start to finish. He was the first American to win the title since 1891, when Joseph Donoghue did it.

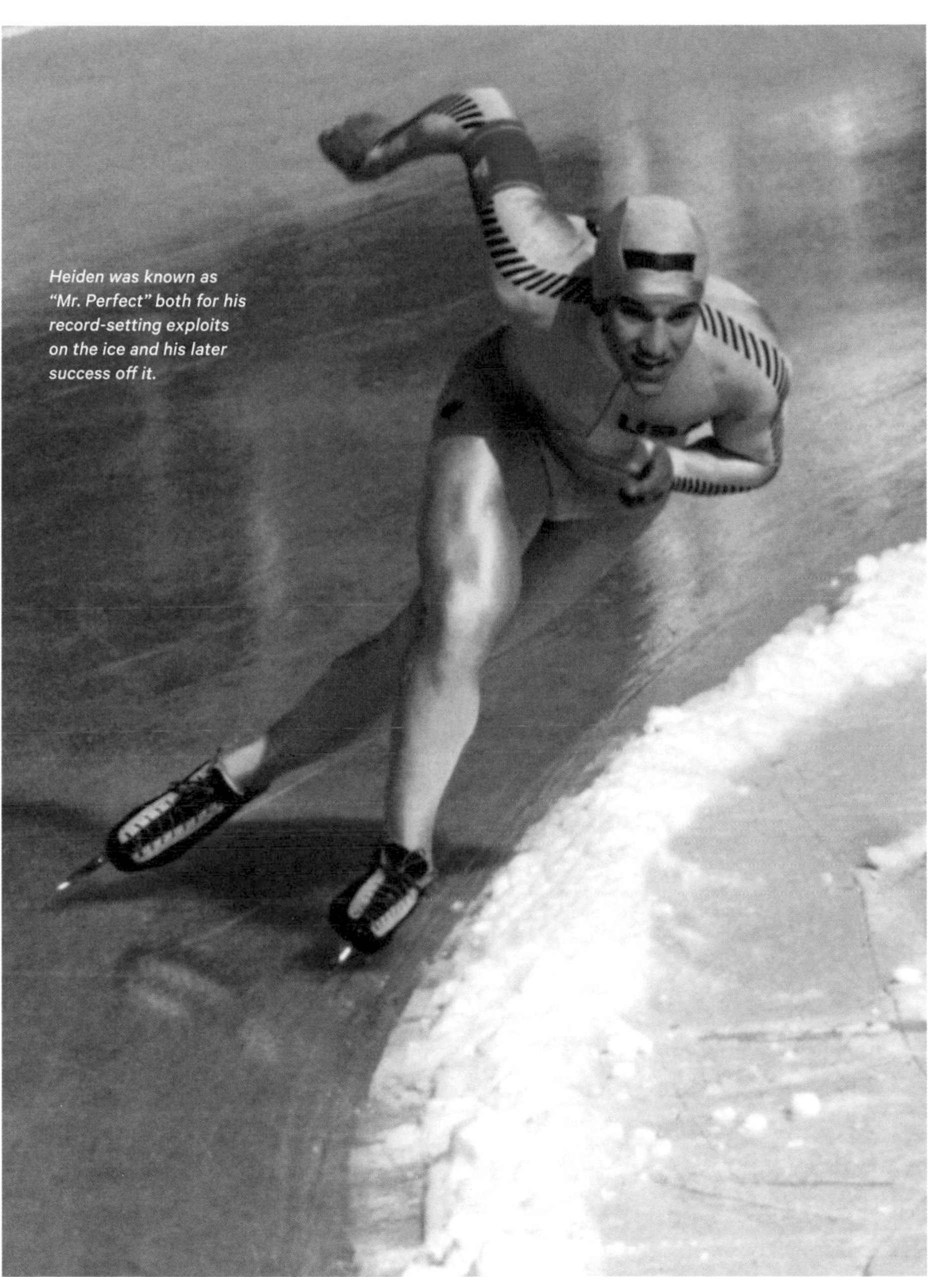

Heiden was known as "Mr. Perfect" both for his record-setting exploits on the ice and his later success off it.

Heiden won three straight world championships and established himself as far and away the best skater in the world. "I don't believe what I am seeing when I see Eric skate," said Annie Henning, a two-time medalist in Sapporo. "He just isn't real. He's as close to perfect as you can get."

Indeed, Heiden seems to exude perfection. Humility? He's got that. He turned down major sponsorships, because he felt he wasn't worthy. "I'm 21 years old," he said. "What do I have to tell anyone?" Practicality? Yeah, he has that too. "Heck, gold medals, what can you do with them? I'd rather get a nice warm-up suit. That's something I can use. When I get old, maybe I could sell them if I need the money." (In fact, while searching for his medals one day, he found one at the bottom of a closet.)

Don't forget that Heiden is incredibly athletic as well. Besides his accomplishments in speed skating, he played two years of varsity soccer at the University of Wisconsin. After Heiden's legendary run at the Lake Placid Games, Wisconsin hockey coach Bob Johnson tried in vain to get him to lace up for his squad. Heiden took up cycling upon retiring from speed skating, and narrowly missed making the 1980 Olympic team. He won the US Pro Championship in 1985 and is a member of the US Bicycling Hall of Fame.

"Heck, gold medals, what can you do with them? I'd rather get a nice warm-up suit."

How about smarts? He's got that in spades, too. Heiden graduated from Stanford medical school, and now works as an orthopedic surgeon in Utah. He also served stints as team doctor for both the Sacramento Kings and the US speed skating team. "Who would you want taking care of you more than a former speed skater?" said J. R. Celski, a three-time speed skating medalist who was in Heiden's care after he suffered a seven-inch gash to his leg.

Everything, from the start it seems, was working in Heiden's favor. And unlike others who came to the Olympics with high hopes only to see them fade away, Heiden delivered. That he chose to step away from the limelight after the Games was not a bad call. No, the guy that seems too good to be true might actually live up to those lofty expectations.

3

WILD AND STRANGE

The Olympics bring together the best athletes in the world for a two-week celebration of all that's good about sports. But that doesn't always mean the sports are played well. From pitifully poor performances to once-in-a-lifetime coincidences to the plain old odd, the Olympics are home to some weird happenings. There have been athletes who didn't quite belong, runners who needed a few unorthodox performance-enhancers to cross the finish line, golfers who didn't know they had won, and a city that lost an Olympics. For all the preparation that goes into creating a site for the Games, and the tireless work that athletes have to put in to realize their dreams, not everything at the Olympics goes smoothly. Sometimes it's a disaster.

One Pitiful Pentathlon

Tunisia's Worst Team Ever

In every Olympic event, someone has to come in last place. With five events in modern pentathlon—pistol shooting, épeé fencing, show jumping, freestyle swimming, and cross-country running—you would think that an individual competitor or team would be able to rise from the bottom of the pack. For the Tunisian squad at the 1960 Summer Olympics in Rome, the bottom began to feel awfully comfortable.

That's right: The Tunisians never finished better than third-worst in any of the events. And they finished last overall in style.

In the freestyle swim, one competitor nearly drowned. In the shooting portion, another was eliminated after firing too close to the judges. In show jumping, they all fell off their horses. At least they got creative in fencing. One Tunisian happened to be pretty decent with an épeé (relatively speaking, of course). Hoping the mask would conceal his identity, he posed as each of his teammates to compete in the round-robin tournament, meant for every competitor to face one another. But the mask could hide only so much and they were eventually disqualified. Two of the last three spots in the cross-country run belonged to Tunisians, although some props are in order for Lakdar Bouzid, who finished 40th out of 58 competitors. (For this group, that's like a gold medal.)

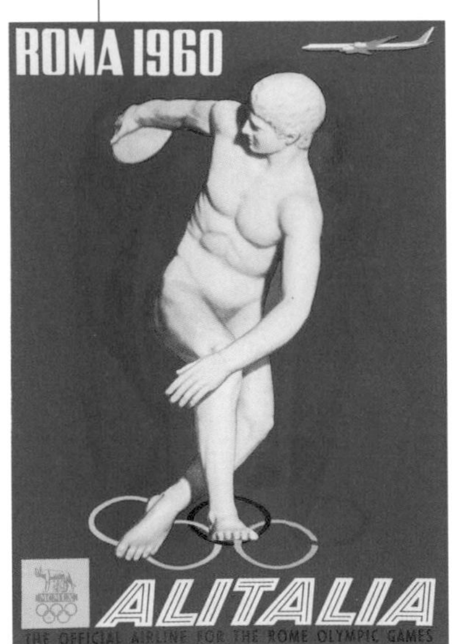

The Olympic poster featured a more competent athlete than the 1960 Tunisian pentathletes.

Although little is known about each individual competitor, we can deduce that the aforementioned drowning swimmer was Ahmed Ennachi, who finished in last place in both the swimming event and the cross-country run. At least Ennachi can cherish this from his otherwise traumatic Olympic experience: He finished 54th out of 58 competitors in the shooting portion.

The (Very) Long and Winding Road

Shizo Kanakuri and the 54-Year Race

The early Olympics were not the most organized affairs. Without big television deals to dictate coverage times and no star athletes to draw crowd attention, events played out in a haphazard fashion. Some competitors didn't even know they had won medals. So if an Olympian in, say, 1912 got lost and disappeared for 50 years, it wasn't entirely out of the ordinary.

Wait, what?

Shizo Kanakuri fell victim to the disarray of the 1912 Games in Stockholm. A top marathoner in his native Japan, Kanakuri had to endure an 18-day journey by boat and the Trans-Siberian Railway to reach Stockholm. It was Japan's first trip to the Olympics. Along the way, team manager Hyozo Omori fell ill, and Kanakuri spent more time tending to him than training. During train stops, he would get in his exercise by running around the stations. When he stepped off the train in Stockholm, he faced 90-degree heat. In fact, 34 of the 68 marathon runners would reportedly suffer from hyperthermia, or extreme overheating.

Shizo Kanakuri finally crosses the finish line in 1967 after originally starting at the 1912 Games.

Midway through the marathon, Kanakuri, who had set a world record during qualifying, was drifting in and out of consciousness. Running through the village of Tureberg, a small Stockholm suburb, Kanakuri noticed a group of people drinking orange juice in a garden. The parched marathoner stopped by and mingled for at least an hour. (There are conflicting reports over whether he stayed there overnight or went to a hotel—either way, Kanakuri had called it quits.) The next day, he left on the first boat back to Japan.

Japanese officials were embarrassed by his failure to finish. Jigoro Kano, Japan's representative to the IOC, wrote in his diary that Kanakuri brought shame to the country. The media in Japan wasn't easy on him, either, scolding him for his choice of Western footwear. They said he wore spikes, but in reality, he wore traditional *tabi*, a two-toed canvas shoe—no easy feat in a 26.2-mile race.

Although the Japanese media were well aware of Kanakuri's travails, the Swedes hadn't a clue. In fact, they had no idea where he even was, and placed him on the missing persons list. Swedish officials couldn't find the runner for more than 50 years, despite the fact that he finished 16th at the 1920 Games in Antwerp and competed again four years later in Paris. Finally, in 1967, the Swedish National Olympic Committee tracked down the 75-year-old Kanakuri and invited him to return to Stockholm to celebrate the 55th anniversary of the 1912 Games. Kanakuri, then a retired geography teacher, accepted.

It took the "father of Japanese marathon" over five decades to finish the race.

Billed as "the missing marathoner," Kanakuri was asked to complete his race to raise funds for Swedish athletes. The septuagenarian runner, competing with good spirit, happily obliged and finished the marathon. The official time? Fifty-four years, eight months, six days, five hours, 32 minutes, and 20.3 seconds. "It was a long trip," Kanakuri told reporters afterwards. "Along the way, I got married, had six children, and 10 grandchildren."

Before he left for Japan, Kanakuri returned to Tureberg and found the garden of Bengt Petre, whose father was the original host. Together they shared a glass of orange juice.

The Wildest Race of All Time

Calamity at the 1908 Marathon

The 1908 Olympic marathon in London featured Sir Arthur Conan Doyle, a fainting pastry chef, Champagne energy drinks, Queen Alexandra applauding from her royal box with the ferrule of her umbrella, and the creation of the official distance of marathons worldwide.

Let's take all that in reverse order. The first modern Olympic marathon, in 1896, was held at 24.85 miles. That distance was chosen to honor

Dorando Pietri (center) gets just the help he needs to cross the finish line first. It was blatant cheating.

Pheidippides, who according to one legend, ran 24.5 miles from the town of Marathon to Athens in 490 BC to announce a victory over Persia. (After delivering the message, he promptly collapsed and died.) The 1908 marathon, however, would be held at 26 miles, 385 yards because Princess Mary wanted her children, including Prince Albert (the future King George VI and father of Queen Elizabeth II), to be able to watch the race from their rooms at Windsor Castle. That increased the distance just a tad to the now-familiar 26.22 miles, today's official standard.

Most competitors in 1908 had never run that far. Charles Hefferon of South Africa was in the lead at 24 miles—he took a glass of Champagne from a fan, thinking he had the race locked up, but suffered from cramps and ended up finishing third. It seems alcohol was the drink of choice for runners during the race. In fact, there was a scientific belief at the time that booze, and Champagne in particular, was a stimulant that soothed the stomach. Everyone was imbibing. The pre-race favorite, Tom Longboat of Canada, withdrew after enjoying a bit too much as well.

It's unclear what caused Dorando Pietri to struggle at the finish. A five-foot-two-inch baker from Capri, Pietri took over first place after Hefferon cramped up. But the Italian was fighting his own battles. It probably didn't help that his pre-race meal was a steak. Whatever the reason, with about 385 yards left, Pietri fainted.

Conan Doyle, 21 years after writing the first Sherlock Holmes novel, was in the stands covering the race for the *Daily Mail*. "Good heavens, he has fainted," he wrote of Pietri. "Is it possible that even at this last moment the prize may slip through his fingers? . . . I do not think in all that great assembly any man would have wished victory to be torn at the last instant from this plucky little Italian."

Pietri would get up with the help of track officials. "I no longer knew if I was heading towards my goal or away from it," he wrote later. "They tell me I fell another five or six times and that I looked like a man suffering from paralysis, stumbling with tiny steps towards his wheelchair."

Pietri, in a famous photo, is seen crossing the finish line with two officials by his side. The crowd was enthralled. The band played "The Conquering Hero." Queen Alexandra cheered. "He has gone to the extreme of human endurance," Conan Doyle wrote. "No Roman of the prime ever bore himself better than Dorando of the Olympics of 1908. The great breed is not yet extinct."

American long-distance runner Johnny Hayes finished the race shortly after Pietri. He had noticed Pietri getting help, which is grounds for disqualification, and launched an appeal. (Hayes, it should be noted, wasn't exactly sober after taking some sips of brandy during the race.) The appeal was successful. Hayes won gold, the Champagne-drunk South African Charles Hefferon won silver, and Pietri, the fan favorite, was disqualified. This led to an outcry. Conan Doyle raised, in today's money, more than $32,000 for Pietri. Queen Alexandra gave him a silver cup. Irving Berlin had one of his first hits based on the runner, titled "Dorando":

Dorando! Dorando!
He run-a, run-a, run-a, run like anything

(Luckily, Berlin would improve his songwriting skills a bit.)

Pietri didn't win the gold, but he made out okay. In November of that year, Pietri and Hayes competed one-on-one at an indoor marathon in New York. It was a sellout crowd in the original Madison Square Garden, and Pietri won by 43 seconds. This time, there was no Champagne or brandy or Queen of England or Sir Conan Doyle. And there was no one aiding his victory.

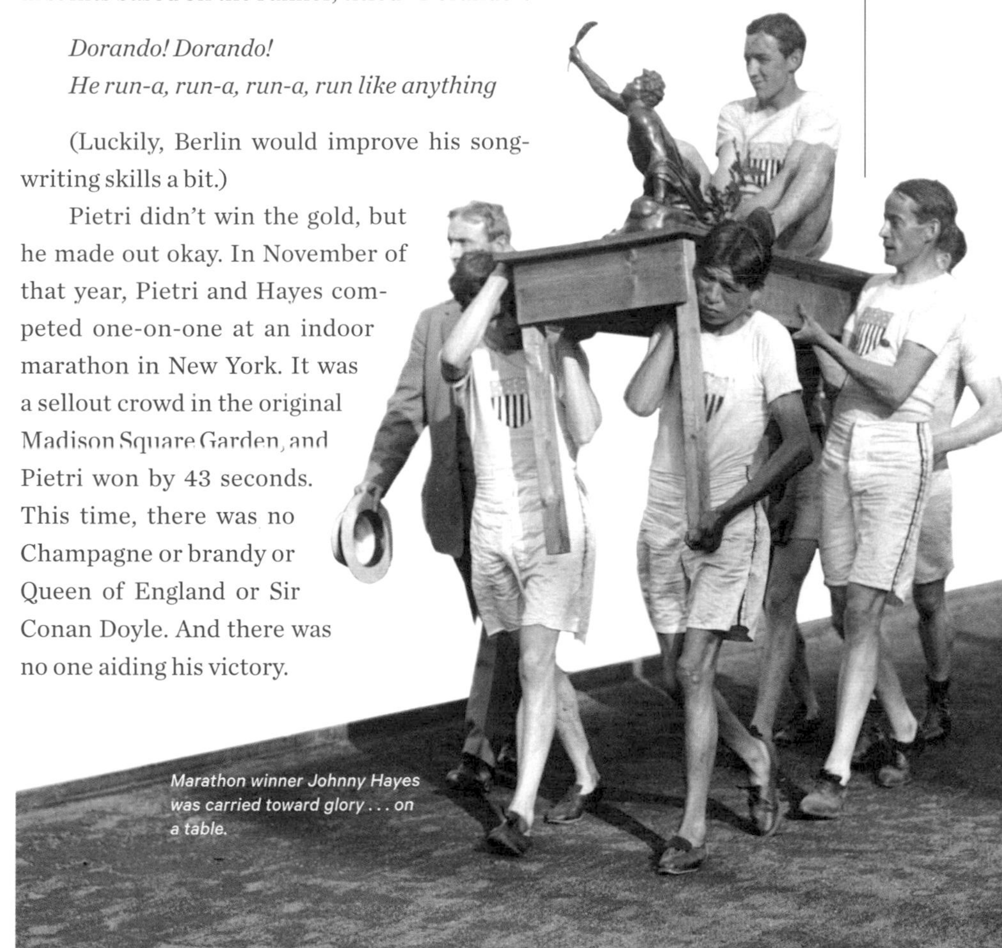

Marathon winner Johnny Hayes was carried toward glory . . . on a table.

An Assortment of Awful Athletes

Even You Can Make the Olympics!

Who gets to be an Olympian? Is it the athlete who has trained all her life to have one moment on the world's stage? Is it the one who sacrificed, worked two jobs, and fought through injuries to make it? Or is it the guy who just gets lucky?

Eric Moussambani might fall into that last category. The 22-year-old from Equatorial Guinea earned a place at the Sydney Games in 2000 as a swimmer because of a wild card system that awarded spots to athletes from developing countries. First Moussambani qualified—then he learned how to swim. In his heat were just three participants, so when two false-started and were disqualified, Moussambani was left to his own devices.

At first, there was laughter. How could you not join in? Fans paid top dollar to see athletes at the height of their abilities, and Moussambani had never swum a 100-meter race in his life. As he flailed about desperately, inching his way toward the finish, laughter soon turned into good-natured cheers. And though his time was at least 30 seconds slower than the gold medal winner's mark way back in 1896, Moussambani became a media phenomenon. Dubbed "Eric the Eel," he was given a translator for interviews, and Speedo brandished him with a new swimsuit and a promotional deal.

Moussambani was in a class by himself—literally.

Lovable losers are lovable for a reason: There's a part of them in all of us. We could be that bad on the biggest stage. We could make a fool out of ourselves. And surely we could get lucky and find ourselves competing under the five rings.

Or we could be Michael Edwards of England, who came in last place in the 70- and 90-meter ski jumps at the 1988 Winter Games in Calgary. He took up the sport on a lark and became a fan favorite, adored as much for his incompetence as for his zeal and nerdy eyeglasses. Frank King, the CEO of those Games, said he "soared like an eagle." But don't fault "Eddie the Eagle" for lack of trying: He trained vigorously by doing 60 jumps a day and was a proficient skier. As actor Steve Coogan, who at one point was set to play Edwards in a movie, put it, "his balls must be made of titanium."

We then look at a sport like luge and think, *Hey, I can do that! I ski occasionally!* We could be like George Tucker, a portly 36-year-old Puerto Rican doctoral student in physics who finished last in luge in 1984 by 14 seconds. The first winter Olympian from the Caribbean, Tucker was a press favorite described by *Sports Illustrated* as "overweight but quick-witted." Or maybe we can be like skier Jamil El Reedy, who grew up in New York but competed as Egypt's sole representative at the 1984 Winter Games. He prepared for the downhill and slalom events by spending 40 days in a scorpion-infested cave in Egypt's Western Desert. Couldn't have been *that* bad. And he didn't even finish in last place!

And surely if Elizabeth Swaney can do it, why can't we? The American-born skier exploited loopholes in the qualifying system to represent Hungary, her grandparents' country, and competed in Pyeongchang in the skiing halfpipe. So what if she couldn't do any tricks, but simply rode up and down the halfpipe repeatedly? The point is she got there—some might say "scammed" her way there, more specifically—to fulfill an Olympic dream. That has to count for something, right?

Indeed, recall the wise words of IOC founder Pierre de Coubertin, who said, "The important thing in life is not to triumph but to compete." Credit these athletes for pushing this statement to its furthest logical limit. After all, they did everything they could, against the odds, to compete against the best. If that isn't good enough for the Olympics, then what the heck have we been watching for the last 124 years?

Here the Eagle soars—only Michael Edwards soared for far less time than his competitors.

The Worst Olympic Committee Ever

The Denver Games That Never Were

In 1970, the IOC awarded Denver the 1976 Winter Olympics. It was meant to honor America's upcoming bicentennial, a celebration on top of a celebration. But two years later, after a lethal combination of poor planning, irresponsible budgeting, and a steady slew of outright lies, the Games were snatched from Denver and given to Innsbruck, Austria.

What the heck happened?

For one thing, the organizers tried to cram everything into a price tag of just $14 million. The previous Winter Games in Sapporo cost $1.3 billion and Grenoble in 1968 was practically a bargain at $250 million. And only $5 million, according to Governor John Love, would come from taxpayers. In a speech to the Colorado state legislature, Love asked, "Is five million . . . too much to spend for the excellence and pride and an international celebration in the hundredth year of Colorado's statehood and the two-hundredth year of our nation?" Clearly this was too good to be true.

In order to sell these as the "Economical Games," the Denver Olympic Organizing Committee (DOOC) relied on financial tomfoolery and far-fetched ideas. What was proposed and what was possible seemed to move further apart each day. They wanted the Olympic Village to be at the University of Denver—but they never bothered to discuss it with the school. Nor did they hatch a plan for what to do with the students, who would be in the middle of their semester. DOOC organizers also claimed that the Denver area had the necessary room to host 100,000 visitors, but hotels had space for only 35,000 people.

One disastrous problem led to another in an absurd comedy of errors.

Further raising eyebrows, the DOOC wanted all events to be near the university, but the downhill skiing events, hosted at Mount Sniktau, was 50 miles away. And, to make matters worse, Mount Sniktau didn't get much snow because it fell on the eastern side of the Continental Divide. (Most Colorado ski resorts are to the west.) Before organizers presented the site to the IOC, they had an artist airbrush snow onto a photo of the mountain.

One disastrous problem led to another, like an absurd comedy of errors. As the skiing venue became impractical, the DOOC turned to other Colorado ski resorts, tapping Steamboat Springs to host some events. But the resort is 160 miles away from Denver, so they proposed an airborne taxi service. Committee head Walter Schirra, one of the original Project Mercury astronauts and the ninth human in space, suggested using DHC-6 Otter planes to ferry people back and forth. Otters, though, hold just 20 people.

Even more complications arose in the small Denver suburb of Evergreen, where the biathlon and ski jump events would be held. Despite the fact that the town's chances of snow in February are just 1 in 25—it's called Evergreen, for crying out loud—the bigger issue was where to put the courses. The biathlon track would have to cut through backyards and schools—not ideal locations for shooting ranges. The ski jump would've necessitated rerouting a residential road and bulldozing a hill.

Then there was the matter of bobsled: As costs soared, building a track looked impossible. The backup plan was even more impossible. After organizers ruled against eliminating bobsled from the competition altogether—a wise choice—they wanted to use the track in Lake Placid, New York. Just one catch: Lake Placid is nearly 2,000 miles away from Denver.

THOSE FAMOUS RINGS

The five Olympic rings logo was originally designed by Pierre de Coubertin in 1913. The idea: the five colors, along with the white background, would represent "the colours of every country without exception." Famed psychiatrist Carl Jung reportedly conceived of the interlocking design, which symbolizes continuity. This, Coubertin said, "is truly an international emblem." The rings made their debut at the 1920 Games in Antwerp.

It became increasingly difficult for organizers to defend their half-baked plan. As new acting governor John Vanderhoof put it ever so delicately, "[The DOOC] were pressed for time, so they lied a bit." Grassroots activists and politicians had had enough and took action. A few state lawmakers began to speak out, and eventually the legislature slashed the DOOC's budget by more than a third. The true cost, it was determined, would not be $14 million. In fact, press housing *alone* would be $26 million. The final tally would also include substantial costs for remodeling, broadcasting, and the Olympic Village.

A group called Citizens for Colorado's Future led a staff of four volunteers to collect 77,392 signatures in opposition to the Games in just one month. Another particularly active local group, the Protect Our Mountain Environment, said they were "simply convinced Colorado would be the laughingstock of the world if it tried to stage the Olympic events."

New IOC President Lord Killanin (second from right) gives Denver the boot in 1972.

These campaigns, spearheaded by an ambitious state legislator, Dick Lamm, forced a vote on a constitutional amendment on whether the state could provide more funds for the Games. Though the DOOC brought in big names like Bob Hope, Bing Crosby, and Jesse Owens to rally support, the measure had little chance of working in their favor, and voters approved the amendment. The IOC quickly took action and removed the Games from Denver. Three months later, they rewarded it to Innsbruck, Austria, host of the Winter Games in 1964. Lamm would be elected governor in 1975 and serve three terms.

Even this immensely troubled history hasn't stopped Denver from trying again. The city put forth a bid to host the 2030 Winter Games. But maybe the ghosts of 1976 came back to the bite them. The US Olympic Committee—headquartered in Colorado Springs, of all places—chose Salt Lake City's bid over Denver's as the official American selection.

OUCH: HIGH-PROFILE RETRACTED BIDS

The triathlon in Central Park. Baseball at Yankee Stadium. Basketball at the Garden. A velodrome in the Bronx; a sailing marina off the Hudson. The proposed plan for the 2012 Olympics in New York City looked, at least on paper, pretty cool.

There was a slight hiccup, however: The city needed a brand-new stadium. There was a proposed West Side Stadium, which would have been the nerve center for the Games. Afterward, it would be the new home of the New York Jets, who would shoulder more than half of the cost. But opposition was fierce. Citizen groups complained about potential traffic; Cablevision, which owned Madison Square Garden, spent $30 million in negative campaign ads. When the local board rejected the state's contribution of $300 million, the stadium—and the bid—were both essentially dead.

New York isn't the only major American city whose residents said no to the Games. Boston was looking to host the 2024 Games but public support declined rapidly, egged on by a local group, No Boston 2024, which loudly protested costs and lack of transparency. The USOC eventually pulled the plug.

There's an overall contradiction here: Some 89 percent of Americans, according to one poll, really want the Olympics in the United States. But only 61 percent want it in *their* city, and only 52 percent want to use taxpayer funds. The message: Oh, sure we want the Games! Just not in my city—nor with my money.

New York City Mayor Michael Bloomberg was thrilled to make the IOC shortlist, but it wasn't meant to be after citizens said no.

The Cheating Marathon

Rat Poison and the Art of Doing Whatever It Takes

If you're going to run a marathon in 90-degree heat, as you negotiate a course riddled with cracked stone pavement, bad footing everywhere, seven hills ranging from 100 to 300 feet, and dogs, cars, and pedestrians in the way, you should at least have ample access to water . . . right?

Wrong. At least not if you're running the marathon in the 1904 Olympics in St. Louis. The race, like the rest of the Games that year, was slapped together quickly, as organizers were focused more on the concurrent St. Louis World's Fair. But there was indeed a marathon, as there has been at every Games before and since. And it was an utter disaster.

Thirty-two runners started the race—just 14 finished it. The course was, as Olympic official Charles Lucas wrote, "the most difficult a human being was ever asked to run over." Behold the calamities that befell these unfortunate souls: With no traffic or crowd control in place, one runner was chased away by wild dogs. Another vomited and gave up. Two ran barefoot, while one more fashion-conscious athlete ran in dress pants and a beret. (Thankfully, a kind fellow competitor cut the pants into shorts for him.) Another nearly died—poor William Garcia, an American, was found lying on the side of the road during the race. He had developed serious stomach issues after inhaling a massive amount of the dust kicked up by cars along the route.

The near-fatality, wild dog chase, and oddly dapper athletic wear weren't the only shenanigans. Take Felix Carvajal, our friend in the beret. A mailman from Cuba, he had raised the funds to travel to the Games by running across the length of the island, some 800 miles. Upon his arrival in the United States, he promptly lost that money in a New Orleans dice game and had to hitchhike to St. Louis. Carvajal seemed more interested in playful hijinks than in winning: During the race, he asked for a peach from a spectator, who refused to give him one. Carvajal snagged two anyway and ate as he ran away. He then stopped at an orchard and scarfed down some rotten apples. He quickly cramped and took a nap. And, in the biggest surprise of all, he finished fourth—just imagine a marathon so dysfunctional that such a man would finish in the top five.

RIGHT: *These 32 runners had no idea what was about to hit them.* **BELOW:** *Hicks, the eventual winner, full of tasty strychnine.*

Then there was the original winner, Fred Lorz. The bricklayer from New York City qualified for the Olympics by finishing in the top eight of a seven-mile race in Celtic Park in Queens. He probably should have trained over longer distances. After running the first nine miles of the 24.85-mile marathon, he fatigued, so his manager picked him up in his car. When the car broke down after 11 miles, Lorz decided to reenter the race near the finish line. He came in first. Though he later claimed it was just a harmless joke, spectators didn't think it was so funny at the time. Alice Roosevelt, the daughter of President Theodore Roosevelt, was about to award Lorz the gold medal when someone mentioned that he had cheated. Lorz, to his credit, fessed up and admitted it was all a ruse. (He did stick with the whole marathon thing and won the Boston Marathon—fairly—in 1905.)

The real winner was Tom Hicks, a brass worker from Massachusetts. He had been in the lead for a good part of the race. With seven miles remaining, he was given a mixture of strychnine and egg whites. (Strychnine was used back then as a stimulant, but it's better known today as rat poison.) It was the first known use of a drug at the Olympics.

As Hicks neared the end of the race, he was administered another dose of the tasty rat poison concoction, this time with a hit of brandy. "Over the last two miles of the road," wrote Lucas, "Hicks was running mechanically, like a well-oiled piece of machinery. His eyes were dull, lusterless; the ashen color of his face and skin had deepened; his arms appeared as weights well tied down; he could scarcely lift his legs, while his knees were almost stiff."

With a mile left, Hicks was close to death. He begged for food and tried to lie down. He walked up hills and then jogged on the way down. Running wasn't working, and it looked more like a shuffle. Eventually, a few of his team members lifted him up and carried him over the finish line. Here, ladies and gentlemen, was your gold medalist. Hicks, though, was physically unable to receive his medal, and doctors rushed him to a nearby gym for a physical examination. After an hour of rest, he was taken to the Missouri Athletic Club, where he promptly fell asleep. He had lost eight pounds.

After running a few more marathons, Hicks moved to Canada, where he became a naturalized citizen. We can only hope that he went on to use rat poison for its intended purpose.

Whoops—Wrong Medal

An Extra Lap Proves Extra Costly

When competing in an Olympic race, the last thing on your mind should be whether the course is up to snuff. You'd be correct to assume that 100 meters is really 100 meters, or that the lanes in the pool are equally spaced, or that the basketball is properly inflated. Well, maybe not. At the 1932 Summer Games in Los Angeles, one person didn't do his job.

It was the 3,000-meter steeplechase, an unusual race where competitors jump over different obstacles, like water pits and hurdles. With each passing lap, an official was supposed to switch the lap number in descending order. The first time the runners passed him, he completely blew it and forgot to update the lap card, so the runners ended up going an extra 3,460-meter-long round. "I yelled at the judges," said American Joe McCluskey. "When they said six laps to go, I yelled, 'Five!' When they said five, I yelled, 'Four!'"

The 1932 steeplechase race got a little harder when an official added an extra lap.

So what's the difference of an extra lap, anyway? It's big. First, it cost Finnish runner Volmari Iso-Hollo a shot at the world record. (He still won gold.) It also cost McCluskey a silver medal. As he crossed the actual finish line, he was in second place, but on the ensuing lap, British runner Tom Evenson passed him.

When McCluskey notified officials of their mistake, they made a tantalizing offer: He could rerun the race the following day at the correct distance. But McCluskey declined. "A race has only one finish line," he fumed.

McCluskey would go onto a storied career in track and field. He won 27 national titles in a variety of distances, and did so without much speed. And though he was elected to the National Track and Field Hall of Fame in 1996, that Los Angeles lap mix-up stayed with him forever. You think you've ever been shafted at work? Try missing out on the right Olympic medal.

General Opium

Patton's First Battle

General George Patton—then just a lieutenant—was lying on the ground, unconscious. "I was out for some hours," he wrote. "Once I came to I could not move or open my eyes and felt them give me a shot of more hop. I feared that it would be an overdose and kill me."

Patton didn't die. He was just completing the running portion of the modern pentathlon at the 1912 Olympics in Stockholm. His trainer administered opium, then legal and thought to boost energy, to revive the collapsed 26-year-old. The man who would later help liberate Europe in World War II was three years out from graduating West Point. He had learned that he would join the Olympic team only two months before the Games began. "Old Blood and Guts" hadn't swum in three years, so while sailing to Europe on the SS *Finland*, he tied one end of a rope to the deck and another around his waist and swam until the chafing got to be too much.

Patton acquitted himself quite well in Stockholm. He finished 11th in shooting, eighth in fencing, sixth in equestrian, and third in the run. But he placed a disappointing 21st in the shooting event; he later claimed, however, that his .38 caliber pistol bullets passed through large holes created by the other competitors' .22 caliber weapons, meaning he hit more targets than he was credited for. Patton finished fifth overall behind four Swedes—if the judges had scored his shots correctly, he might've won a medal.

Patton qualified for the 1916 Games, but those were canceled because of World War I. Whether he would've won an Olympic medal is anyone's guess. But it is clear that the hard-charging manner he later showed on the battlefield came through on the playing field.

LEFT: *"Old Blood and Guts" was a particularly strong fencer and runner.*

SEMPER MEDALIS

The US Army has an Olympic division. Okay, not quite, but there is the World Class Athlete Program to support Olympic dreams. It's simple: Any active-duty soldier good enough to make the Olympics can receive top-notch training and coaching while serving. Though it's been in effect only since 1997, the results so far have been impressive. Army specialist Paul Chelimo won silver in the 5,000 meters in 2016, Army Major Christopher Fogt won a medal in bobsled in 2014, and Army Major Michael Anti won silver in the 50m rifle in 2004. American service members have found tremendous success in Olympic Games. Since 1948, soldiers have won more than 100 medals.

Just a Sip

Brewskies, Pistols, and the First-Ever PED Ban

Who among us hasn't taken a sip—or two, or three—of alcohol to calm the nerves before a big moment? It's called liquid courage for a reason. So Hans-Gunnar Liljenwall, a Swedish pentathlete at the 1968 Summer Olympics in Mexico City, did what any anxious person might do. He took a big ol' swig of beer before the pistol-shooting event.

Okay, it wasn't just one swig. He reportedly drank two beers, which, even if it didn't get him drunk, was probably not the best idea before taking control of a firearm. His timing was even worse: In 1967, the IOC banned all performance-enhancing drugs, alcoholic beverages included. Liljenwall tested positive for ethanol and became the first athlete to be officially disqualified for performance-enhancers. Not only was he booted out of competition, but he also cost the Swedish team their bronze medal. (France was bumped up from fourth to third.)

In 2017, the World Anti-Doping Agency, which governs drug use in sport, removed alcohol from the prohibited substances list. Somewhere, Liljenwall, who was 76 at the time, was smiling—or supremely angry.

Found Love in a Hopeless Place

Forbidden Romance of the 1956 Olympics

In its modern incarnation, the Olympic Village has become legendary as a haven of sex and lawlessness (read: Ryan Lochte). But the amorous atmosphere isn't known for being particularly conducive to lasting romance. And at the 1956 Summer Olympics in Melbourne, true love would seem to be a difficult proposition between athletes from countries on opposite sides of the Cold War.

Harold Connolly was a hammer thrower from Boston. He excelled at his sport despite a withered left arm that was four and a half inches shorter than his right, and a left hand that was two-thirds the size of his right. He took up the sport while at Boston College, in part to strengthen that arm. "The thought of being patronized made me sick," he once said. "I wanted to play by the rules, not rules adapted for me because I was disabled."

Connolly, who would go on to set six world records from 1956 to 1965, won gold in the event in Melbourne. He wore his trademark ballet slippers to help with his footing. While at the Games, Connolly met Olga Fikotova of Czechoslovakia. Fikotova had been competing in discus for only two years when she, too, won gold. The two quickly fell in love.

Fikotova and Connolly quickly became the Golden Couple—both metallurgically and otherwise—after the 1956 Games.

Connolly proposed a few months after the Games, and both athletes were told to keep things low-key. The Americans approved of the union—Secretary of State John Foster Dulles, a Cold War hawk not exactly known as a romantic, said, "We believe in love." The Czechs, however, seemed worried that Fikotova would defect and "sell out to American glitter," so the couple had to appeal to Czechoslovakian president Antonin Zapotocky.

The government eventually granted permission and the two married in Czechoslovakia. Among the 30,000 witnesses packed into Prague's Old Town Square was Emil Zatopek, the legendary runner. The pair returned to the United States, settling in Santa Monica. Connolly taught high school English; Fikotova attended medical school. They were married for 16 years and had four children before divorcing in 1973.

Connolly and Fikotova both returned to the Olympics after 1956. Connolly competed three more times, finishing as high as sixth in 1964. Fikotova was denied permission to compete for the Czech team—from 1960 to 1972, she competed for the United States, finishing as high as sixth in 1968. In 1972, she was the country's flag bearer.

THE WILD VILLAGE

Athlete safety is always of the highest priority at the Olympics. Perhaps that's why Olympians had their choice of 110,000 condoms provided to them at the 2018 Games. (That works out to 37 per athlete.) But that's nothing—there were 450,000 condoms in Rio in 2016.

Why so many? Turns out athletes have a little extra energy to burn off. American swimmer Ryan Lochte estimated that 70 to 75 percent of Olympians are getting busy during the Games. (We shudder to think of his London experience: "My last Olympics, I had a girlfriend—big mistake. Now I'm single, so London should be really good. I'm excited.") Added British table tennis player Matthew Syed: "Olympic athletes have to display an unnatural level of self-discipline in the build-up to big competitions. How else is this going to manifest itself than with a volcanic release of pent-up hedonism?"

In 1988 in Seoul, there were so many condoms found on the roof of an Olympic Village building that the organizers banned outdoor sex. (That rule didn't follow for future Games, where US soccer star Hope Solo said she saw people getting "down and dirty" everywhere, including "on the grass.") Stay safe, Olympians!

Loathsome Losers

How to Succeed in Badminton Without Really Trying

The point of the Olympics is to win. Right? Well, not necessarily if you're a badminton player. The sport has a weird quirk when it comes to Olympic play: With a round-robin format in the preliminary round that determines seeding for the knockout round, it can sometimes be advantageous to lose in the earlier qualifying rounds.

Here's what happened at the 2012 Summer Games in London. In the women's doubles, there were 16 teams. Eight would qualify for the next round. Some teams had already qualified for that round, despite having one preliminary game remaining. That's when insanity ensued.

The Chinese twosome didn't want to face the other Chinese pair, which was ranked second. The Koreans, it turned out, *also* didn't want to face that Chinese pair, because of how good they were. So the teams made a heroic

Olympic judge Thorsten Berg threatens Indonesian and South Korean players with a dreaded black card.

effort to look awful and lose. They served into the net. They served below the net. The longest rally lasted four shots. Fans booed. "I'm sorry, it's blindly obvious what's going on," the BBC's announcer said. "It's as if neither player wants to win the match. Tonight has left me with a very nasty taste in the mouth." The Chinese lost, but things would get even worse from there.

An hour later, the Indonesian and South Korean teams played. The Indonesians wanted to lose to avoid later facing a good Chinese team—the South Koreans wanted to lose to avoid facing the other Korean team, a talented squad who would reduce their medal chances. So they, too, did their best to lose. This time, the head ref Thorsten Berg got involved. "It looked pretty awful," he said. "This was not right. I told them, they were making a serious mistake."

Sometimes it pays to lose: Each team made a heroic effort to appear completely incompetent.

After a few more serves, Berg noticed that his warning had fallen on deaf ears. So he pulled out a black card, which signals disqualification. The players weren't DQ'd yet, but the threat was imminent. "They should play or they would be in deep shit," Berg put it plainly.

Play didn't seem to improve at all and the Indonesians lost. These world-class athletes looked like it was their first time holding a racquet. But all of these teams, in the end, would lose. They were immediately disqualified for "conducting oneself in a manner that is clearly abusive or detrimental to the sport." The Chinese team that no one wanted to face took home gold. But the biggest winners might have been the Russian team, who suddenly leapfrogged to their first-ever badminton medal, a bronze.

The Badminton World Federation responded by changing the rules so that all teams finishing in second place would go through another draw to figure out who they would play in the knockout round. No players involved in the fracas were further disciplined beyond the disqualification. Yu Wang, one of the Chinese players, rebounded nicely winning gold at the 2013 world championships. And Jung Kyung-eun, from the South Korean team, won bronze at the 2016 Olympics in Rio. Maybe it does pay to lose?

You Get a Silver! You Get a Silver! Everybody Gets a Silver!

Second Best . . . Times Three

At the 1968 Winter Olympics in Grenoble, the US women's speed skating team got into a bit of a pickle. First, Jeanne Ashworth, who won bronze in that event in 1960, took a tumble in a time trial and couldn't skate. Her 18-year-old replacement, Jenny Fish, made the team only as an alternate. Meanwhile, Dianne Holum, a 16-year-old from Illinois and the team's best hope for a medal, got hit by a nasty flu bug that was floating around the

From left: Jenny Fish, Mary Meyers, and Dianne Holum. Second place isn't so bad when you can share it with friends.

Olympic Village. Then there was Mary Meyers, who had admittedly lost her passion for the sport and was ready to move on to another career.

Meyers was first to go, and she finished with a respectable 46.3 seconds. She seemed relieved to get it over with. "Speed skating is a sort of love-hate relationship," she said. "I like the skating part but I cannot stand the getting in shape part. I can never go through it again."

Up next was Holum, whose classmates at Regina Dominican High prayed together in an assembly at school before the race. They also sent a rather unholy cable to Grenoble: "Dianne, the members of the junior class are hoping you will beat their [expletive] off." Holum, full of flu medicine in her system, went next and finished in . . . 46.3 seconds.

Then it was Fish's turn. And wouldn't you know it: Fish clocked in at, you guessed right, 46.3 seconds. That time earned silver and no bronze was awarded. (Lyudmila Titova, from the Soviet Union, won gold.) The three Americans cozied up on the medal stand. "We planned it that way," Fish said.

Holum would go on to take bronze in the 1,000 meters as well. She also won a gold and a silver in 1972 in Sapporo, where she was the flag bearer, and later helped coach five-time gold medalist Eric Heiden. Her daughter, Kirstin Holum, participated in speed skating in the 1998 Games in Nagano.

Neither Fish nor Meyers competed in another Games. But a medal shared three ways—well, it's certainly better than nothing.

BEST EVER?

Somehow this one seems a bit off. Melankomas of Caria was an ancient Olympic boxer, who, believe it or not, went undefeated in AD 49 despite never hitting an opponent or being hit by one. He did it with incredible endurance and by staying quick on his feet. Apparently he could fight all day long, and waited for his opponents to tire out. (The original rope-a-dope!) According to one legend, he went two straight days with arms in the air, never putting them down.

High-Tech Tomfoolery

The Tale of the Unnecessary Cheater

Boris Onischenko was a world-class pentathlete. The three-time medalist entered the 1976 Summer Games in Montreal as a favorite after winning both a silver medal as an individual and a gold in the team event in 1972. So why would he go to such elaborate lengths to cheat this time?

Ironically enough, the Ukrainian-born world champion's strongest discipline was fencing. He started the day off incredibly well, leading the Soviet team to beat the British handily. But the Brits noticed something was off. "Onischenko scored a hit, but we could not see how he managed it," said Mike Proudfoot, the team manager.

Onischenko kept racking up the victories—until he faced off against his friend Jim Fox, one of the best pentathletes in British history. When Onischenko reached out to hit Fox, the scoreboard lit up. (For those who might need a refresher: In épée fencing, a point is counted when the tip of the weapon has been depressed from the force of hitting an opponent, which sends a signal to an electric system.) But Fox had leapt backward and yet somehow didn't feel anything. "It was like waving a magic wand," he said.

The world-class pentathlete didn't need a rigged blade to succeed—he was good enough to win gold.

Fox had suspected something was awry while watching Onischenko's bout with another fencer. The Brit noticed that the opponent seemed to have backed away from the weapon without being hit, yet the Soviet still got a point. Fox and Onischenko had known and competed against each other for years, so he decided to confront his friend. "I said: 'Something is wrong here.' He said: 'Yes, I know I didn't hit you,' and tried to change his weapon."

Fox immediately called for an investigation of what he thought was just a faulty épée. His most worthy adversary couldn't possibly be cheating . . . right? When officials examined the weapon, they found something incredible. Buried in the handle and hidden under leather was a complex wiring system. Onischenko could press a pad in the handle to score a hit.

"It was a real engineering job," Proudfoot said. "Not just a ham amateur's effort."

Onischenko was eventually disqualified. But to make matters even stranger, as the officials examined the blade, they allowed him to compete with another one. And he went 5–2. Onischenko didn't need the rigged blade to succeed—he was good enough to win, even to be a potential Olympic champion. "He is a great fencer," said Fox. "The need to win is too great for some people."

Onishchenko immediately returned home to Kiev, and his two teammates continued on. Pavel Lednev won silver in the individual, and there is no indication that he or the other Russian used rigged equipment. The press called the disgraced pentathlete "Disonischenko." Two months later, Soviet leader Leonid Brezhnev reportedly berated him in person. He was dismissed from the Red Army and fined 5,000 rubles. He had to give back all his medals, began working as a taxi driver, and since the Montreal Games, has lived in obscurity.

An official catching Boris Onischenko red-handed—his weapon hid an elaborate scheme to help him cheat.

ANCIENT CHEATING HISTORY

The history of cheating in the Olympics is, unfortunately, long and varied, with gold medals stripped and entire countries banned. But it ain't exactly anything new. Olympic athletes have cheated since the very beginning way back in ancient Greece.

Nero, the tyrannical, sex-obsessed, and completely shameless Roman emperor, enjoyed many varied pursuits, athletics among them. Desperate to race chariots in the Olympics in AD 67, he bribed officials to delay the Games by two years so that they would happen during his already planned trip to Greece. Upon his arrival, Nero paid some more so that he wouldn't have to actually compete against anyone. It's no surprise, then, that the emperor—after taking a potion made from wild boar's manure—won gold in the four-horse chariot race. All this despite falling off his horse and failing to even finish.

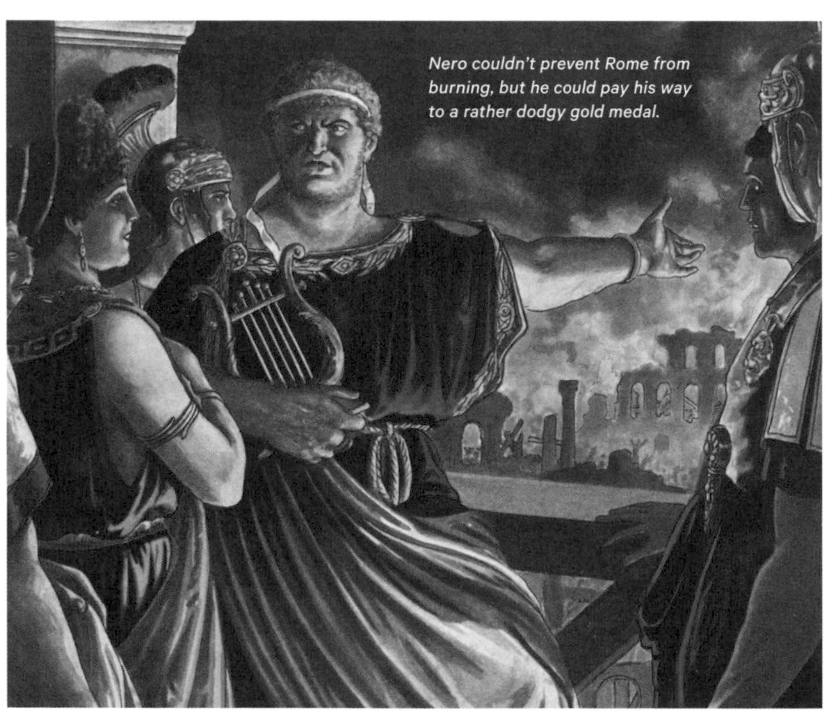

Nero couldn't prevent Rome from burning, but he could pay his way to a rather dodgy gold medal.

Better Than Nothing?

The Shortest World Record Ever

If you owned something for 1.2 seconds, and then it was gone forever, was it ever really yours? How about just 0.4 seconds?

Russian pentathletes Olga Rukavishnikova and Olga Kuragina pondered these very inquiries into time and space at the 1980 Olympics in Moscow. Both were finishing up the final event in the pentathlon, the 800-meter run. Kuragina finished first, crossing the line in 2:03.6. That gave her a total of 4,875 points, which bettered her own world record. But just 1.2 seconds later, her teammate Rukavishnikova crossed the line, with 4,937 points. A new record!

Before either of the Olgas had a chance to even register what they had accomplished, their teammate Nadezhda Tkachenko crossed the line in 2:05.2. That was just 0.4 seconds after Rukavishnikova, giving Tkachenko a grand total of 5,083—a *new*, new record.

Officially, Rukavishnikova and Kuragina never held the record. The International Association of Athletics Federations, track's governing body, counts records as complete only after all competitors have finished. Still, a world record is something to celebrate—even if you hold it for less than a blink of an eye.

The Big Owe

Financial Mayhem at the 1976 Summer Olympics

Hosting an Olympics is not a cost-effective proposition for a city. The average Summer Games incur overruns at 176 percent above budget; the average Winter Games are a relative bargain at 142 percent. It's almost certainly a losing deal. But there are reasonable overruns and then there are potentially catastrophic overruns. In 1976, the budget for the Montreal Summer Games was utterly out of control. By the end, the City of Saints had set a new Olympic record: *720 percent* over budget.

And here's the worst part: The organizers were completely confident that the project would be self-financed, paying for itself through the sale of commemorative coins, stamps, and lottery tickets. Said mayor Jean Drapeau, "The Olympics can no more run a deficit than a man can have a baby." Yeah, he probably wishes he could have that statement back.

The budget was originally set for $120 million (in Canadian dollars) to pay for things like the stadium, the velodrome, and the Olympic Village. But the project was riddled with mismanagement through every step of the process. Construction began on the Olympic Park, which housed many of the venues, 18 months behind schedule after a 155-day construction worker strike. They had good reason to draw up a picket line: By the time of its completion, 11 workers had died in accidents.

Then there was gross corruption. The contractor, Regis Trudeau, built a $163,000 chalet for Gerard Niding, the right-hand man to Mayor Drapeau. Trudeau and Niding eventually entered no plea to fraud, bribery, and breach of trust, though eventually Trudeau was forced to present the bill to Niding. "The construction of the Olympic Park and stadium," original architect Roger Taillibert told French-language magazine *Le Devoir*, "showed me a level of organized corruption, theft, mediocrity, sabotage, and indifference that I had never witnessed before and have never witnessed since."

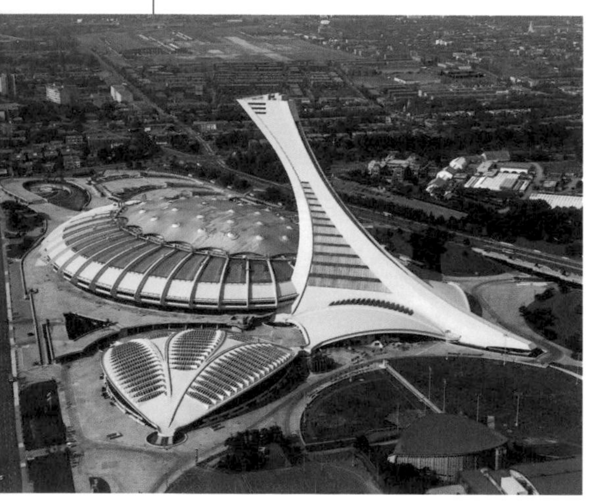

The Big O became a Big Headache for Montreal taxpayers, to the tune of $1.3 billion.

To get it done in time, 3,000 laborers had to work nearly around the clock. But at last, on July 17, 1976, the opening ceremony commenced, marking the start of the 31st Olympiad. The Games themselves were still thrilling. Decathlete Bruce Jenner became a star, gymnast Nadia Comaneci nailed the first perfect 10, and the Americans won seven medals in the boxing competitions. Canada, meanwhile, became the first host nation not to win a gold medal on home soil.

So how did the whole self-financing thing shake out? Nope,

MOST EXPENSIVE OLYMPICS

The Olympics aren't a cheap show to put on. You have to build new stadiums, facilities, housing, and more. Some Games, though, really know how to spend. Here are history's costliest:

1. **Sochi 2014:** $49.96 billion
2. **Beijing 2008:** $42.58 billion
3. **Athens 2004:** $18.22 billion
4. **Nagano 1998:** $17.59 billion
5. **Barcelona 1992:** $15.4 billion
6. **London 2012:** $13.98 billion
7. **Rio de Janeiro 2016:** $13.2 billion
8. **Pyeongchang 2018:** $13 billion
9. **Vancouver 2010:** $8.33 billion
10. **Seoul 1988:** $7.69 billion

It took a lot of rubles to pay for the Sochi Games.

that didn't work. With a final price tag of $1.3 billion in Canadian dollars, it would take the city 30 years to pay off the mounting debt.

The brand-new Olympic stadium didn't hold up well, either, even though it was used to house the Montreal Expos for 27 more years. In 1991, a 55-ton beam fell off. In 1999, the roof tore under a pile of snow. It was nicknamed the Big O, but locals preferred to call it the Big Owe. A report that looked into the stadium fiasco placed most of the blame squarely on Mayor Drapeau. But he consistently found ways to keep his political fortunes alive, remaining in office for another decade.

Today, things are picking up around the stadium. The city spent $7 million on a new esplanade, and they've hosted exhibition sporting events and concerts. Sightseers can enjoy an observation bank, and parts of the complex are being opened up to office space. The Big Owe owes no more. But if there's one thing Quebecers—and indeed, the world—have learned, it's that as sure as a man cannot have a baby, the Olympics will always have a deficit.

Duck, Duck, Gold

Fowl Play at the 1928 Olympics

What happens when an unstoppable force meets an immovable object? Let's say you're unstoppable force Bobby Pearce, a top contender in single sculls rowing at the 1928 Olympics in Amsterdam. Nothing could ever stop you, right? Wrong.

Pearce, an Australian who carried the flag at the opening ceremony, had made it past the first two rounds without a sweat. Midway through his quarterfinal against Frenchman Vincent Saurin, Pearce met his immovable object: a family of ducks passing from one end of the shore to another.

What do you do? Row on through and go for gold, ducks be damned? Or stop and wait for the family to reach its new home? Pearce did the only thing a true Olympian could do. He stopped and waited.

"I heard wild roars from the crowd along the bank of the canal," he said in an interview 48 years later. "I could see some spectators vigorously pointing to something behind me, in my path. I peeked over one shoulder and saw something I didn't like, for a family of ducks in single file was swimming slowly from shore to shore. It's funny now, but it wasn't at the time, for I had to lean on my oars and wait for a clean course."

As Pearce waited, Saurin took advantage. The Frenchman rowed past Pearce and took a five-length lead. But Pearce wasn't in trouble—he calmly caught up to Saurin over the last 1,000 meters and finished nearly 30 seconds ahead. Pearce went on to win gold easily in the final, setting a world record that lasted for almost 60 years. The duck-loving rower would return to the 1932 Games in Los Angeles, and again stood atop the podium with a gold.

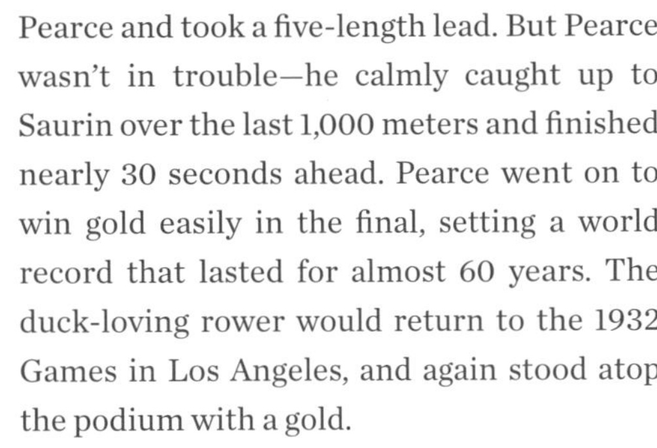

Pearce's son, however, had a slightly different take on his dad's benevolence for waterfowl: "If the race had been close he would have gone right through the ducks."

Pearce in his single scull. Ducks not pictured.

Benevolence to birds aside, Pearce was an incredibly talented rower who won back-to-back gold medals in 1928 and 1932.

Check Your Work

Anders Haugen and the Medal-Costing Math Mistake

Imagine if your whole life's course was changed by a single mathematical error. Anders Haugen knew the feeling all too well.

Born in Norway, Haugen moved to the United States at age 20 in 1908 and worked as a bricklayer. He was already well versed in ski jumping, a popular sport in his native country. Haugen set three world records, and along with his brother, Lars, won 11 combined US ski jumping championships. By the time the first Winter Games came around in 1924, Haugen was 36 years old, leaving him little opportunity for Olympic glory. But when he finally got his shot at the Games, glory would be snatched away from him.

Haugen was all smiles before the 1924 Winter Olympics, but surely the mathematical manipulations left him miffed for life.

Before the event began, Lars warned Anders, "You may out-jump all of them, but you won't win. The judges won't let you." Europeans resented an American encroaching on their sport, and it showed. Haugen made a spectacular jump in Chamonix, and the US coach was certain of a victory, but Haugen knew the deck was stacked against him. Despite having the longest jump of the competition at 50 meters, the American was significantly docked points for form.

Even with the judges' bias, Haugen had earned enough points to win a bronze medal. But a rare mathematical error placed him in fourth. For 50 years, no one noticed or figured it out. In 1974, Jakob Vaage, a Norwegian ski historian—a most Scandinavian job, to be sure—reviewed the results of the 1924 Games and noticed that his countryman Thorleif Haug, who won three gold medals at those

Games, was wrongly awarded Haugen's bronze. After Vaage campaigned to correct the error, the mistake was reversed. In Oslo, Haug's daughter Anne Marie gave 86-year-old Haugen the bronze medal he should've had for a half century. He remains the first and only American to win a medal in ski jumping.

"When the competition began in 1924, I was thirty-six," said Haugen after receiving the medal. "The others were in their twenties and I told them not to worry about trying to beat me because I was old by their standards. But I out-jumped 'em."

SIBLINGS WITH MEDALS

Some families just seem to have the right Olympic genes. There's a long history of siblings competing at the Olympics. In fact, at Rio in 2016, 36 sets of siblings competed. Of course not all of them are successful, but here are a few of the families with a lot to celebrate:

Edoardo and Dario Mangiarotti: Fencing, Italy, 16 medals

Ole Einar and Dag Bjørndalen: Cross-country Skiing, Norway, 14 medals

Sawao and Takeshi Kato: Gymnastics, Japan, 14 medals

Vilhelm and Eric Carlberg: Rifle, Sweden, 13 medals

Raimond and Piero D'Inzeo: Equestrian, Italy, 12 medals

Jack and Shirley Babashoff: Swimming, USA, 11 medals

Venus and Serena Williams: Tennis, USA, 9 medals

Mike and Bob Bryan: Tennis, USA, 5 medals

Jocelyne and Monique Lamoureux: Hockey, USA, 6 medals

Phil and Steve Mahre: Skiing, USA, 3 medals

Gaston, Jacques, and Amédée Thubé: Sailing, France, 3 medals

William and Lottie Dod: Archery, England, 2 medals

Dave and Mark Schultz: Wrestling, USA, 2 medals

Keeth and Erinn Smart: Fencing, USA, 2 medals

Rough (Home) Crowd

The Pros and Cons of Playing Host

In addition to the worldwide attention and prestige that comes from hosting an Olympics, there's a more metallic benefit. Research has shown that playing host provides a tangible advantage to winning more medals.

Just look at the raw numbers: In Summer Games from 1952 to 2012, all but two host countries improved their medal count, most of them significantly. And it goes back even further. In 1904, Great Britain won just two medals competing abroad in America—four years later, with the Games in London, the Brits won 146. The trend makes sense, considering sympathetic home crowds can give athletes a psychological boost. It's also cheaper to send a larger delegation, and these athletes are in familiar environments.

Research has shown that hosting the Olympics boosts a country's medal count—usually.

Of course, not every country gets this bump. Take France, which hosted the Games in 1924 in Chamonix and won just three bronze. (Okay, we can give them a break—it was the very first Winter Games.) Four years later, Switzerland, hosting the 1928 Winter Games in St. Moritz, regressed from three medals in 1924 to just one.

Canada probably has had it the worst. The Great White North hosted the Games in 1976—and though they collected 11 medals, more than double their 1972 total, they became the first host country in Summer Olympics history to not win a single gold medal. As one Canadian sportswriter wrote, "A lot of you guys watch the Olympics like it's a kids' game down at the local field, and you're the angry parent who keeps swearing at the ref. Canada is the one who brings orange slices for everyone and just hopes nobody gets hurt."

It certainly didn't get much better in 1988, either. Hosting the Winter Games in Calgary, the Canadians managed just five medals and no gold. Twenty-two years later, however, the Canadians turned it around. They won 14 gold medals in Vancouver—the most in a single Winter Games ever.

From Olympian to Offender

Humberto Mariles's Life of Crime

A Mexican horseman known for his toughness and flair, Humberto Mariles had what would seem to be the perfect life. He was a powerful general in the army. He won three medals at the 1948 Summer Olympics, two of them gold. And then he escaped to Texas and embarked on what can only be described as the oddest life of crime ever.

Mariles first ran afoul of the law, he claims, in an act of self-defense. While driving home from a party in his honor on the night of August 14, 1964, a car forced him to pull over. The other driver approached Mariles, brandishing a towel and shouting obscenities. Mariles took out his pistol and fired, killing his assailant. Although there's no proof of motive, some believe that Mariles was being persecuted. Before the shooting, Mariles got involved in a dispute with unknown antagonists, who killed 24 horses on Mariles's property by poisoning them with arsenic and hydrocyanic acid. Okay then!

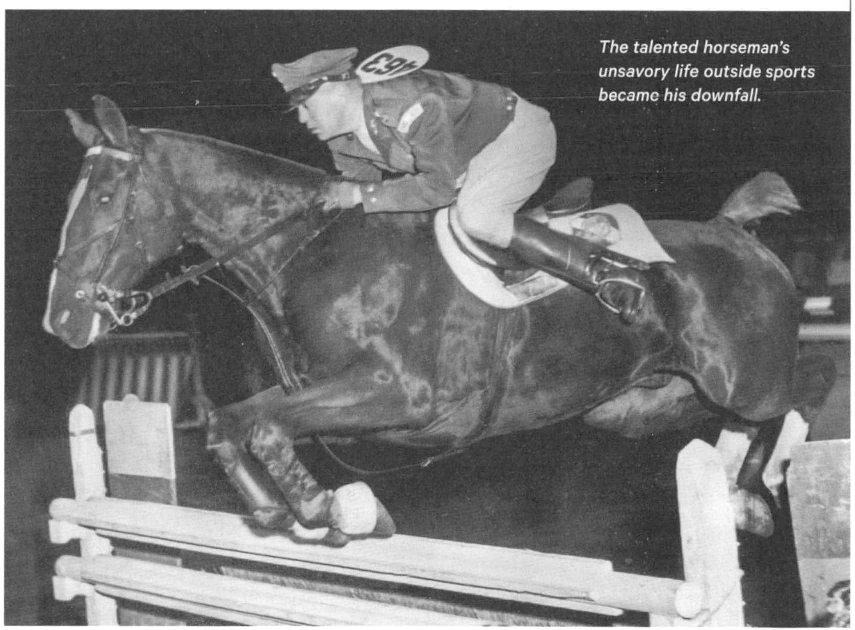

The talented horseman's unsavory life outside sports became his downfall.

As a result of the incident, Mariles was sentenced to 10 years in jail in 1966. He served six years before being released by presidential pardon. But that wasn't the end of his troubles. In 1972, he was one of eight arrested in Paris as part of an international drug ring when police confiscated 132 pounds of heroin. Mariles, who at the time of his arrest told reporters he was working for the Mexican Tourist Commission, admitted to owning the suitcases but claimed he didn't know what was in them. A week later, Mariles died in a French prison while awaiting trial.

There remains quite an air of mystery around the horseman. Whom had he angered? How had he come to be part of an international drug ring? Who kills a dang horse, for crying out loud? Those questions will forever be unanswered. But there's no doubting this: For an otherwise staid sport, equestrian may forever have its most interesting—and controversial—figure in Humberto Mariles.

MOST WANTED OLYMPIANS

Sometimes the greatest athletes in the world can end up on the wrong side of the law. In fact, a handful of Olympians have been arrested for gravely serious crimes. Take, for example, **Wolfgang Schwarz**, an Austrian figure skater who was convicted on human trafficking charges in 2002. Or **James Snook**, an American shooting gold medalist who was convicted of murder in 1929 (and, as far as we know, the only Olympian to be executed). And, of course, there's the infamous **Oscar Pistorius**. The South African "blade runner," who competed with prosthetic legs in the Paralympics, shot his girlfriend to death in their home in 2013. He claimed he mistook her for an intruder, but he was instead found guilty of culpable homicide.

Now that we've got the really heavy stuff out of the way, there are those Olympian crimes that aren't quite so intense. **Arne Borg**, a popular five-time medal-winning Swedish swimmer in the 1920s, was arrested after attempting to avoid conscription by going on vacation. At the 1988 Games in Seoul, **Troy Dalbey** and **Doug Gjertsen**, who each won two gold medals in swimming, were arrested after stealing a marble lion's head from their hotel. And they weren't the only Americans behaving badly in South Korea that year: **Johnny Gray**, a middle distance runner, was arrested after kicking a taxi.

Competitive Bliss

Power-Couple Camilla Andersen and Mia Hundvin

Imagine if Michael Phelps and Ian Thorpe, two of the best swimmers in the world who often went head-to-head for Olympic glory, got married. Now picture just that, but in the cutthroat world of Scandinavian handball, and you might get a slight idea of the media frenzy that erupted when Camilla Andersen and Mia Hundvin got hitched.

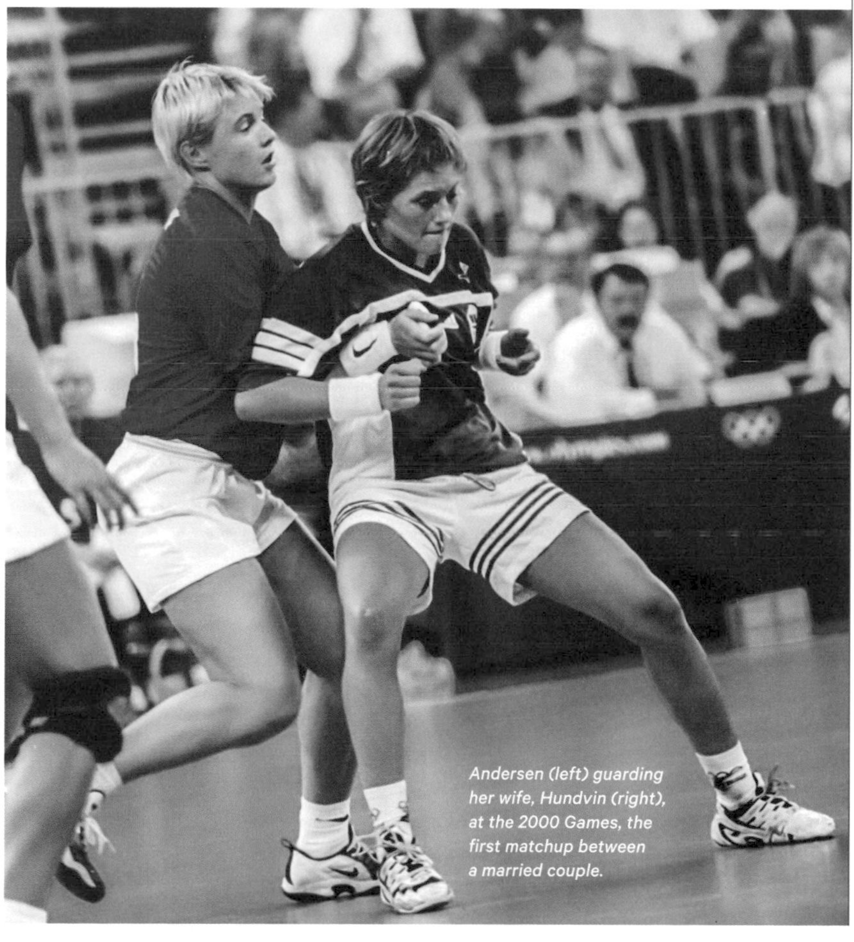

Andersen (left) guarding her wife, Hundvin (right), at the 2000 Games, the first matchup between a married couple.

Andersen, who at one point held the ranking of second-best female handball player in the world, was a key member of Denmark's 1996 gold medal team. Hundvin was Norway's rising star, eager for her first medal. Handball might not be a big deal in America, but the union between handball stars—and one including Hundvin, who had been voted as Norway's sexiest woman—was electric in Scandinavia. The pair became a media sensation.

"I am crazy about Mia and I am proud to be married to her," Andersen told a Danish magazine. "On one hand, I want to shout it out to the world, and on the other hand, I do not want to see myself on the front pages." (It should be noted that she was on the cover of that particular magazine.)

There was lurid debate in the papers during the lead-up to the 2000 Games. Would they take it easy on each other on the Olympic court? Would they collude? Would they spill secrets? "Should I go hit Mia to prove they're wrong?" Andersen asked. For her part, Hundvin didn't seem too worried: "The more you know someone, the more you want to beat them. It's like when you play your wife in cards—don't you want to beat her?"

The union of two handball stars was a media sensation in Scandinavia.

Norway would defeat Denmark in the matchup of the married—the first of its kind in any event in Olympic history—but Andersen and the Danish team got the last laugh. They repeated as gold medal winners, and Norway finished with a bronze. Much to the dismay of both handball fanatics and romantics everywhere, three years after the Sydney Games the couple got divorced.

4

FIRSTS

Spectacular, unimaginable feats of athleticism unfold before our eyes at every Games. World records are shattered; underdogs beat powerhouses. But even as we come to expect the unexpected, there is a first time for everything at the Olympics. With every first, a new character in the Olympic movement is born.

Of course, it's not just a matter of who crosses the finish line in first place. It's about who represents their country for the first time, who blazes a trail for others of their sex or religion. It's about the athletes committed to doing something magical—victory or not—on the largest stage. The people put themselves in the spotlight—and make the world a better place.

PHILIP BOIT
Kenya's First Winter Olympian

KENYA | CROSS-COUNTRY SKIING | 1971–

NAGANO 1998 • SALT LAKE 2002 • TURIN 2006

Kenya, by virtue of the equator running right through the middle of the country, does not experience a cold winter. Lowest temperature on record? Forty degrees. Balmy! So the idea of Kenya becoming a winter sports factory seems rather unlikely. But that hasn't stopped skiers from trying.

In a move that was part marketing campaign, part science experiment, Nike sent two Kenyan long-distance runners, Philip Boit and Henry Bitok, to Finland in 1996 to learn how to compete in cross-country skiing. Nike paid a reported $200,000 for coaching and lodging. Was it a gimmick? Tough to tell. It of course brought attention to Nike, though not all of it positive. (One headline blared: "Just Do It? Just Let Them Be.") There's some wisdom in the idea of distance runners with extraordinary cardiovascular health trying to ski, which requires similar forms of endurance. But, you know, there's the whole *using skis* part getting in the way. It's one thing to have superhuman endurance; it's another to translate that into wielding a piece of athletic equipment.

Bitok gave up skiing after a few races and returned to his farm in Kenya. Boit, however, adapted relatively quickly. He fell often, and struggled particularly in rough conditions. His skiing style was still clunky, and his talent not necessarily Olympic-level, but he managed to qualify for the Games in 1998, becoming the first Kenyan to appear in a Winter Olympics.

In Nagano, Boit was up against a legendary skier who also recorded an Olympic first. Bjorn Daehlie of Norway won the 10 km classic style easily and became the first man to amass six career gold medals at the Winter Games. Daehlie would finish his career with 12 total medals, eight of them gold. Boit, on the other hand, did not have an easy time of it. It was raining that day, which made the snow accumulate on the skis, and he broke into an illegal skating style. He fell down repeatedly, and ran into the course-lining flags. But somehow he finished. And waiting for him at the line was Daehlie.

Daehlie and his team had heard about Boit. Kings of the cross-country world, the Norwegians took an interest in the experiment and wanted to see if the newbie could excel at their sport. Daehlie could've left the site to prepare for the medal ceremony, but curiosity and admiration prevailed. "I felt really impressed that he was able to finish the race in these conditions and I wanted to wait to have him over the finish line, this African, brave skier," he said.

The two hugged, and Daehlie claims that Boit, ever the fierce competitor, told him, "I will beat you in Salt Lake." That meeting was the start of a lifelong friendship. A few weeks after the Games, Boit's son was born. His first name? Daehlie. Now a young man, Daehlie Boit and the Norwegian for whom he is named have since met up numerous times.

Norwegian legend Daehlie (left) helped newbie Boit (in front) regain his balance at the finish line.

As for Philip Boit, he continued his skiing career for many years, an incredible feat given his inexperience and unfamiliarity with the sport. That he didn't finish last in the race, and that he was able to compete without embarrassing himself, is a testament both to his natural athletic ability and to his determination to learn the sport. In Salt Lake in 2002, he showed improvement, finishing 64th in the sprint skiing event, ahead of five other racers. In 2006, he finished 91st in the 15 km, again ahead of five others. Boit retired after the 2011 season and is now an adviser to his country's Olympic committee.

Did the Boit experiment work? Yes and no. He became an Olympian, after all. He wasn't very good, of course, at least relative to the top skiers he raced against. He didn't quite inspire a legacy of Winter athletes in his home country, either. But after Kenya missed out on the 2010 and 2014 Games, Sabrina Simader qualified for the alpine downhill in 2018. Slowly, perhaps, Boit's impact is being felt.

NAWAL EL MOUTAWAKEL
The First Muslim Woman to Win Gold

MOROCCO | TRACK AND FIELD | 1 MEDAL | 1962–

LOS ANGELES 1984

After she crossed the finish line in Los Angeles and sobbed into the red flag of her country, Nawal El Moutawakel was taken into a side room. "The king is on the phone," she was told.

Dialing in from Morocco was King Hassan II, calling to congratulate El Moutawakel on becoming the first Moroccan gold medalist and the first woman from a majority Muslim country to take home gold. "The entire country is going wild," he said. "This victory has made us all so happy and proud of you." He also declared that every girl born that day should be named Nawal.

Life changed dramatically for the 400-meter hurdle champion in 1984. She became a hero for Muslim women around the world. When fans wrote to her, they would simply address an envelope to "Nawal El Moutawakel, Morocco," and the letters would always arrive. "Women would write to me and thank me for what I did for them through sport," she said. "Ladies with and without the veil told me I'd liberated them."

A knee injury saw her retire from track a few years later at age 25. But she returned to Morocco with a sense of purpose—and the goal of using her newfound fame to help others. She became the country's national athletic director, and then a member of the Moroccan Olympic Committee. In 1998, she was named the first Muslim woman on the IOC. She was later in charge of evaluating potential cities for the 2012 and 2016 Summer Games.

One victory by a Muslim woman would not lead to more immediate opportunity and freedom for women across the region. But El Moutawakel's medal did help break barriers for her cohort. Nike made its own athletic hijab. And at the 2016 Games, 14 Muslim women won medals, including American sabre fencer Ibtihaj Muhammad. The obstacles, as El Moutawakel once said, are always in the way. But she charted a new path for Muslim women everywhere to "get over the hurdles and keep running."

El Moutawakel ran a joyous victory lap after becoming the first Muslim woman to win a gold medal.

ALICE COACHMAN
The First African American Woman to Win Gold

USA | TRACK AND FIELD | 1 MEDAL | 1923–2014

LONDON 1948

Alice Coachman grew up the fifth of 10 children in a poor black family in deeply segregated Albany, Georgia, during the 1920s and '30s. After watching a boys' track-and-field meet, she became infatuated with high jumping, but the local gym barred her from training there. Coachman was undeterred, improvising however she could to practice, running and jumping barefoot on dirt roads and using ropes and sticks for high jumps.

Coachman quickly developed into a superb high jumper, beating most boys her age. She won 10 straight Amateur Athletic Union high jump championships from 1939 to 1948. A natural all-around athlete, she also won five straight AAU 50-meter dashes from 1943 to 1947. She won three straight collegiate national championships at the Tuskegee Institute and later Albany State, and also played basketball.

Coachman had to wait eight long years in the prime of her career for her first Olympic appearance, since the 1940 and 1944 Games were canceled because of World War II. At the 1948 Games in London, her event was the last on the track-and-field schedule. With a

LEFT: *Coachman stood tall on the podium, but returned to America as a second-class citizen.*

THE FIRST PRIZES

Winners at the ancient Olympics were awarded money—and later on, a lifetime of free meals—but not medals. The medal ceremony is an innovation from the first modern Games in 1896, and the traditional trio of gold, silver, and bronze was introduced in 1904. Medals also didn't originally dangle from the winner's neck. From 1904 to 1956, the medal was attached to a ribbon, which was affixed to the athlete's chest with a pin. That was the standard until the Rome Games in 1960, when organizers designed a laurel leaf chain, which gave way to the necklace-style ribbons we see today.

jump of five feet, six and one-eighth inches, the 24-year-old not only took gold, but also became the first African American woman to win an Olympic gold medal. "I made a difference among the blacks, being one of the leaders," she told the *New York Times* in 1996. "If I had gone to the Games and failed, there wouldn't be anyone to follow in my footsteps. It encouraged the rest of the women to work harder and fight harder."

Even after she received her medal from King George VI, the racism that scarred her early life and athletic career remained. Back in Albany, after the segregated parade in her honor, blacks and whites could not sit next to each other at the city's auditorium. The mayor refused to shake her hand, and she had to leave through a "blacks only" side door.

Coachman's gold medal win in London was her last athletic competition. She retired to Georgia, teaching in elementary and high school and starting the Alice Coachman Track and Field Foundation. But she continued forging new paths: She was the first female African American to endorse an international product, when she signed on to promote Coca-Cola. She was featured on billboards with another hero: Jesse Owens.

LAMINE GUEYE
The First Black African Skier

SENEGAL | SKIING | 1950–

SARAJEVO 1984 • ALBERTVILLE 1992 • LILLEHAMMER 1994

The father of Senegalese downhill skiing comes from a country without a ski hill. Well, there's one hill, but it's only 820 feet high. (For comparison's sake, Snowbasin, the peak used for downhill events at the Salt Lake City Games, stands at 9,350 feet.) Neither is there a word for *downhill* in Wolof, the most common Senegalese language. But to Lamine Gueye, that little bump in the earth—and lack of linguistic options—wasn't a reason to stop. If anything, it was motivation to make history.

Gueye, the grandson of the longtime president of the National Assembly (also named Lamine Gueye) had developed an interest in skiing as a boy while studying in Switzerland. Later, while living in France, he ran into the vacationing Senegalese president, Leopold Sedar Senghor. With a dream of skiing in the Olympics, the 19-year-old persuaded Senghor to authorize paying for his trip to the 1984 Games in Sarajevo. He became the first black African to compete at a Winter Olympics. (South Africa had previously sent an all-white delegation of figure skaters in 1968, and Uganda-born Tofiri Kibuuka competed in the 1976 Winter Paralympic Games.)

Winters in Senegal can reach 80 degrees, but Lamine Gueye was determined to make Winter Olympic history.

Despite having to explain to some of his countrymen what snow was, Gueye, after just 14 months of training, finished in 51st place out of 60 in the men's downhill and 57th out of 76 in the giant slalom. "I was so afraid I almost threw up," he said. Gueye learned to ski as a 10-year-old in boarding school, but that hadn't quite prepared him for the terror of standing at the top of the hill at the Olympic Games. "You're thinking, 'I'd rather be somewhere else, anywhere else but here,' he said. "You're praying they cancel the race for some reason."

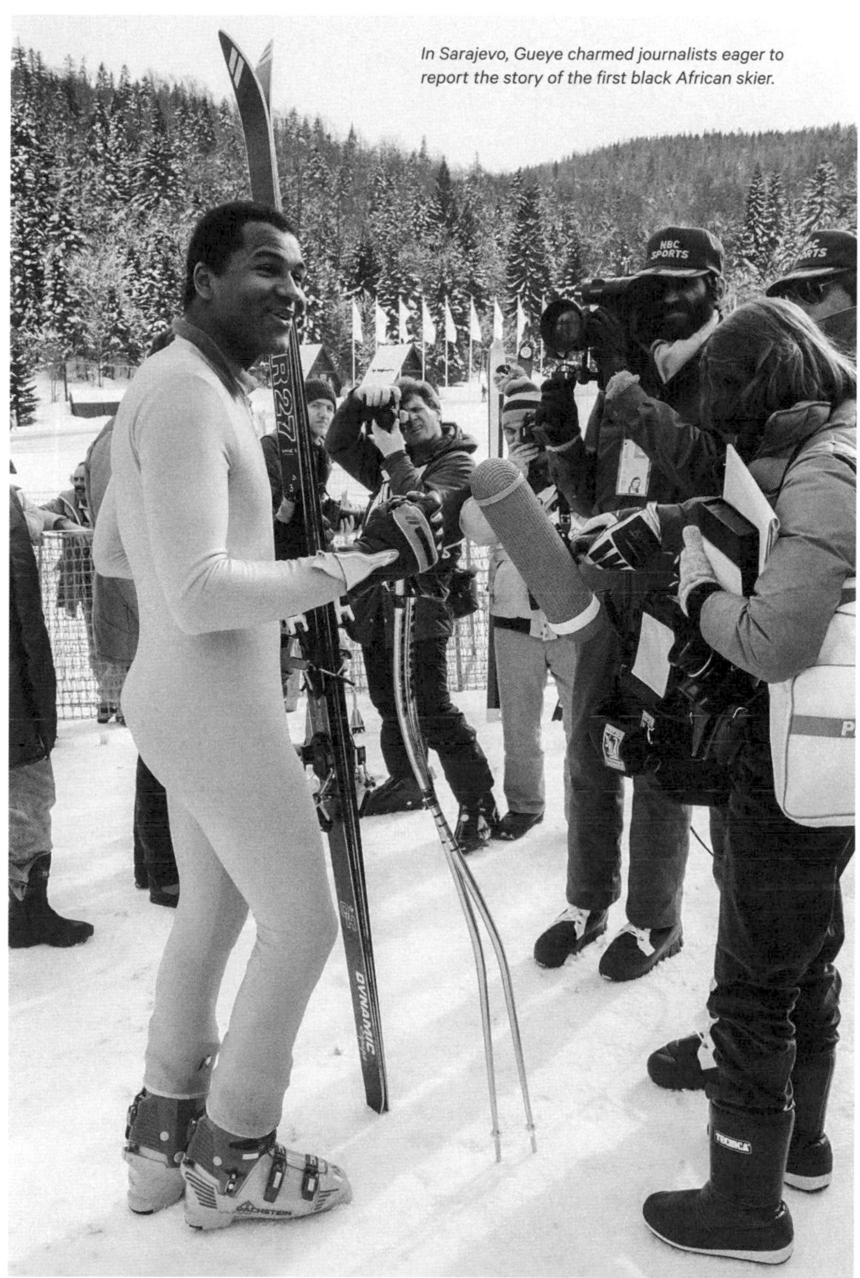

In Sarajevo, Gueye charmed journalists eager to report the story of the first black African skier.

Gueye's persistence paid off. He returned to the Games in 1992 along with Senegalese alpine skier Alphonse Gomis. (They even secured slick purple-and-gold ski suits.) Gueye has since spawned a legacy of African Winter athletes. In 2010, Kwame Nkrumah-Acheampong—a.k.a. the Snow Leopard—competed in the slalom for Ghana and became a media sensation. In 2018, Nigeria and Eritrea made their Winter Olympic debuts, and the Nigerian women's bobsled team was a media darling.

Gueye, a man from a country with barely a hill, where winter temperatures can hit 80 degrees, found his way to the top of a ski slope and performed admirably. More important, he inspired a generation of those from his continent to do the same. If that's not the Olympic spirit, then what is?

AGUIDA AMARAL
Timor-Leste's First Olympian

TIMOR-LESTE | TRACK AND FIELD | 1972–

SYDNEY 2000 • ATHENS 2004

Her home was burned down. She lost most of her possessions, including her only pair of running shoes. Then she learned she was pregnant. But Aguida Amaral continued running—this time barefoot.

Amaral is from East Timor, a tiny nation in Southeast Asia that voted for independence from Indonesia in 1999. That did not sit well with the Indonesians, who had brutally occupied the country since 1975. In response, Indonesian forces tortured and killed thousands. Amaral, along with thousands of others, went into hiding.

All that turmoil did not stop Amaral and three other East Timorese athletes from keeping their Olympic dream alive. After the United Nations sent a peacekeeping force into the country, Indonesia finally relinquished control in October 1999 and the IOC allowed the athletes to compete under the Olympic flag as "individual Olympic athletes." (First created for athletes from former Soviet republics, this classification is meant to aid cash-strapped or politically unstable countries that don't have the resources for their own Olympic Committees.)

After arriving in Sydney, Amaral still needed shoes. The marathoner had trained without footwear, running first alongside roads and then on the beach. She received an impromptu shoe-fitting when Kevan Gosper, an IOC delegate from Australia, asked Amaral to stand on a white sheet of paper and traced her foot with a red pen. Soon after, her shoes arrived.

All the East Timorese athletes—including weight lifter Martinho de Araújo, boxer Victor Ramos, and fellow marathoner Calisto da Costa—marched in the opening ceremony. In the Olympic stadium, they danced and waved to their friends and family back home. Amaral finished the marathon in 43rd place, nearly an hour off world record pace. When she entered the stadium, she ran 150 meters before collapsing to the ground, her hands together in prayer. She then was told that she had to run one more lap. That didn't stop the crowd from cheering like crazy. "Yes, when I heard them, I got so happy," she said. "It was like a dream."

At the 2004 Games in Athens, Amaral and marathoner Gil da Cruz Trindade became the first athletes to officially represent the independent nation of Timor-Leste in the Olympics. (The country was renamed in 2002.) She held the nation's flag in the opening ceremony. "I am happy," she said, "because I see all the flags from the other countries, and now I can see my flag." Though her time was eight minutes slower than it was in 2000, she still finished. "I needed to keep going," she said. "Quitting was not an option."

RIGHT: *Amaral said a prayer after finishing the 2000 marathon in a time of 3:10:55.*

THOMAS BURKE
The First "Fastest Man Alive"

USA | TRACK AND FIELD | 2 MEDALS | 1875–1929

ATHENS 1896

As the 100-meter dash began in Athens in 1896, the Greek spectators were confused by the American team's exuberance. The US track delegation, mostly made up of Bostonians, were chanting, "B! A! A! Rah! Rah! Rah!" It was enough that the Greeks didn't know BAA stood for Boston Athletic Association—they had never really heard cheers quite like that in an athletic competition. But in time, they joined in.

"All at once, they seemed to grasp the meaning of our effort," wrote Ellery Clark, an Olympian that year who won gold in the high jump and long jump. "We had, by good fortune, chanced to please the popular taste, and the cheer from that moment until we left Athens was in constant demand." It helped, too, that Americans dominated the track-and-field program, winning nine of the 12 events, and medaling in all but two.

Thomas Burke in 1896

One of the more successful athletes was Thomas Burke. A champion 400m runner, the Boston University law student hadn't run too many 100-meter races. Despite his inexperience, and the new challenge of running clockwise—standard in Europe but not in the United States—Burke won both the 400 and the 100, becoming the first "fastest man alive."

Upon his return home, Burke and other members of the BAA, who so enjoyed watching the marathon in Athens, decided to create a version of their own at home. In April 1897, the BAA Marathon was held. Today, it's known as the Boston Marathon, the oldest annual marathon in the world.

The First American Female Swimmers

USA Swimming Makes Waves in 1920

They were called "mermaids," and not affectionately. When USA women's swimming first competed at the 1920 Games, male spectators seemed more interested in their appearance than their athletic skill. But that didn't stop these trailblazers from eschewing the "aesthetically pleasing" sports like archery and sailing.

After a men-only affair in the first modern Olympics in 1896, women made their debut in the 1900 Paris Games under the utterly bizarre stipulation that they couldn't participate in any events that might make them visibly perspire. Of course, Olympic founder Pierre de Coubertin didn't want women to compete at all. "I do not approve of the participation of women in public competitions," he said. "In the Olympic Games, their primary role should be to crown the victors."

Though Coubertin wasn't in charge of the 1900 Games, the 22 women who were allowed to compete didn't have much to work with. They played in just tennis, golf, and croquet (a one-time-only Olympic sport). In 1908, 44 women competed, but only in the sports that supposedly didn't cause sweating. (Oddly, that again included tennis, which typically leaves one completely drenched in sweat.)

The first Olympics to feature female swimming was 1912 in Stockholm. The Americans refused to send a delegation because they required women to compete in long skirts. Women did swim in the United States—in fact, there were marathon swimming events from Manhattan to Coney Island, watched by some 20,000 people—but with ridiculous dress codes enforced. Any women swimming recreationally in public had to wear full outfits, including skirts, which led some to drown when the cloth ensnared them.

The United States Olympic Committee finally relaxed their rules in 1920, and the mermaids made their Olympic debut at the Antwerp Games, their talents unleashed for the world to see—and finally freed from the long skirts. They wasted no time in absolutely demolishing the competition, winning seven medals in the three women's events, including a sweep of the 100- and 300-meter freestyle.

The inimitable Ethelda Bleibtrey (far left) took gold in the 1920 women's 100-meter freestyle.

The team's leader, Ethelda Bleibtrey, was a force to be reckoned with, and the *New York Times* called her "the world's great woman swimmer." She never lost a race as an amateur, and won national championships from 50 yards to three miles, a truly impressive range. (She also had a distaste for the rules on modesty. As a 17-year-old in 1919, she was arrested for swimming without stockings.) In Antwerp, with the swim events taking place in a tidal estuary, Bleibtrey won three gold medals in the 100-meter free, 300-meter free, and 4 x 100 relay. She set world records in each of them, and remains the only athlete to sweep all the swimming events at a single Games. "Swimming is the best sport in the world for women," she said.

Bleibtrey became a worldwide star. She surfed with the Prince of Wales and was congratulated by King Albert of Belgium. She toured the Panama Canal and Australia. She was credited with rescuing a woman and her two children from drowning in Narragansett Bay, Rhode Island, in 1925. Ever the rule breaker, she was arrested again three years later for swimming in the Central Park reservoir. Suffice it to say she's one of the original badasses.

Bleibtrey wasn't the only great American swimmer in the 1920 Games. She shared the medal stand with relay teammates Irene Guest, now a member of the International Swimming Hall of Fame; Frances Schroth, who won three medals; and Margaret Woodbridge, who had set national records in the 200- and 500-yard freestyle.

The US swimming team would, of course, continue its dominance throughout the decades. Of the women with the 15 most medals in Olympic swimming history, eight are Americans. US women have won a medal at every Olympics they have participated in.

At first they were ignored. They were told not to participate, but they persisted. And now, American female swimmers are the best in the world.

MARGARET ABBOTT
The First Female American Victor

USA | GOLF | 1 MEDAL | 1878–1955

PARIS 1900

1 0 0

True story: A woman entered an Olympic competition on a lark and won gold. The kicker? No one even mentioned it was the Olympics. Even more unbelievable, no one told Margaret Abbott that she had become the first American woman to win an Olympic gold medal. Cruel? Not exactly. It's just that the 1900 Olympics in Paris were a total mess.

Women have long participated in golf. Way back in the sixteenth century, Mary, Queen of Scots, hit the links quite often. In 1891, Shinnecock Hills Golf Club on Long Island first allowed women to compete in America, and three years later, the first amateur ladies tournament began. Abbott, who grew up well off, started playing in 1897 at the Chicago Golf Club. At five foot eleven inches she was quite athletic and showed an immediate aptitude for the game, winning the 1898 Deering Cup competition on "ladies day."

Abbott had gone to Paris in 1899 to study art with the likes of Auguste Rodin and Edgar Degas, not necessarily to hit the links. Her journey to Olympic glory was as haphazard as the Paris Olympics themselves. Unlike today's highly choreographed, multibillion-dollar spectacles, these Games looked like they were planned overnight. They fell at the same time as the lavish world's fair, called the 1900 Paris Exposition, which was the much bigger attraction, drawing some 50 million visitors.

In fact, the Olympics were more commonly referred to as the Games of the Exposition, just another part of the fair's schedule of events. Alfred Picard, the exposition organizer, thought the Olympics were an anachronism, an affront to the new, modern Paris. The Games were so disorganized that they almost caused the downfall of the whole Olympic project. "It's a miracle," Pierre de Coubertin said, "that the Olympic movement survived that celebration."

Well-known graphic artist Charles Dana Gibson drew this portrait of Abbott in 1903.

So it's no surprise that Abbott thought the women's golf event in Compiegne—a small town 50 miles north of Paris best known for being the site of the Armistice signing in 1918—was just a local tournament that she could enter for fun. The twenty-year-old had no conception of the Olympics, nor the trailblazing history she was making. No, this was just a sunny day in France!

Abbott won gold in the nine-hole tournament, shooting a 47. (It was an American sweep; Polly Whittier won silver and Abbie Pratt took bronze.) Abbott's mother, Mary, also competed, tying for seventh and shooting a 65. The Abbott women are, to this day, the only mother-daughter duo to compete in the same event at the same Olympics.

THE FIRST OLYMPIC POOLS

You would think that swimming events at the Olympics have always taken place in a standardized, chlorine-filled pool. You would be wrong. The first Olympic pool was introduced at the 1908 Games in London; natural water sources had been used for all previous swimming events (including such beloved bodies of water as the Mediterranean Sea in 1896, the Seine River in 1900, and a lake in St. Louis in 1904).

But it's not that pools weren't around. In fact, the first man-made pool dates back to 2600 BC. Pools just weren't particularly popular, given how expensive it was to operate them in the early 1900s. With the introduction of chlorine and filtering technology, however, pool water could be recycled. Now, the "Olympic-sized swimming pool"—50 meters long, 25 meters wide, no more, no less—is as iconic as the rings or medals. Indeed, researchers believe that the faulty pool in Rio gave some swimmers, depending on the lane, a speed boost. (Not sure the Seine comes with that feature.)

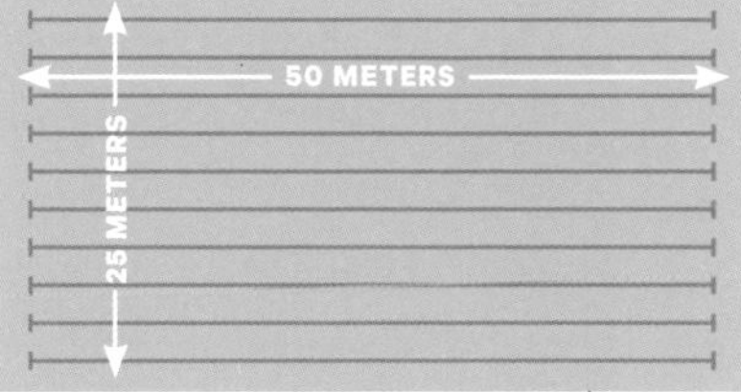

Abbott received a gilded porcelain bowl for her win. And then she largely disappeared from history—little is known about her post-Olympic life. She died in 1955, at age 76, with no idea she was an Olympic champ—or even an Olympian. In 1973, however, Paula Welch, a professor at the University of Florida, came across her name at US Olympic Committee headquarters. (In keeping with all the other blunders of 1900, Abbott's name was misspelled "Abbot.") From there, Welch started a long, 10-year journey to track her down. When Welch reached Abbott's son, Philip Dunne, he had no idea that his mother had even competed in the Olympics.

The whole debacle is a testament to just how messy the early Games were. (Anyone trying to simply walk onto an Olympic course today would be arrested in short order.) And it is truly a shame that Abbott could never appreciate her own achievement and singular place in history. Even so, she will forever be the first American woman to win gold—or porcelain, in her case—in the Olympics.

ALVIN KRAENZLEIN
The First Quadruple-Gold Winner

USA | TRACK AND FIELD | 4 MEDALS | 1876–1928

PARIS 1900

Alvin Kraenzlein's biggest contribution to the Olympic movement might be his development of the modern hurdling technique. Countless hurdlers from around the world have used it at every Olympics since. You know the one: leading a straight leg over the hurdle while suspended in midair. The guy responsible for that? Kraenzlein.

A college superstar in track, Kraenzlein set world records in the 120-meter high and 220 low hurdles. He helped the University of Pennsylvania win four straight intercollegiate championships. Mike Murphy, his coach, called him the "world's best all-around athlete of his time."

At the 1900 Games in Paris, Kraenzlein cemented his claim as the world's finest. He won four gold medals in track and field—the 60-meter dash, the 100-meter hurdle, the 200-meter hurdle, and the long jump. He became the first athlete to collect four individual gold medals at a single Games, a record that held until 1936, when Jesse Owens matched it.

Though he was trained as a dentist, Kraenzlein decided to go into coaching. In 1913, he agreed to coach the German team for a whopping $50,000. Just as his tenure was beginning, he was told to evacuate before the war started. He returned home and spent some time with the Cuban track-and-field team before dying unexpectedly at age 51.

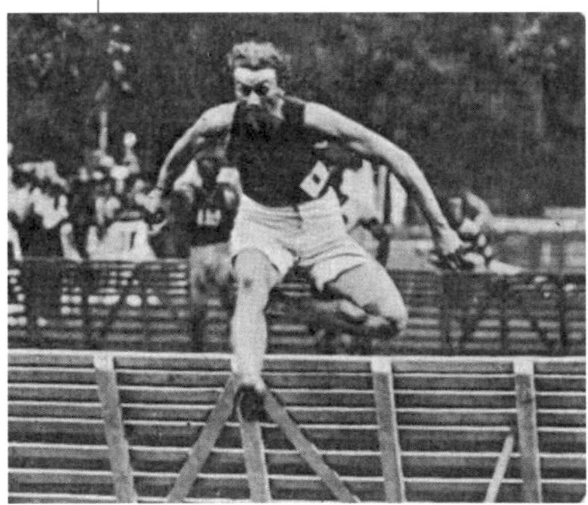

LEFT: *Kraenzlein developed the leg kick technique that remains the standard today.*

LONG JUMP, BIG FIGHT

Just because countrymen become teammates doesn't mean that they always get along. After all, they're often fighting for the same medal. Literally. In fact, the long jump at the 1900 Games almost descended into fisticuffs—depending on whom you believe. Alvin Kraenzlein's main competitor in the long jump was Myer Prinstein, then the world record holder. Prinstein, a member of the Syracuse University team, was barred by the school from competing on Sundays, the day of the final in Paris. As such, the teammates had made a gentlemen's agreement wherein both would rely on their qualifying numbers as their final score rather than compete for a final time on Sunday. For whatever reason, Kraenzlein decided to compete anyway, setting an Olympic record in the process. What happened next is in dispute: Some say Prinstein punched Kraenzlein in the face, but others insist that someone managed to stop him. Either way, Prinstein turned out just fine. He still won silver in the long jump and finished his Olympic career with three gold medals.

JOHN TAYLOR
The First African American Medalist

USA | TRACK AND FIELD | 1 MEDAL | 1882–1908

LONDON 1908

1 0 0

The first African American to win a gold medal at the Olympics was the son of former slaves. John Taylor broke a major color barrier in sport, but his historic accomplishment at the 1908 London Olympics wasn't fully embraced back in America. Indeed, Taylor has never been widely known in modern times.

Born in Washington, DC, Taylor settled with his family in Philadelphia, where he quickly established himself as one of the top athletes in the area. At the University of Pennsylvania—which saw its first African American student graduate in 1883—he was the collegiate champ in the quarter mile in 1903 and helped the school win a national championship in 1907. Taylor probably would've been a contender at the 1904 Olympics in St. Louis had he even known the Games were happening in the first place. He entered the 1908 Olympics in London, however, and Taylor became the first African American to represent the United States in international competition. Little did he know he'd be part of one of the weirdest, most controversial races in Olympic history.

There were four competitors in the 400-meter final. Three, including Taylor, were Americans; the fourth, Wyndham Halswelle, was a Brit. John Carpenter, from Cornell, led in the final stretch. But as he moved to the outside, he got in front of Halswelle, obstructing his progress. The officials called off the race immediately, and Carpenter was disqualified. A re-race was awarded, but the Americans, in solidarity for the call against Carpenter, decided not to run it. So Halswelle ran the race himself, winning gold in the only walkover in Olympic history.

Taylor has never been widely known in modern times, despite breaking a major color line.

Taylor wasn't done, however. He won gold in the medley relay four days later. (Though in practice it was a 4 x 400 relay, the first two runners ran 200 meters; the others were a 400 and 800. The practice ended after the 1908 Games.) After the win, Taylor became one of the most famous people in the United States, particularly among African Americans. But his meteoric rise was cut tragically short. Four months later, he succumbed to typhoid pneumonia, dying at age 26.

We can't know if Taylor would've gone on to win more Olympic medals, or if his name would've been up there with the likes of Jack Johnson, Muhammad Ali, and Jackie Robinson as brilliant, world-shaking African American athletes. But Harry Porter, the 1908 high jump gold medalist, thought that he was already at that level. "It is far more as the man that John Taylor made his mark," Porter wrote in a poignant letter to Taylor's parents. "Quite ostentatious, genial, kindly, the fleet-footed, far-famed athlete was beloved wherever known."

Taylor, seen here at the 1908 Games, died of pneumonia shortly after returning home.

EDDIE EAGAN

The First Two-Sport Star

USA | BOXING/BOBSLED | 2 MEDALS | 1897–1967

ANTWERP 1920 • PARIS 1924 • LAKE PLACID 1932

We can start, if you like, with his intelligence. Or we can start with his right hook, or even his accidental gold medal. Wherever you start, and however you tell the tale, you're bound to end up with the same conclusion: whatever Eddie Eagan did, he did it incredibly well.

Born to a working-class family in Denver, Eagan certainly had the smarts. He attended Yale, graduating in 1921. He then went to Harvard Law School but dropped out after a year . . . because he was awarded a Rhodes Scholarship. (If that's not an academic mike drop, then what is?) It was during his time at Yale that Eagan won his first gold medal. Yes, the brainiac was a damn talented boxer who "never relented in his attack" and "gave no quarter to his opponent," as the *New York Times* reported. The boxing event at the 1920 Games, held in the main hall of Antwerp's Zoological Gardens, saw Eagan win all his matches by decision.

The light-heavyweight from Yale took gold in 1920.

After Antwerp, and while still at Oxford, Eagan embarked on an unofficial world tour, taking on all comers. "In every country Eddie challenged the amateur champion," said his wife, Peggy. "He finished the tour undefeated. So when you talk about undefeated championships, my husband was one of them." He also trained with Jack Dempsey, and later worked with Gene Tunney before his controversial Long Count Fight in 1927, one of the most famous bouts in boxing history.

Eagan's world tour did not turn into further Olympic success in 1924; he was knocked out in the first round. He hung up the gloves for good and

Left to right: Billy Fiske, Eddie Eagan, Clifford Gray, and Jay O'Brien at the 1932 Winter Games

went on to a legal career, but he soon began feeling a little "cobwebby." The Olympics were calling to him again. Here's the thing: You have to be a ridiculously talented athlete to take up a new sport just three weeks before the Olympic Games. Even if you stink, it's an impressive feat. But when you join the defending gold medal–winning bobsled team on a whim, you're talking about an athlete for the ages.

It appears that the head of US Bobsled, a friend of Eagan's, invited the superathlete to join out of desperation when a participant dropped out at the last minute. Eagan joined a four-man team led by Billy Fiske, who won that event as a 16-year-old driver in St. Moritz in 1928. A blizzard probably didn't help calm the nerves of Eagan, who sat in his first bobsled *ever* in Lake Placid. But he and his merry band of bobsledders—also including

40-year-old Clifford "Tippy" Gray and 49-year-old Jay O'Brien, on the brakes—defied what we think of preparation. Though the group saw one of the blades climb onto the lip at the edge of the course—"picture a steel comet with four riders hurtling through the air," Eagan said—they still held on for a comfortable two-second win.

With the dicey victory, Eagan became the first (and only, to date) person to win gold medals in two different sports in the Summer and Winter Games. "That run will always be vivid in my memory," he once said. "It took only about two minutes to make, but to me it seemed like an eon."

After that magic win in 1932, Eagan worked as an assistant US attorney for the Southern District of New York, became a lieutenant colonel in the US Army Air Corps during World War II, and later worked in the Eisenhower administration. After dying of a heart attack at age 69, he was one of the 21 inaugural inductees into the US Olympic Hall of Fame.

Was he myth? He certainly was a legend. Eagan was one of those rare individuals who seems to accomplish just about anything they want to. His mind was sharp, his jaw was strong, his sense of adventure knew no bounds. And he's the owner of an Olympic record that will likely last for a long time.

DUAL-SEASON OLYMPIANS

Though winter and summer sports seem to have just about nothing in common, there is a long history of summer athletes trying their hand at cold-weather sports, and vice versa. Track athletes in particular seem to have an affinity for bobsled.

Although Eddie Eagan's dual-season golds stand alone, he isn't the only athlete to win medals in multiple sports, in multiple seasons. **Jacob Tullin Thams**, a Norwegian, won gold in the ski jump in 1924, followed by silver in 1936 in sailing. In 1988, **Christa Luding-Rothenburger**, from Germany, won two gold medals in speed skating, and then a silver in sprint cycling. **Clara Hughes**, a Canadian, won two bronze in cycling and then four medals in speed skating. **Lauryn Williams**, from the United States, won gold in the 4 x 100 relay and then silver in bobsled.

BOB MATHIAS
The Original Teenage Wonder

USA | DECATHLON | 2 MEDALS | 1930–2006

LONDON 1948 • HELSINKI 1952

The man once called the "greatest athlete in the world" began life as a sickly boy prone to nosebleeds. He was anemic, confined to bed 12 hours a day, and had to take iron and liver pills. How the heck, then, did he come to take on the world's hardest sport? How did he become the youngest gold medalist in track-and-field history? And how did he do it after learning the event existed only three months earlier?

The story goes like this: Bob Mathias would outgrow his anemia and turn into a talented athlete. During high school in Tulare, California, Mathias's coach, Virgil Jackson, told him to give decathlon a try. "That's great, Coach," Mathias replied. "It sounds like fun. But just one question: What's a decathlon?"

He had never run 400 or 1,500 meters in a competition. He had never broad jumped or pole-vaulted, or even seen a javelin for that matter. So of course, he won the first meet he entered. The local Elks club raised the cash for Mathias to head to the Olympic trials in New Jersey, where he bested Irving Mondschein, a three-time national champion. The 17-year-old was London-bound.

Seventeen-year-old Mathias competes in the discus in 1948.

Even for an experienced decathlete, the 1948 Olympics would be a true test of endurance. On both days of the competition, it was pouring rain and freezing cold in London. In between events, Mathias sat on the wet ground and covered himself in a blanket. This was, after all, a bare-bones affair, part

of the cash-strapped "Austerity Games." The 1,500 meters was lit by headlights on cars, the javelin foul line illuminated by a flashlight. Mathias's overall exhaustion made the event an unbelievable slog. But just three months after starting the discipline, with the help of a creative and dedicated coach, the teenage wonder won. "I've never worked longer or harder," he said.

Mathias returned home a hero. President Truman greeted him, and he received marriage proposals from 200 women. Back in Tulare, thousands lined the streets for nine miles. Still utterly drained from the grueling conditions in London, Mathias was more interested in finally getting some sleep.

After the gold medal win cemented him as the greatest athlete in the world, Mathias enrolled at Stanford in 1949 and joined the football team. In a game against the University of Southern California, with a Rose Bowl berth on the line, he ran a 96-yard kickoff return for a touchdown. Before his Olympic return in 1952, he played against Illinois in the Rose Bowl, the nation's first nationally televised college football game. (He's also the only person to compete in the Olympics and the Rose Bowl in the same year.)

In Helsinki, Mathias won again easily despite pulling a muscle in his thigh. He earned his second gold medal and set a record with 7,887 points in the process, winning five of the 10 decathlon events. He retired soon afterward at age 21, having won all 11 competitions he'd entered during his brief but stellar career. The Olympic superstar quickly cashed in with numerous advertising campaigns and starred as himself in *The Bob Mathias Story*. He went on to serve in Congress, representing his hometown, for eight years.

Decathletes are often referred to as the world's greatest athletes. The event is the ultimate test of strength and speed. Mathias, the back-to-back victor, was clearly the world's greatest athlete at the time. And then he retired at only 21 years old. It's tantalizing to think that had he competed in the 1956 Games at age 25, he might have won a third-straight gold, an unprecedented feat. He wouldn't have just been the best athlete in the world; he may very well have been the best athlete ever.

OPPOSITE: *Mathias vaults his way to another gold in Helsinki despite pulling a thigh muscle.*

AMERICAN DECATHLON DOMINATION

Of the 23 decathlons featuring American competitors, the United States won at least one medal in 19 of them. (They missed out in 1964, 1972, 1984, and 1988.) The Americans won gold 14 times, including six straight from 1936 to 1960, and collected multiple medals six times, including a sweep in 1936 and 1952.

The United States is still crushing the competition—Americans have won gold in the last three Olympics, to date.

US GOLD MEDALISTS, DECATHLON

1912: Jim Thorpe
1924: Harold Osborn
1932: Jim Bausch
1936: Glenn Morris
1948: Bob Mathias
1952: Bob Mathias
1956: Milt Campbell
1960: Rafer Johnson
1968: Bill Toomey
1976: Bruce Jenner
1996: Dan O'Brien
2008: Bryan Clay
2012: Ashton Eaton
2016: Ashton Eaton

Two-time gold medalist Ashton Eaton in Rio

VICKI DRAVES
The First Asian American Female Gold Medalist

After the 1948 Olympics in London, it seemed like Vicki Draves would be the next big star. She became the first woman to be awarded golds in two different diving events and the first Asian American woman to win a medal. *LIFE* magazine featured Draves in its pages, and named her and decathlete Bob Mathias the top two American athletes of the Games. But the magazine, in keeping with the sexism of the day, called her the "Olympics' prettiest champion." "Had there been a beauty contest at last year's Olympic Games," *LIFE* wrote in its May 16, 1949, issue, "the raven-haired girl shown here would have won it just as she won both of the women's diving championships."

Female Olympians have endured a long and difficult road toward recognition for their athletic talent. At those 1948 Games, Dutch track star Fanny Blankers-Koen, who won four gold medals, was nicknamed "The Flying Housewife." (Most media thought her career was over when she had her first child in 1942.) There were far fewer female events than male ones—in gymnastics, for instance, the women only competed in the team all-around, while men did six individual apparatuses.

To many men in the media, Draves was seen more as a pretty face with star potential. She was offered roles in four movies, including two in the Philippines, where her father was born. She could easily have been one of the first breakout stars in Olympic history. She turned it all down. "MGM and 20th Century Fox had their eyes on her," her husband and coach, Lyle Draves, said. "They wanted to make a south-sea island girl out of her—to wear a sarong and all this stuff—but she didn't want any part of it."

Despite her prodigious talent, Draves, at heart, was a shy girl from San Francisco. Born Victoria Manalo, she didn't learn to swim until about age 10,

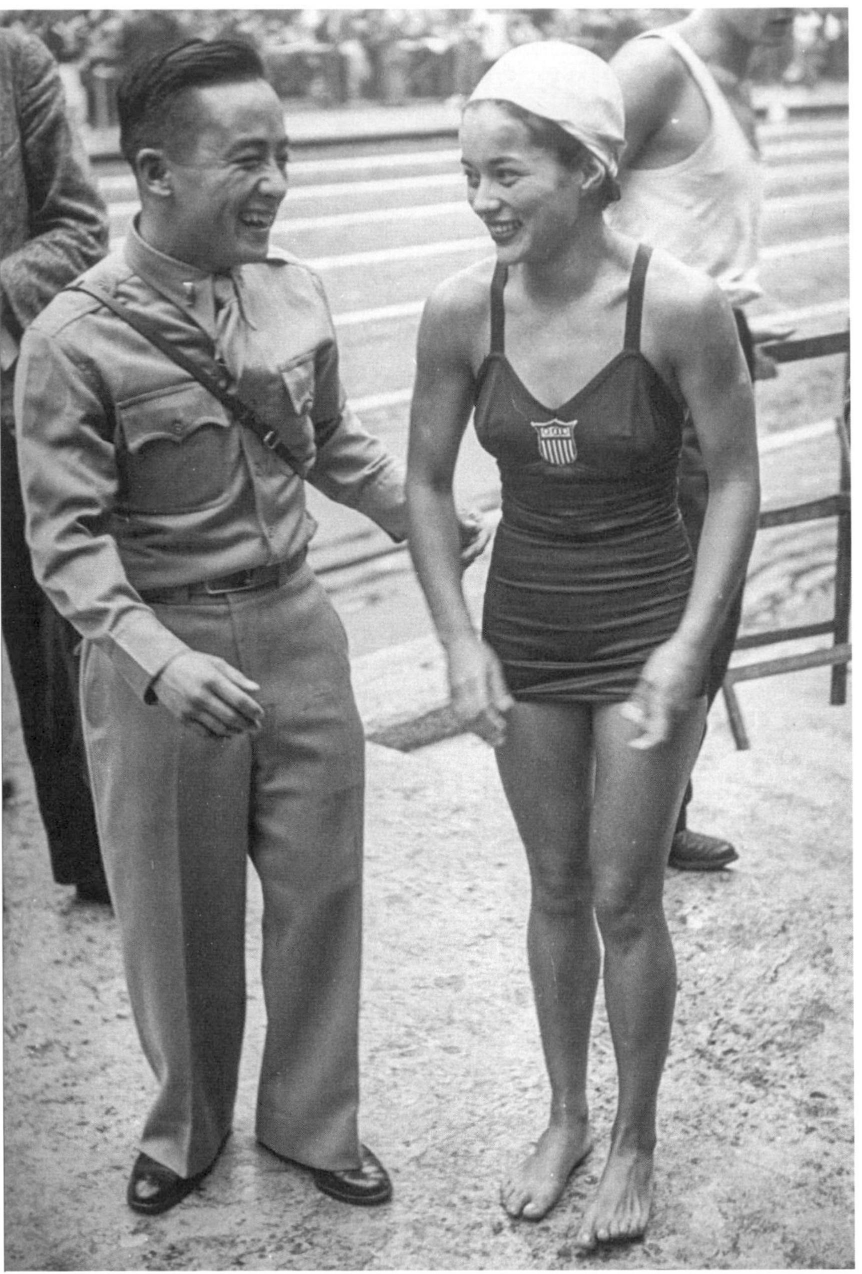

and even then, she admitted, she was afraid of the water. She dreaded school, where she faced prejudice from classmates. At first, Draves's high school coach, Phil Patterson, wouldn't allow her to be part of his swim club at the Fairmont Hotel. Even so, he recognized her talent and instead created a new segregated club called the Patterson School of Swimming and Diving. "I think he was a prejudiced man," she said of him in 2005. "It wasn't special for me. It was his way of separating me from the others." She even had to use, at Patterson's request, her white mother's maiden name, Taylor. She wouldn't use her Filipino name until three years later, for fear of racism and being excluded from events. By that time, at age 21, she had won her first national championship.

She met her next coach, Lyle Draves, after the national Amateur Athletic Union championships in 1944 and married him two years later. She entered the Olympics under the tutelage of her husband, who, upon first seeing her, knew instantly she would become a champion. Of course, he was right. But Vicki Draves, even standing on the platform, had to fight her own doubts.

It wasn't easy climbing up the ladder for the final dive in the 3m springboard, in which she would need to be flawless to overtake first place. She was so nervous that she would shake before each dive. "I can't do this," she told her friend and fellow gold medalist Sammy Lee, the first Asian American man to win gold. "I am not going to make it." But as champions do, she nailed it. After the Games, Draves turned pro, and toured around the world with gold medal–winning swimmer Buster Crabbe, the *Tarzan* and *Flash Gordon* actor. But mostly she stayed out of the spotlight. She and her husband opened a training program in California, and she worked as a secretary.

Draves was a quiet girl who very easily could've been a big star. Instead, she took her two gold medals and her infectious smile and lived a quiet life in California. But then again, wasn't her Olympic outcome predestined? After all, Victoria, in Roman mythology, is the goddess of victory. And *Manalo*, in Tagalog, means "win." With that lineage, how could she not come in first?

OPPOSITE: *Draves, seen here with fellow gold medalist Sammy Lee in 1948, helped push boundaries for Asian American athletes.*

SAMMY LEE
The First Asian American Male Gold Medalist

USA | DIVING | 3 MEDALS | 1920–2016

LONDON 1948 • HELSINKI 1952

Wednesday was something called "International Day" at the Brookside Park pool in Pasadena. For just one day of the week, black, Latino, and Asian families could enjoy the facilities. The city drained the pool and refilled it afterward for the white males. This is where Sammy Lee first began to swim and dive. And it's where he developed the large chip on his shoulder that propelled him to Olympic glory.

Lee was born in Fresno, California, the son of Korean immigrants. Everywhere he went in his childhood, he was reminded of his second-class status as an Asian American. He couldn't practice diving at private clubs, which were closed to Asians. "It disgusted but never discouraged me," he said. "It made me tougher."

Lee served as a lieutenant in the Army Medical Corps during World War II, when more than 100,000 Asian Americans, mostly of Japanese ancestry, were interned in camps throughout the country. All Lee wanted was to be accepted as an American—while never hiding his Korean heritage. When he first met his coach Jim Ryan, the former diver said he'd turn "that Jap" into the world's best. Lee, all five feet of him, grabbed the six-foot-four-inch, 275-pound Ryan by the belt. "I'm not a Chink, I'm not a Jap, I'm a Korean," he said. Ryan soon became a trusted ally and teacher. The prejudice fueled Lee, making him determined to prove that even in a racist America, he could do anything.

After earning his medical degree in 1947, Lee went to the London Games the following year. In the 10m platform competition, he scored two 9.5s and a 10, and did a three-and-a-half somersault—three-and-a-half full revolutions of the body—which was unheard of at the time.

Lee makes a gold medal–winning dive in Helsinki in 1952.

When he first hit the water, he thought he had done a belly flop. Boy, was he ever glad to be wrong. Lee became the first Asian American man to win a medal. (Vicki Draves, an American diver of Filipino descent, won her medal in the women's event a few days earlier for another Olympic first.) Lee would also take a bronze in the 3m springboard.

Still an active service member, Lee had thought he was going to serve in the Korean War. His superiors told him to instead seek glory in the 1952 Games. "Major Lee," they said, "we've got only one doctor who can win an Olympic gold medal. We've got hundreds of doctors who can repair the wounded. You can go, but you better win."

Of course, he won—adding another gold to his résumé.

But Lee, even as a distinguished veteran, doctor, and two-time gold medalist, couldn't escape the prejudice that marked his early life. Upon returning to California after the Games, he unsuccessfully attempted to buy houses in Garden Grove and Anaheim. In a typical case of racist housing segregation known as redlining, real estate agents refused to sell Lee and his wife a house, claiming it would devalue the properties. Lee wrote to a CBS journalist, and subsequent news coverage shed a light on the Olympian's plight, drumming up support in the community. A sympathetic Jewish developer, who said he too had known such discrimination, sold the Lees a house. "My belief in the American people is substantiated," Lee said.

Lee was determined to prove that even in a racist America, he could do just about anything.

After retiring from competitive diving, Lee continued swimming a few laps a day, even into his nineties. In 1990, he stood on the 10-meter platform at the Rose Bowl Aquatic Center. It was the opening of the new, lavish pool complex replacing the race-restricted Brookside Park of his childhood. Lee, taking a look from his 10-meter perch, liked what he saw.

How flabbergasted Lee must have been, standing 32 feet in the air above a pool that used to be open to him only on Wednesdays, now a place accessible to swimmers and divers of all races and sexes. How great it must have felt to know that, because of people like himself, the door had been flung wide open. That he, and all the others, were American, too.

GEORGE EYSER
The First American Gymnastics Star

USA | GYMNASTICS | 6 MEDALS | 1870–1919

ST. LOUIS 1904

If you happened to be a German immigrant at the turn of the twentieth century, chances are you had some experience in gymnastics. Popular exercise clubs called *Turnvereins,* or Turner halls—gymnastics unions that later became hubs for political activity—came to America with the waves of Germans who arrived throughout the nineteenth century. In St. Louis in the 1890s, for example, there were as many as 11 Turner halls.

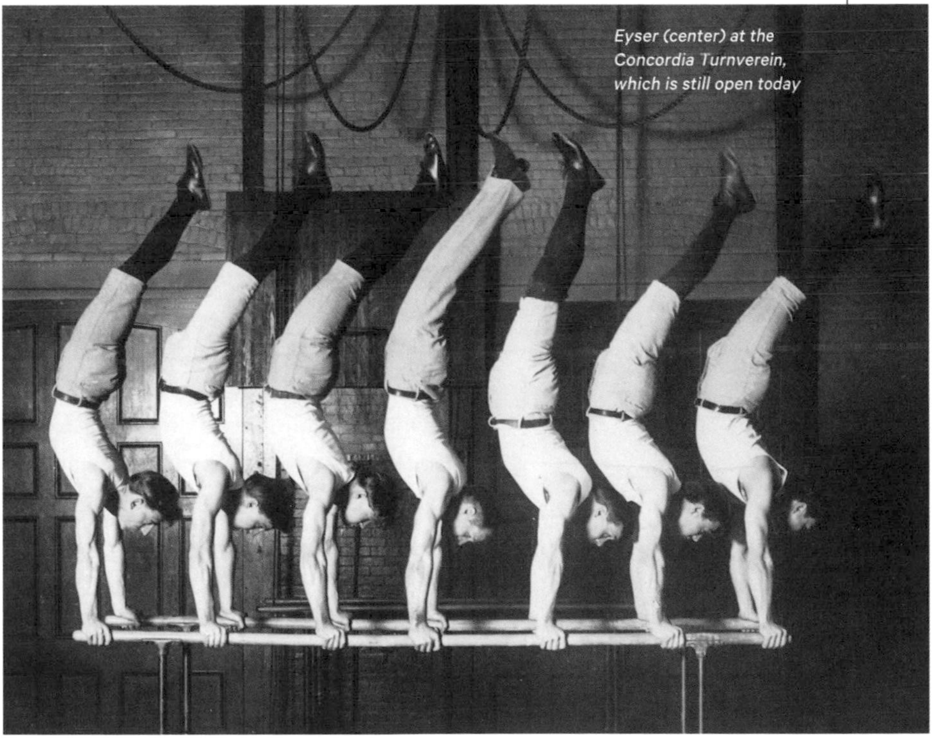

Eyser (center) at the Concordia Turnverein, which is still open today

One mainstay of the St. Louis gymnastics scene in the 1900s was George Eyser. He emigrated to the United States in 1884 as a 14-year-old and joined the Concordia Turnverein, which is still standing today. At one point in his youth, Eyser lost most of his left leg to amputation after a train ran over it. He was fitted with a wooden prosthesis that fortunately allowed for jumping and running. Despite that hardship, he became one of the best gymnasts in the country, a remarkable feat given the inflexibility of prostheses back then.

His time in the Turnverein prepared him well for the 1904 Olympics, which, lucky for him, were taking place right at home in St. Louis. These were the third-ever Olympic games, and the first held in the United States. (It was also the first Games in which gold, silver, and bronze medals were handed out—previously, winners were given trophies.) Unlike today's highly structured spectacles, the early Games were haphazard and spread out over months. There were two gymnastics competitions. The first, the International Turners' Championship held in July, featured the all-around, triathlon, and team events. (Triathlon at that time featured the long jump, shot put, and 100-yard dash.) The more traditional Olympic Gymnastics championship, held later in October, featured the individual apparatuses seen today.

Eyser (center) poses at the International Turnfest in Frankfurt in 1908.

Eyser would probably like to forget his performance in the Turners' Championship. In the all-around he finished tenth. The triathlon was worse—he finished dead last. But three months later, and with a fresh slate, Eyser rose to the challenge. On October 29, Eyser won an astounding six medals, three of them gold, for the most ever in a single day. He finished first in the parallel bars, the vault, and the rope climb. (Yes, *that* rope climb from your PE nightmares.) He also took home two silvers in the pommel horse and what was known then as the combined four-event all-around, and nabbed a bronze in the horizontal bar.

A BRIEF HISTORY OF THE POMMEL HORSE

The pommel horse, that odd, leather-covered apparatus where male gymnasts move their hands in circles as if they were on fire, has a long and distinguished history. Soldiers in ancient Rome used a wooden version to practice mounting and dismounting horses. Alexander the Great and his Macedonian army were also said to have used it in their military preparations. In the 17th century, it was reclaimed as an athletic endeavor—called equestrian acrobatics—in academies for knights. By the 1800s, fake horses—complete with head and mane—found their way into competitions. This version was used as late as the 1936 Games.

Though today's pommels are made of leather and rubber, a small subset of people have taken it to the next level. In a sport called equestrian vaulting, athletes perform gymnastics moves on actual, living horses. (Giddy-up.) Bringing it to the Olympics might finally liven up an otherwise staid equestrian program.

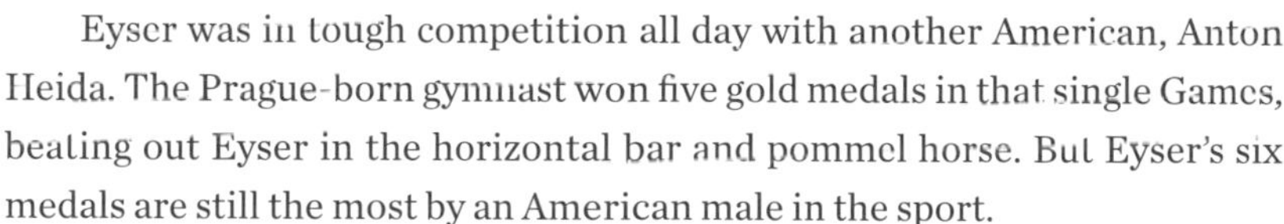

Eyser was in tough competition all day with another American, Anton Heida. The Prague-born gymnast won five gold medals in that single Games, beating out Eyser in the horizontal bar and pommel horse. But Eyser's six medals are still the most by an American male in the sport.

Eyser was also the first person to compete with an artificial leg in the Olympics, a mark that would stand for 104 years until Natalie du Toit of South Africa swam in the 10 km marathon in Beijing. Despite all the history-making, little is known about Eyser's post-Olympic life. He was still a member of the Concordia Turnverein at least as late as 1908, and records show he worked as a bookkeeper. But Eyser's greatest accomplishments came on one warm fall day in October, when a gymnast with a wooden leg transcended his limitations to reach Olympic glory.

DEBBIE MEYER
The First Three-Time Swimming Gold Medalist

USA | SWIMMING | 3 MEDALS | 1952–

MEXICO CITY 1968

While training in Colorado Springs ahead of the 1968 Summer Olympics, Debbie Meyer received a card in the mail from her father. "Happiness," it read, "is a gold medal." A few weeks later, after returning home from the Games, Meyer scribbled over the card and sent it back. "Happiness," it now said, "is three gold medals."

Meyer, at just 16 years old, had won triple-gold in swimming at the Mexico City Games, prevailing in the 200, 400, and 800 freestyle. And she did it all while battling a bad stomach bug. "She was a hell of an athlete," said her coach, Sherman Chavoor. "She was in a class by herself." Meyer, showing the priorities of a teenager, said, "After this, I am going to go home and stuff myself."

She became the first female swimmer to win three gold medals at the same Games, a feat that went unmatched until Katie Ledecky collected four in 2016. Between 1967 and 1971, Meyer set 20 world records. But at age 19, before she got the chance to defend her titles at the Munich Games, she decided to retire. The drive just wasn't there anymore. "I have been to the Olympics and don't want to work that hard to get there again," she said. "My mind tells me to get moving, but my arms won't go."

Meyer's retirement didn't start off well after she broke her ankle while skiing. She then struggled with body image. She saw people staring at her as if she was the same stellar athlete that she had been, despite, in her view, her body not matching the expectation. While recovering from her ankle injury, she continued her normal 6,000-calories-a-day diet, but without the same amount of exercise, and gained 50 pounds. "I started building fat on fat and I was so ashamed of myself. The more ashamed I got, the more I ate." At UCLA, she sat in her room trying to avoid the thin girls around her.

But after college, Meyer got a job doing something she loved: swimming. She became a coach at Stanford and joined Speedo's promotion department. She also worked with her former coach Chavoor at the Arden Hills club in Sacramento. "You can't imagine how nice it was to be waking up in the morning and going to a pool again," she said.

Today, Meyer still coaches in California. But her achievements as a 16-year-old are never far away. When she drives to practice, the license plate on her car reads "3 GOLD 68."

Meyer winning gold in the 400-meter freestyle, her second of three in 1968

CHARLES JEWTRAW
The First Winter Medalist

USA | SPEED SKATING | 1 MEDAL | 1900–1996

CHAMONIX 1924

When Charles Jewtraw walked in the small opening ceremony of the 1924 Olympics in Chamonix, France—the first ever Winter Games—he was an awestruck 24-year-old. He looked around and saw 294 athletes from 18 countries milling about. Some of the athletes were carrying all their own equipment—one even lugged a heavy bobsled. They were just regular folks: mountain guides, local athletes, and firefighters. Even the tourists, said a member of the Swedish ski team, "seemed more interested in the social whirl than in the Olympic sporting life." Jewtraw may have been in complete awe, but the modest opening ceremony crowd of 2,089 seemed to indicate that Chamonix itself wasn't particularly impressed by the brand-new Winter Olympics.

Though the 1924 Games paled in comparison to today's extravaganzas, it was all a bit much for Jewtraw, who felt unprepared and overwhelmed by every little detail in France. A national champion in speed skating, Jewtraw had by that point pretty much retired from competition and was gearing up for college when he was invited to join the American delegation in France. "I hadn't trained at all," he recalled. "I didn't want to go. My tutor convinced me I should. I was so sick crossing the ocean that I kept praying the ship would sink."

LEFT: *Jewtraw, much to his own surprise, won the first gold medal at the first Winter Games.*

AMERICA'S FIRST ICE QUEEN

The most decorated US female figure skater got her start at the 1924 Winter Games. Beatrix Loughran began by winning silver in ladies' singles—then called "fancy skating"—in Chamonix. At one point, the judges had her and Austrian Herma Szabo in an even tie before giving Szabo the gold. Loughran followed that medal with a bronze in 1928 in St. Moritz and a silver in pairs with Sherwin Badger in 1932 in Lake Placid. She is one of only three Americans to win three medals in figure skating, and she took home six national titles as well. Loughran was also a Broadway actor and had a career as a coach, working with her niece, three-time national champion Audrey Peppe.

Jewtraw wasn't nervous the day of the race—in his mind, he couldn't possibly win. He had a point. The first race was the 500 meter—in the United States races went up to only 440 yards. (That's about a 100-yard difference.) He had never skated against the clock, never competed in a one-on-one heat, never changed lanes midway. As he lined up, he said to himself, "For my country and my God, I'll do my best."

He skated the 500 meters in just 44 seconds, winning by .2 seconds. Because it was the first race of the entire Olympic slate, Jewtraw went down in history as the first-ever Winter Olympic gold medalist. The American team flooded the ice and surrounded him. "They hugged me like I was a beautiful girl," he said. "I ask you, how many people have a moment like that? I did."

Unlike today's winners, fame and riches didn't await Jewtraw upon his return home. He worked at Macy's in New York City, and faced hard times and unemployment during the Great Depression. In 1938, he began working long hours as a custodian and a part-time instructor at a rink in the city. He donated his gold medal to the Smithsonian Museum in 1957 and eventually retired to Palm Beach, Florida, where he died in 1996. "Fame doesn't bring all that one might think," he said. "That gold never changed me at all. I never meant to capitalize on it. But then I never had a chance to, did I?

BETTY ROBINSON
The First World's Fastest Woman

USA | TRACK AND FIELD | 3 MEDALS | 1911–1999
AMSTERDAM 1928 • BERLIN 1936

In her fourth-ever official race, Betty Robinson, a 16-year-old from Illinois, won the first women's 100-meter dash at the 1928 Olympics in Amsterdam in world-record time. Three years later, she was dead. Then she woke up.

Robinson's near-death in a plane crash was only one in a series of dramatic moments for the trailblazing runner, and her rise to prominence followed an unusual path. Just a few months before the Games, Robinson had shown no interest in running. "I had no idea that women even ran then," she said. "I grew up a hick." But then, the story goes, a high school teacher saw her running to catch a train and thought she had some talent. She was quickly Olympic-bound.

This was the first time that women competed in sprinting events, and Robinson benefited from crucial mistakes made by her competitors. The world record holder, Myrtle Cook of Canada, as well as top contender Leni Schmidt of Germany, false-started in the final and were disqualified. Robinson finished in 12.2 seconds, equaling the world record.

In Amsterdam, Robinson made quite the impression on General Douglas MacArthur, then the president of the American Olympic Committee. He wrote of "that sparkling combination of speed and grace by Elizabeth Robinson which might have rivaled even Artemis herself on the heights of Olympus." Upon returning home, she had ticker-tape parades in New York and Chicago. She received a silver cup from her high school and a diamond watch from her hometown of Riverdale.

Then, tragically, she died.

Okay, not quite. In 1931, Robinson was flying in a biplane with her cousin when they crashed outside Chicago. Both survived—though she suffered a concussion, her left leg broken in three places, a broken left arm, and severe cuts over one eye. When a passerby found them, he mistook her for dead and brought her to the morgue. Luckily, the undertaker noticed Robinson was breathing and called for the doctors who saved her life.

After a long, arduous recovery, her left leg had become a half inch shorter than it was before the crash. Robinson was able to walk and run again, but she couldn't assume the crouch stance needed at the start of a track race. But that didn't stop her. At the 1936 Olympics in Berlin, the US team established Robinson as the third runner in the 4 x 100 relay race—meaning she could start from a standing position while she waited for the baton. Though the Germans were ahead at the time, Robinson kept it close, and the Americans took the lead in the final leg to win gold.

Robinson was inducted into the National Track and Field Hall of Fame in 1971, but isn't as well known as some of her fellow female track stars. But for Robinson, a naturally modest person, that she was known at all was a surprise. "I still can't believe the attention I get for something I did so long ago," she said.

Robinson (center) was a natural, beating out Canadians Bobbie Rosenfeld and Ethel Smith in just her fourth-ever race.

AL OERTER
The First Four-peater

USA | TRACK AND FIELD | 4 MEDALS | 1936–2007

MELBOURNE 1956 • ROME 1960 • TOKYO 1964 • MEXICO CITY 1968

If the word *longevity* ever applied to one athlete, that person would probably be Al Oerter. A computer executive by day, discus thrower by night, Oerter was the first to win gold medals in four straight Olympics (since matched by Carl Lewis). But he was also *really* good, for a *really* long time.

Take Oerter at age 43, when he decided, 11 years after his fourth gold medal in Mexico City, to make a comeback. In May 1980, he threw a 227-10½, a personal best, more than six feet farther than the gold-medal-winning throw in 1976, and nine feet more than the eventual title-winning throw at the 1980 Games. In 1982, while filming an ESPN show, he threw the discus more than 240 feet, which would have been a world record. A year before the 1984 Games in Los Angeles, he threw 222-9, which would've won gold. (He missed these Games because of a strained Achilles tendon, old age seeming to finally catch up to him at 47 years old.) "These are the Olympics," he once said. "You die before you quit."

Oerter's decades-spanning, record-setting, incredibly successful career started on a lark. Growing up in West Islip, New York, he threw his first discus at age 15 after one landed beside him as he ran near the school's track practice. He threw the discus back, and it flew so far that the coaches made it clear he had to compete. (Replace that discus with any flying object and you can easily imagine Oerter dominating the javelin or shot put, excelling as a pro pitcher or quarterback.) Four years later, he threw an Olympic record in Melbourne to win his first gold, and was so nervous that he almost fainted on the medal stand. In Rome, in 1960, he won gold again.

In between Olympics, Oerter was emphatic about not being a full-time athlete. "Professional sport is just a big carnival," he said. "All that greasy-kid-stuff business. I could never do that. More stunts, more zanies, all to make more money—they should carry Actors' Equity cards." But the Olympics

Oerter, seen here in 1956, winning the first of four straight gold medals

always kept him coming back. He didn't compete for money. The Olympics meant something more than just dollar signs to Oerter—it was an ideal to strive for. "There is something about the Games that gets in your blood," he said. "All those people from those various nations, all with the same purpose. The crowds, the training, the competition, the pressure. I know it may sound dumb, but I can really get charged up about the Olympics."

It was that charge that led Oerter to a tough victory in the Tokyo Games in 1964. Two years before, he pinched a nerve in his neck that rendered his left side numb and multiple doctors told him to quit. He didn't listen. Then, six days before competition in Tokyo, he slipped and tore cartilage in his rib cage. With shots of Novocain and a massive amount of tape wrapped around his body, he was still able to pull off gold.

"There is something about the Games that gets in your blood . . . I can really get charged up about the Olympics."

Oerter repeated in 1968, winning an historic gold with an Olympic-record throw. Mexico City would prove to be his final Games, but thereafter he never stopped pushing to compete. He thrived at the World Veterans' Games—of course—winning the 1989 event by more than 30 feet. And he loved every moment. "This is more like the Olympics than the Olympics," he said. "None of the drugs, politics, or money. Just people who enjoy competition without being desperate or unwell about it."

A self-described highly nervous person, Oerter found another post-Olympic outlet in painting. He founded Art of the Olympians, a foundation that showcases Olympic values through the arts. It features works by Peggy Fleming, Florence Joyner, Rafer Johnson, Bob Beamon, Birgit Fischer, and Shannon Miller, all gold medal winners.

In 2003, Oerter, who long suffered from high blood pressure, had fluid build up in his heart and it stopped beating momentarily. He denied a heart transplant. "I've had an interesting life," he said, "and I'm going out with what I have." He died in 2007.

What he had was determination, a whole lot of longevity, and yes, the heart of the champion.

The 1928 Summer Olympics

Multiple Firsts at the "Parking Lot Games"

We've all been through it: Traffic is a mess and you're searching frantically to find a parking spot. You're circling again and again, waiting for any sign of relief. Finally, when you find that open spot—and see that beautiful white on blue P—you can breathe a sigh of relief. And then you should thank the Olympics.

Yes, the international sign for parking was created for the 1928 Summer Games in Amsterdam. With the lot next to the stadium able to hold just 2,000 cars, the Amsterdam organizers knew they would need far more space. After adding more spots around the city for 3,500 cars and 2,000 bikes, they just needed an identifier. Hence, the blue parking sign we all know and love.

As if changing the face of parking forever weren't enough, the 1928 Games saw a few other momentous firsts. How about the Olympic flame, that symbol of the torch races from Antiquity? Yep, that started in the Netherlands. Women made their track and field debut in five events, much to Pierre de Coubertin's dismay. Oh yeah, and there was this: The US delegation received 1,000 crates of Coca-Cola, marking the first time that the drink sponsored the Games. Though Coke is probably not the drink of choice for most Olympic athletes, it is the longest continuous sponsor of the Olympics. Guess you can thank the Dutch for that one, too.

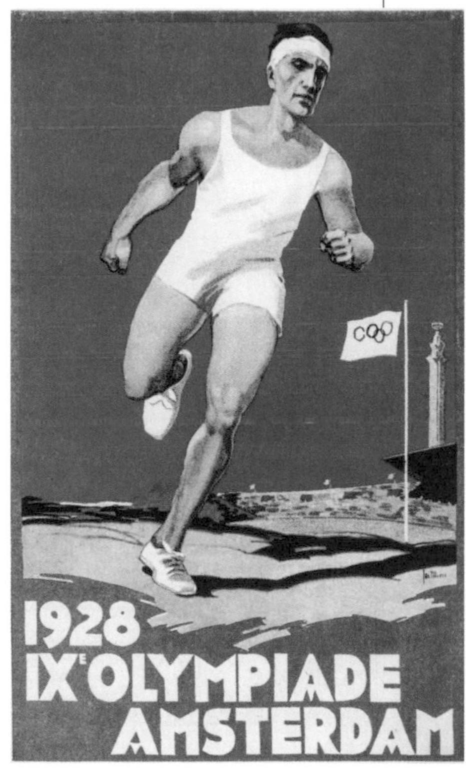

A Dutch poster for the 1928 Summer Olympics

The 1932 Summer Olympics

The Innovation Games

The 1932 Summer Olympics in Los Angeles introduced a slew of innovations that have since become staples. Perhaps the biggest advance was the very first Olympic Village. Though the 1924 Olympics in Paris was the first to offer lodging for some athletes, the 1932 Games expanded the concept to accommodate all male competitors in a self-contained, full-service village close to the Los Angeles Coliseum. (The female athletes, meanwhile, stayed at the nearby Chapman Park Hotel.) It wasn't a popular idea. There was concern that the men wouldn't get along in such close quarters. As far as we know, however, no international fistfights broke out.

The village, built specifically for the Games, contained 550 portable bungalows, each 24 by 10 feet, on a 321-acre lot meant to host 1,836 men. For about $2 per day, athletes had access to five dining halls, a post office, radio station, fire station, movie theater, and hospital. "I'll never forget the elation

An overhead view of the new Olympic Village in Los Angeles. Everything a (male) athlete would need was housed here.

of living at the Olympic Village in Baldwin Hills," said Frank Wykoff, who won gold in the 4 x 100 relay. "Being able to visit throughout the village, trying to overcome the language differences with representatives of 56 nations was a rare delight."

The village wasn't the only first in 1932. Automatic timing (as opposed to hand-kept) made its debut, as did the photo-finish Kirby Two-Eyed Camera, which could decide close track races to within one-hundredth of a second. The schedule was modernized as well—the Games themselves lasted for just 16 well-planned days. Previous Olympics had taken months to complete but after Los Angeles, the two-week period became customary. The Los Angeles Games also introduced one of the Olympics' most iconic elements: the three-tiered podium. For the first time, the gold medalist reveled at the top, head and shoulders above the second- and third-place finishers, who stood on progressively lower steps.

The 1932 Games were a bit hamstrung by the larger economic peril gripping thc world. Only 37 countries competed, down from 46 in 1928. It was a sign of things to come—with World War II looming on the horizon, competition began at the height of the Great Depression. Grim economic realities would make the next few Olympics a bit more modest.

THE FIRST PODIUM

Ever wonder why, during the medal ceremony, athletes stand on podiums? The answer isn't quite as sexy as you might think—if you were envisioning ancient Greece, try Ontario. At the 1930 British Empire Games in Hamilton, Canada (later known as the Commonwealth Games), a podium was used for apparently the first time in sports history. IOC president Henri de Baillet-Latour, who happened to be attending, liked what he saw and made sure it was instituted at the next Games.

At the 1932 Winter Olympics in Lake Placid, after winning the 500-meter speed-skating race, the United States' Jack Shea became the first gold medalist to receive a medal on the stand. It didn't go so smoothly, however. The silver medalist, Norway's Bernt Evensen, stood in the bronze position, with Canada's Alexander Hurd in the silver medal spot.

ROBERT GARRETT

The First (Accidental) Discus Winner

USA | TRACK AND FIELD | 6 MEDALS | 1876–1961

ATHENS 1896 • PARIS 1900

Robert Garrett, a scion of old money from Baltimore, won the first-ever discus event at the 1896 Olympics in Athens. A few weeks prior, he had no idea what a discus even was.

A shot-putter at Princeton, Garrett first learned of the Games from a classics professor at the school. He then found an illustration of an ancient Greek discus in an old textbook and had a blacksmith create a metal replica. Discus itself wasn't all that popular at the time; it had been resurrected from its ancient form only in the 1870s. At 30 pounds, Garrett's discus was a good six times heavier than the 4.4-pound one he would use in Athens. (Nowadays, a discus is usually made up of a combination of plastic, wood, fiberglass, and carbon fiber, affixed to a metal core.)

Garrett practiced his new sport on the deck of the ship taking him to Europe. He arrived in Athens barely in time. The American delegation didn't know that Greeks still used the Julian calendar, so they rushed frantically from their port of entry in Naples to Athens. (We told you the early Games were a disorganized mess.) Like a baseball player emerging from the on-deck circle after practicing with an extra-heavy doughnut, Garrett set a world record, beating the silver medalist by more than two feet. "Nobody was more surprised than I was when they gave me the prize," he said.

Garrett also took gold in the shot put, his more familiar sport, and won silvers in the high jump and long jump. He returned to the Olympics in Paris in 1900, winning bronzes in shot put and the standing triple jump. After his athletic career, Garrett went on to finance important archaeological digs in the Middle East and collected historic manuscripts and texts. Hopefully his measurements on the digs were a little more accurate than his discus making.

Garrett had never seen a proper discus before reaching Athens, but he quickly adapted to win gold in 1896.

JAMES CONNOLLY
The First Medalist . . . in Anything

USA | TRACK AND FIELD | 4 MEDALS | 1868–1957

ATHENS 1896 • PARIS 1900

The first Olympic gold medalist in a millennium and a half didn't receive a gold medal. Though Pierre de Coubertin wanted to award gold medals to each top winner, Prince Constantine of Greece thought that it would appear as if the best athletes were getting paid. They reached a compromise: Winners got a silver medal and an olive branch. Second place got bronze medals. Third place got nothing. (Harsh.)

So a silver medal is what James Connolly received after winning the triple jump—or, as it was known back then, the "hop, step, and jump"—on the opening day of the 1896 Games. This most historic Olympic victor was a 27-year-old high school dropout who had managed to make it into Harvard. He barely made it to Athens. On the trip over, Connolly's wallet was stolen during a stopover in Naples. Police wanted him to stay in Italy for prosecution of the criminal, but Connolly wouldn't have it. With the train literally leaving the station, he ran and leapt on, and was pulled through a compartment window.

It's a good thing he got to the Games. In addition to the gold, Connolly won two other medals, including silver in the high jump. He also won a silver in 1900 in the triple jump. He returned to the Olympics again in 1904, though this time covering the Games as a journalist. He went on to become a prolific writer, publishing 25 novels and hundreds of short stories.

LEFT: *James Connolly took home the first-ever gold medal—even though it was made of silver.*

JOHN & SUMNER PAINE
The First Sibling Medalists

JOHN PAINE: USA | SHOOTING | 1 MEDAL | 1870–1951

ATHENS 1896

SUMNER PAINE: USA | SHOOTING | 2 MEDALS | 1868–1904

ATHENS 1896

There was no rivalry between the first pair of siblings to win medals at the Olympics—just a lot of brotherly love. John and Sumner Paine were skilled marksmen from Boston whose father was a general in the Union army. The Paines arrived in Athens for the 1896 Games with some 3,500 rounds of ammunition but would need just 96 bullets to win both events. In the 25-meter military pistol event, John Paine won handily, beating his older brother, who won a silver, by 62 points.

Someone seemed to have taught these two manners—before the first competition, they agreed that whoever won an event first would drop out of

SISTERS IN CRIME

At the 1984 Games, Puerto Rico's Madeline de Jesús felt a pull in her hamstring. This presented two problems: She couldn't finish the long jump, and she wouldn't be able to help her team in the 4 x 400 relay later in the schedule. But maybe that second issue wasn't so problematic after all. Luckily for de Jesús, her identical twin sister Margaret, also a 400-meter runner, was in the stands as a spectator. Why not try the old switcheroo? Posing as her sister, Margaret ran in the qualifying heat for the relay, and it worked—until they were found out. Once their coach discovered the ruse, he refused to let his team run in the final. The Puerto Rican Olympic Committee banned the de Jesús sisters for life.

the next one. So in the 30-meter free pistol event, Sumner won a gold of his own while his younger brother stood on the sidelines.

Though Sumner would die just eight years later from pneumonia, John kept the Olympic legacy alive. One hundred years after his win in Athens, his great-granddaughter Cecile Tucker competed in rowing in Atlanta. If that's not the longest time to pass between relatives competing, it's sure up there.

ALEKSANDR DITYATIN
The First Eight-Medal Winner in One Olympics

SOVIET UNION | GYMNASTICS | 10 MEDALS | 1957–

MONTREAL 1976 • MOSCOW 1980

3 6 1

Before Michael Phelps won his octet of medals in 2004, Aleksandr Dityatin was the first to do it. Well, given that 65 nations boycotted the Moscow Games, including the United States, the comparison doesn't quite hold up. But at the 1980 Summer Olympics, Russian gymnast Aleksandr Dityatin won a record eight medals, the most of any single Olympics: three gold (in the team, all-around, and rings), four silvers, and a bronze.

Had Dityatin still been able to snag eight medals with no boycott, it's likely he would be one of the most famous and celebrated Olympians of all time. That asterisk in the record books, combined with the fact that he couldn't defend his

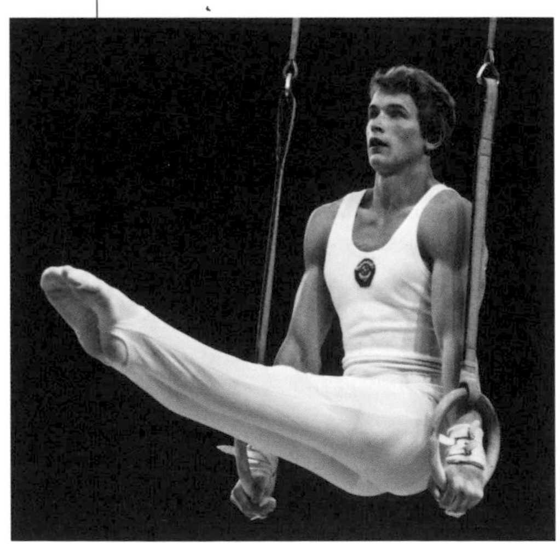

LEFT: *Dityatin did his damage while many countries were boycotting, but he still collected eight medals.*

crown in 1984 when the Soviets boycotted the Games in Los Angeles, has reduced Dityatin to a footnote in Olympic history. (He is, for what it's worth, quite famous in Russia.)

In fact, most people didn't remember Dityatin until Michael Phelps tied the single-Olympics record with eight medals in 2004 and again in 2008. (Rick Reilly, writing in *Sports Illustrated,* dismissed Dityatin's achievement as "beating three Latvians and a trained goat.")

Even so, one thing can never be taken away from the Russian, boycott or not: Dityatin, on the vault, recorded the first-ever perfect 10 by a male gymnast at the Olympics.

FUN WITH FLAGS!

The Los Angeles city flag is elegant and simple. It features three notched stripes of green, gold, and red: green for olive trees, gold for orange groves, and red for vineyards. If you're a Los Angeles native, it's possible you haven't even seen it. But the world got a good, long gander at it in 1980. As the boycotted Moscow Games came to a close, a sticky situation arose. Traditionally, the next host country is honored in the closing ceremony and their flag gets waved. In an awkward twist, however, the United States, leader of the Moscow boycott, was set to host next in Los Angeles in 1984—what were the Soviets to do?

Simple: Raise the flag of Los Angeles. After all, the Soviets didn't have a problem with L.A. per se, just the country the City of Angels happened to be in. And so the flag of Los Angeles got perhaps more international shine than at any time before or since. And then, instead of handing the Soviet flag to L.A. mayor Thomas Bradley, as would be customary, IOC president Juan Antonio Samaranch waved the Olympic flag. Ouch.

EMIL ZATOPEK
The First Distance King

CZECHOSLOVAKIA | TRACK AND FIELD | 5 MEDALS | 1922–2000

LONDON 1948 • HELSINKI 1952 • MELBOURNE 1956

Of all the great Olympic champions, Emil Zatopek could be the nicest. Make no mistake, "nice" doesn't mean he was a weak competitor—he won five medals, four of them gold. After all, the Czech runner is the first, and only, person to win the 5,000 meter, the 10,000 meter, and the marathon all at the same Games, achieving the incredible feat at the 1952 Summer Olympics in Helsinki. All of those races, by the way, were Olympic-record times—and it was the first marathon he had ever run.

"There is not, and never was, a greater man than Emil Zatopek."

But it's what Zatopek did off the track that might define his Olympic legacy most. One of his rivals, Fred Wilt, an American, said he was "perhaps the most humble, friendly, and popular athlete in modern times." Zatopek gave one of his gold medals to Ron Clarke, an Australian distance runner who set many world records but never won a gold of his own. ("There is not, and never was, a greater man than Emil Zatopek," said Clarke.) When he entered the stadium at the end of the marathon, his victory certain, some 70,000 people chanted his name. "At that moment," said Juan Antonio Samaranch, who would become the president of the IOC in 1980, "I understood what the Olympic spirit means."

Indeed, it was Zatopek's spirit that carried him through. He wooed his wife, Dana Zátopková—herself a two-time medalist in javelin—with folk songs. He met athletes from around the world, and tried to learn their languages by memorizing dictionary pages. (He eventually became fluent in eight languages.) He refused to attend the Helsinki Games until his friend, a middle-distance runner who was left off the Czech team because of his father's antigovernment stance, was allowed to compete. Legendary for his rigorous dedication to running, Zatopek trained in army boots and wore

Zatopek crosses the finish line in the 10,000 meter in London with his trademark expression of agony.

three tracksuits at a time; he would jog in place for hours, and ran with Dana on his back. He always looked like he was in tremendous pain when running. He joked, "I am not talented enough to run and smile at the same time."

Zatopek supported the liberal movement in Czechoslovakia against the Soviets, and his status as an Olympian didn't save him from political banishment. He was kicked out of the Communist Party in 1968 and given menial jobs. Still, despite what looked like a fall from grace, Zatopek kept going. Even as he worked as a garbage collector or a street sweeper, there was always an admiring fan, ready to lend a helping hand.

Zatopek was officially "rehabilitated" in 1990 by Czech President Václav Havel before passing away in 2000. Hundreds of friends, luminaries, and fellow athletes attended his funeral, held at Prague's National Theatre, his escape from pariah status complete.

Zatopek (right) beat Alain Mimoun of France (center) by just 0.8 seconds in a thrilling finish to the 5,000-meter race in 1952.

5

DISCONTINUED SPORTS

Most viewers tune into the more unusual Olympic sports just once every four years. How much curling can one consume on a regular basis, anyway? Events like biathlon or race walking may look a bit odd, but they're often more popular globally than in the United States. (And we could all use a little more curling in our lives.)

Some events—particularly in the early days of the Games—were a mix of traditional sports and misplaced add-ons. That, in turn, made the final product comically out of place in an athletic competition. There's a reason the early Olympics were so poorly organized and so scattershot: The events were all over the place! Then there are "demonstration sports"—unofficial events getting an Olympic tryout to gauge their potential success and popularity. (It doesn't always work out so well.) All of these odd sports have been discontinued from the Games. But they will forever remain part of the rich Olympic legacy.

Club Swing

Swinging for Glory

Indian clubs were popular pieces of exercise equipment in the nineteenth century. Similar in size and appearance to bowling pins, they were swung one or two at a time in different patterns—up and around the shoulder, over the head, behind the back. The clubs originated in India, as early as the third century, as a way for soldiers to improve strength. The practice then moved to Europe, and spread to the United States as an aerobic exercise. Americans loved it, though enthusiasm for the sport petered out by the 1950s.

Club swinging—no, not swinging in a club—was also an Olympic sport. It appeared just twice, in 1904 and 1932. In both Games, the competitor had to stand still and swing the clubs for as long as possible. This meant swinging it around the body and over the head, as well as in a circular direction. (You can observe the fine art of club swinging in the 12-second 1891 film *Newark Athlete,* the oldest film in the National Film Registry.)

Americans absolutely dominated Olympic club swinging. At both Games, the United States swept. In 1904, Edward Hennig was the gold medal winner. A gymnast from Ohio, he also won gold that year in the horizontal bars, and competed in the pommel horse, all-around, and gymnastics triathlon (a one-time event that was like a compressed all-around, consisting of the pommel horse and horizontal and parallel bars). Hennig was the most successful club swinger of all time—over 47 years as an active competitor, he won 13 national titles, including his last at age 71.

The 1932 gold medalist hitchhiked home after the medal ceremony.

Club swinging didn't appear again until the 1932 Summer Games in Los Angeles, the next time the Olympics were on American soil. It was again a red, white, and blue rout. George Roth took gold. Unemployed during the Great Depression, Roth would steal food from the Olympic Village for his family. After winning gold and participating in the medal ceremony, he walked out of the stadium and hitchhiked back to his home in East Hollywood, never to be heard from again, not unlike the sport in which he conquered.

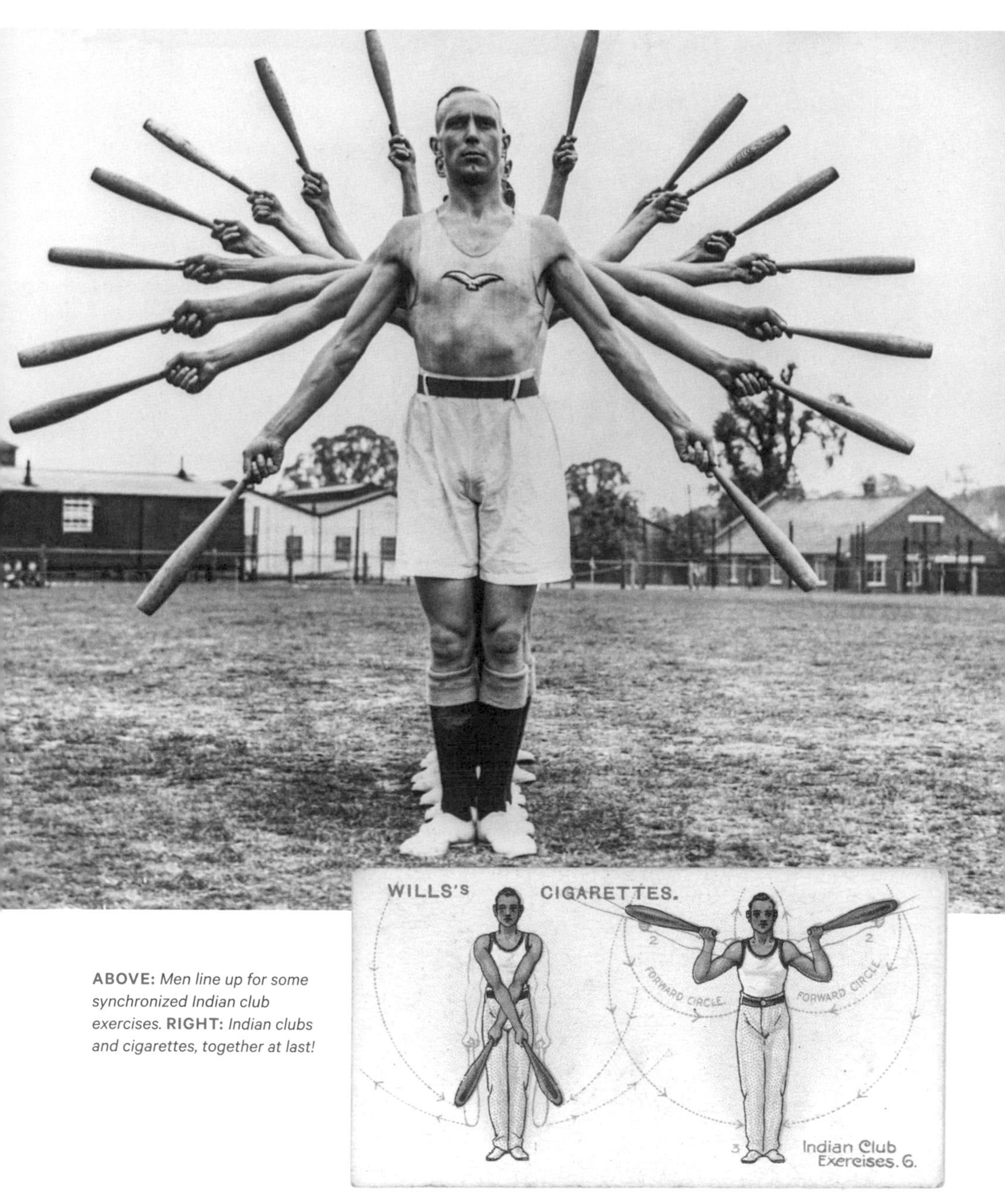

ABOVE: *Men line up for some synchronized Indian club exercises.* **RIGHT:** *Indian clubs and cigarettes, together at last!*

Swim Obstacle

Look Out Below!

Fred Lane, an Australian swimmer, pulled off a unique double gold at the 1900 Paris Games. His first gold, on August 12, 1900, was in the 200-meter freestyle. Swimming in the River Seine, Lane crushed the second-place finisher by six seconds. Later that day, Lane took to the Seine for another 200-meter competition. This one, though, was a little different. It was still swimming, but with a twist: The swimmers had obstacles in the way.

The 200-meter swimming obstacle was held just this once at the Paris Games—and probably for good reason. There were three obstacles spaced over the 200 meters. First, the swimmers had to climb over a pole. Then they had to pull themselves up and over a row of upside-down boats stationed in the water. That was followed by swimming *under* another row of boats.

Lane won with a respectable time of 2:38.4. In 1902, he would become the first man to swim the 100-yard freestyle in under a minute.

Underwater Swim

The Longest Float

The 1900 Paris Games saw an underwater swimming competition, the first—and only—of its kind. It worked like this: Two points were awarded for each meter swum, and one point for each second underwater. Only 14 swimmers, 10 of them French, took part. And apparently there was a bit of strategy involved. The third-place finisher, Peder Lykkeberg of Denmark, swam much farther than the 60 meters that gold medal winner Charles Devendeville did. But because Lykkeberg swam in a circle instead of a straight line, he was credited for only 28 meters, and lost despite staying underwater for nearly 30 seconds longer than Devendeville. Heartbreaking!

The event was reportedly poorly attended, and pretty much as silly as it sounds. But that hasn't stopped kids from enjoying their summer break by seeing just how long they can hold their breath underwater. (By the way, kids, Lykkeberg's time to beat is one minute and 30 seconds.)

Tandem Bicycle

Two Wheels, Four Legs

British songwriter Harry Dacre was half crazy for Daisy Bell—so madly in love, in fact, that though he couldn't afford much, he could buy "a bicycle built for two." The couple would go in tandem as husband and wife, and pedal down the road of life.

We're not sure if there was the same type of affection at the Olympics, where tempers flare, dreams are dashed, and some athletes might happily trade their spouses for a gold medal. But there was a sport that featured a bicycle built for two. It's exactly what you would think: two racers on a tandem bike, best time wins. The 2,000-meter tandem first appeared in 1908, then resumed in 1920, where it would go on through the 1972 Games.

It's not clear why tandem bicycle stopped, but the sport does live on in the Paralympics. Track cycling events have two competitors, who must be perfectly in sync. On the front of the bike is the pilot, who is sighted, and on the back is a visually impaired cyclist, bringing the thrill of fast-track cycling to all—or at least pairs.

André Auffray (left) and Maurice Schilles (right) of France won gold at the 1908 Olympics.

Plunge for Distance

Where the Least Athletic Are King

There was once an Olympic sport that, according to the *New York Times,* favored "mere mountains of fat who fall in the water more or less successfully and depend upon inertia to get their points for them."

Yes, welcome to plunge for distance, which made its first and only appearance at the 1904 Olympics in St. Louis. The objective: Dive into the water. And then . . . just see what happens. Athletes were judged by how far they floated without moving any part of their body within 60 seconds. (The world record is 86 feet, 8 inches, set by Frank Parrington in 1933, which, you have to admit, is kind of impressive.) The Americans swept—easy to do considering only Americans competed—though the winning distance was more than 17 feet off the world record at the time.

This feels like a sport any one of us could do . . .

The event, as one could expect, was widely mocked. The Amateur Athletic Union wanted to eliminate the sport from its ranks, panning it is as "a type of contest requiring neither athletic ability, nor especial skill of any kind." By 1925, it was removed from the NCAA. Indeed, it's difficult to determine just how much athletic ability is required to outplunge the greatest, but at least one of the Olympic medalists was most assuredly a fine athlete. Bronze medal plunger Leo "Budd" Goodwin also took home a gold in the water polo event, and he was an early sports star in America. Goodwin won 19 national swimming championships and was even featured in trading

FUTURE OLYMPIC SPORTS

Lightsaber duels. Break dancing. Three-on-three basketball. Monobob. Three of these things are future Olympic sports—can you guess which one isn't? (If you picked lightsaber duels, you would be correct—but fret not! The French fencing body has recognized lightsaber as an official sport.) Are any of these even sports? Maybe. Monobob (a one-person bobsled) and 3-on-3 basketball probably come the closest, and break dancing is one heck of a workout.

As the Olympics looks to broaden its reach, IOC will try to include more events to appeal to more people. That means newer and obscure-looking sports. If you're a fan of wushu (a martial art), netball (essentially basketball with more players), power kiting (we'll leave that to the imagination), ultimate Frisbee (favorite of bros everywhere), or orienteering (calling all navigators), you missed out. But that's no reason to stop trying!

cards, which were placed in cartons of Mecca cigarettes. His card called him "in all probability the best all-round swimmer in the United States." (He also won a Congressional Gold Medal for bravery after a sea rescue in Newport News, Virginia.)

Though the sport is now out of fashion, one last link remains. David Parrington, the grandson of Frank Parrington, world record holder and International Swimming Hall of Famer, is the head coach of the diving team at the University of Tennessee. David teaches the plunge to his athletes and encourages them to watch how plungers enter the water to mimic their technique. He admits, however, that his charges "are not too good at it" and the fine art of distance plunging appears to be fading fast. But plunging runs deep in the Parrington family. While David has yet to reach his grandfather's distance, his personal best of 75 feet would've taken the 1904 gold medal in a landslide.

Pistol Dueling

Remember the Ten Duel Commandments

If only Alexander Hamilton and Aaron Burr had held off on their duel for 102 years, they could've earned a medal.

Yes, dueling was an Olympic sport for one sweet spring in 1906. But it was a little different from every noble's favorite form of violent conflict resolution. At the 1906 Intercalated Games, competitors shot at dummies dressed in coats held at distances of 20 and 25 meters. In 1908, dueling returned as an unofficial demonstration sport. This time it looked a bit more familiar: Competitors actually shot at each other. (Thankfully, the bullets were made of wax.) They wore heavy, protective equipment, including a hand guard and a helmet with a glass window. They called it "bloodless dueling."

As you might imagine, dueling dissipated after the 1908 Olympics. But perhaps the dream is still alive: before the 2000 Games in Sydney, a poll of Australians showed that 32 percent were interested in seeing the sport resurrected. Not to mention, the musical *Hamilton* is all the rage. Hope springs!

The winning French team would've shot just about anyone for gold.

Live Pigeon Shooting

A Truly Depraved Event

Way back in the eighth century BC, pigeons were used to carry messages out into the country, spreading news of the latest results in the Olympic Games. So it shouldn't come as *too* much of a surprise that pigeons would be used in the modern Olympics as well. Except we don't think the ancient Greeks quite had this in mind.

At the 1900 Games in Paris, organizers used live pigeons in the trap-shooting event, whereby targets are launched in the air and the competitors shoot them down. The idea was simple: Kill as many birds as possible. Each competitor saw six birds released at the same time, and he was eliminated whenever he missed two. Some 300 pigeons were killed, and Belgium's Leon de Lunden narrowly outshot France's Maurice Faure 21 birds to 20.

The bloodshed must've been too much to witness, as this was the last time live animals were used. Today, the event is simply called trap, and the targets are clay. The 1900 pigeon shoot marked the only time in Olympic history when animals were killed on purpose—the dove blaze of 1988 notwithstanding.

Donald MacIntosh of Australia bagged 18 pigeons on his way to a less-than-heroic bronze medal.

Running Deer

Testing Accuracy on the Move

Unlike its disturbed cousin, live pigeon shooting, the running deer shooting event skipped the involvement of any live animals. Fortunately, no deer were harmed in the making of this Olympic event, and the "deer" were cardboard cutouts. They moved across a distance of 75 feet in four seconds and the competitor, depending on the discipline, would have either one or two shots. There have always been shooting events at the Games, but it was definitely a good idea that the Olympic movement moved away from the whole killing-animals thing—fake or not.

Last held in the 1952 Summer Games in Helsinki, the event forged the legacies of some terrific athletes. The greatest Olympic running deer shooter of all time might have been Oscar Swahn, the oldest athlete to win an Olympic gold. In all, the Swede won three golds, a silver, and two bronzes in the running deer. He first struck gold in 1908 at age 60 and his last medal came at age 72 at the 1920 Olympics in Antwerp. (His son Alf was no slouch, either—he won nine medals in a variety of shooting events, although his last medal was at the practically adolescent age of 44.)

Oscar Swahn (second from right) gave new meaning to staying active in retirement.

Another multiple medalist was Walter Winans, who won gold in the double-shot at the 1908 Games in London and silver in the team single-shot at the 1912 Games in Stockholm. The noted marksman won 12 consecutive British championships and apparently killed 2,000 big-game animals. (Oh, that few?) He also—believe it or not—won gold in art. Yes, at the 1912 Games, Winans won the top prize for his sculpture *An American Trotter*. Talk about a unique medal haul. He died atop his horse, Henrietta Guy, during a race in London in 1920. The grandson of a railroad magnate, Winans was independently wealthy, and a *New York Times* obituary wrote of his "lack of interest in business." So he spent his days shooting, racing horses, and making sculptures. Nice work if you can get it!

THE GREAT DOVE BLAZE OF 1988

Doves, everyone's favorite symbols of peace and love, are no strangers to the Olympics. Officials have released doves at most opening ceremonies since at least 1920 as a gesture of international goodwill. In 1960 in Squaw Valley, for instance, some 2,000 doves were released. But if you're going to release an enormous flock of our fine feathered friends, you have to be careful. In 1988 in Seoul, disaster struck.

Instead of flying out of Olympic stadium as hoped, some of the doves found their way to the edge of the unlit cauldron. And so when three Koreans fired it up, well, let's just say the doves were in the way. It's not clear how many doves were burned, but it was enough to classify it as a mass killing, broadcast for the whole world to see.

After the disturbing events of 1988, Olympic organizers wisely changed tack. Some countries have stopped using the real McCoy. In Turin in 2006, a team of acrobats formed a dovelike shape. In London in 2012, performers dressed as doves rode through the stadium on air-suspended bikes. When South Korea hosted the Games again in 2018, they went with a group of people standing in the shape of a dove instead.

Rope Climb

From Gym Class to Medal Stand

While most of us stood anxiously at the bottom of the rope in gym class, waiting for the wretched nightmare to be over, there was always the one classmate who bolted up the rope like it was no problem. That kid, surely an alien among us, would've fit right in at the early Olympics.

That's because the rope climb—yes, that PE horror—was an Olympic sport. And this was no one-off. The event appeared in five Olympics as part of the gymnastics competition, ending after the 1932 Games in Los Angeles. The rope ranged from 25 to 32 feet long and the first rope climbers were judged on both speed and style. (At the 1896 Games, for instance, athletes earned points for their ability to configure their body in an L-shape.)

The United States won its first rope climb gold in 1904, when one-legged gymnast George Eyser collected one of six medals in a single day. An illustrious era peaked in 1932, when the Americans swept and Raymond Bass took home gold. He later served as a rear admiral in the navy and was inducted into the U.S. Gymnastics Hall of Fame. Though Bass has his theories about why the rope climb disappeared—"I presume [the IOC] voted out the rope climb because they didn't care much for the U.S. getting 1-2-3," he said in 1982—the all-time great continued climbing ropes, often at random gymnastics events, as he aged. "Even up into my fifties, they would call me out of the crowd without notice, drop a rope, and make me climb it," he said.

Though not *quite* the same, sport climbing is making its way into the Olympics. Contested for the first time at the 2020 Games in Tokyo, the event has three disciplines: bouldering, where the object is to climb up as many different routes as possible; lead, which tests how high athletes can climb in six minutes; and speed climbing, where two climbers go against each other. At least one pro climber, Eric Horst from the United States, swears by the rope climb and thinks it should make an Olympic comeback.

And who knows: If sport climbing takes off, maybe we'll see rope climbing return to the Games. If that happens, surely gym classes everywhere will reintroduce the challenge—which, for some if not most of us, could be a very bad thing.

Georgios Aliprantis of Greece conquered a 10 meter rope in 11.4 seconds for gold at the 1906 Intercalated Games.

Basque Pelota

Bleeding for Victory

If you've seen a game of jai alai, you will probably recognize Basque pelota. With roots in the fourteenth century, the sport exists these days mostly in northern Spain and southern France. The idea is to take a ball—similar to a baseball in weight and texture—and slap it as hard as you can against a wall, all while barehanded. Teams gain points when opponents can't get to the ball before it hits twice on the ground.

Sound painful? Well, it is. Some modern players make small cuts on their hands with a razor to draw out blood to bring relief. (Others now use a racquet or wooden basket, fortunately.) Perhaps that's why Basque pelota got only limited action in the Olympics—and even then it was barely played.

Pelota had one official appearance at the 1900 Paris Olympics and three runs as a demonstration sport, most recently in 1992 in Barcelona. A sport that regularly induces bleeding seems like a long shot to return to the Games, but Dominique Boutineau, the former president of the International Federation of Basque Pelota, has hope. "The dream of everyone," he once said, "is that one day Basque pelota can get into the Olympics."

That dream, it seems, applies to about five people.

LEFT: *Applaud this pelota player for having the smarts to not use his bare hand.*

Special Figures

The Skating/Sketching Hybrid

Special figures was a discipline of figure skating in the early twentieth century. The idea? Trace precise geometrical patterns on the ice with only one blade. If you're assuming this event was just about carving pretty pictures in the ice, then think again. It required a terrific balance and control.

The 1908 Olympics in London were the first in which figure skating events were contested. (This preceded the Winter Games, which began in 1924.) There were the typical skating events that we see today—memorably, Ulrich Salchow, whom the jump is named after, won gold in men's singles. And then there was figure skating's odd cousin, special figures. Nikolai Panin won the contest, earning Russia its first gold medal in history. (He also competed in the 50-meter rifle competition at the 1912 Games—quite a unique combination of talents.)

Still doubting? Lace up a pair of skates and try for yourself. A whole lot of falls are in your future.

Auto Racing

Olympics Meets Open Road

The debate rages on: Was auto racing officially part of the 1900 Paris Exposition or the Olympics? Either way, we know there were 16 events in a wide variety of categories based on type of car, weight, and distance, including such favorites as delivery van, taxi, fire truck, and seven-seater car. The events weren't well documented, but clearly there was some type of home team advantage, as the French won all but three of the medals.

Of course, at the time automobiles themselves were relatively new. Karl Benz had developed the first gasoline-powered car in 1885. This wasn't NASCAR—the 1901 Mercedes topped out at just 53 miles per hour. We don't know much about the drivers, either, but one name is definitely recognizable: Louis Renault. The founder of the Renault automobile company won in the small-car race.

Firefighting

We Didn't Start the Fire—Oh Wait, We Did

That there would be an athletic competition involving firefighters isn't entirely crazy. As any beefcake calendar will prove, these guys are in great shape—strong, fast, with top-notch endurance. That's why there's the World Firefighters Games, a quadrennial, international event featuring sports such as basketball, cycling, judo, marathon, and rugby. Missing from the list: actual firefighting. Makes sense—can you imagine staging a controlled fire and seeing who can put it out first? Actually, yes. Or at least the organizers of the 1900 Olympics in Paris did.

There's almost no available information about the demonstration sport itself, but we do know that there were two competitions: amateur and professional. A group of Portuguese volunteer firefighters won the amateur, and a group from Kansas City beat out an Italian squad for gold in the professional. As A. G. Spalding, the founder of the eponymous sporting goods company, wrote in a summary of the Games, the KC pros used their "famous engine and hook and ladder company No.1." And how!

Like so many events at the wacky 1900 Games, firefighting did not last. We can only hope that genuine firefighting will show up again at the World Firefighters Games.

Dumbbells

No Dumb Sport Here

Of all the incredibly odd sports to appear at the early Olympics, lifting some big ol' dumbbells at least seems reasonable. The 1904 Games in St. Louis featured two dumbbell disciplines as part of the weight-lifting competition. One was the two-handed lift (essentially a barbell); the other was the all-around.

These lifters weren't your run-of-the-mill meatheads at the local gym. The all-around in particular seems like a legitimate test of strength. There were 10 events, ranging from lifting a dumbbell from the ground to the shoulder with one hand, to pushing it up slowly above the shoulder, to a simple curl. The final event was up to the contestant. American gold medal winner Oscar Osthoff, while "potting up in a bridge," as he called it, lifted 177 pounds six times with two hands. He would go on to play four sports at the University of Wisconsin and won all–Big Ten honors in football.

One of the others to excel at the event was American Frank Kugler, who won bronzes in the two-hand lift and all-around. He cleaned up at the St. Louis Games, winning silver in freestyle wrestling and bronze in the tug-of-war. He remains the only Olympian to win medals in three different sports at a single Games.

It's not clear why the dumbbells fell out of favor, though a 16-year gap in weight lifting after the St. Louis Games might explain it. Given the raft of grunting lunks at every gym in the country, surely there would be enough interest to bring it back. Whether we want to see a bunch of gym rats compete for a medal is another story.

All-around silver medal winner Fred Winters gets swole in St. Louis.

Solo Synchronized Swimming

The Battle for Self-Control

How hard can it be to stay in sync . . . with yourself? Quite hard, apparently. The sport's name isn't as contradictory as it sounds—the athlete is supposed to stay in sync with the music. That's the idea behind solo synchronized swimming, which made its Olympic debut in 1984 and lasted until 1996, when it became a nine-person team event. It's quite popular in Russia, winner of five-straight gold medals in the team event. Seems pleasant enough, but one Olympic contest came with some big-time drama.

Canada's Sylvie Frechette, the favorite at the 1992 Games, lived up to all the hype with her gold medal performance. But a judge mistyped her 9.7 score as 8.7, putting Frechette in second for a silver. The beneficiary of the blunder was the United States' Kristen Babb-Sprague, one half of an athlete-couple who might have had the best year of any marriage ever. A few months after Kristen won gold, her husband, Toronto Blue Jays catcher Ed Sprague, won a World Series ring. In 1993, however, the IOC ruled that Frechette should be awarded the gold. (Babb-Sprague got to keep hers anyway.)

Of course, synchronized swimming—renamed "artistic swimming" in 2017—continues on, with both team and duet events. It's a lot more difficult than you might imagine. Picture an early-morning water aquatics class, only you're not in the shallow end and the entire group has to stay perfectly in sync. Maybe it is pretty darn athletic after all.

TRUMPED-UP SPORT

Herodorus of Megara was absolutely gargantuan, and he used that size to become . . . the loudest trumpet player in the land. Which was perfect for the Herald and Trumpet contest in the ancient Games. How did you win? It's pretty technical: Competitors were judged on clarity of the blast and the precision of the notes. Herodorus was so good that he won 10 times between 328 and 292 BC. He also helped King Demetrios invade Argos by playing his horn so loudly that the townspeople fled. Somehow that doesn't strike one as medal-worthy.

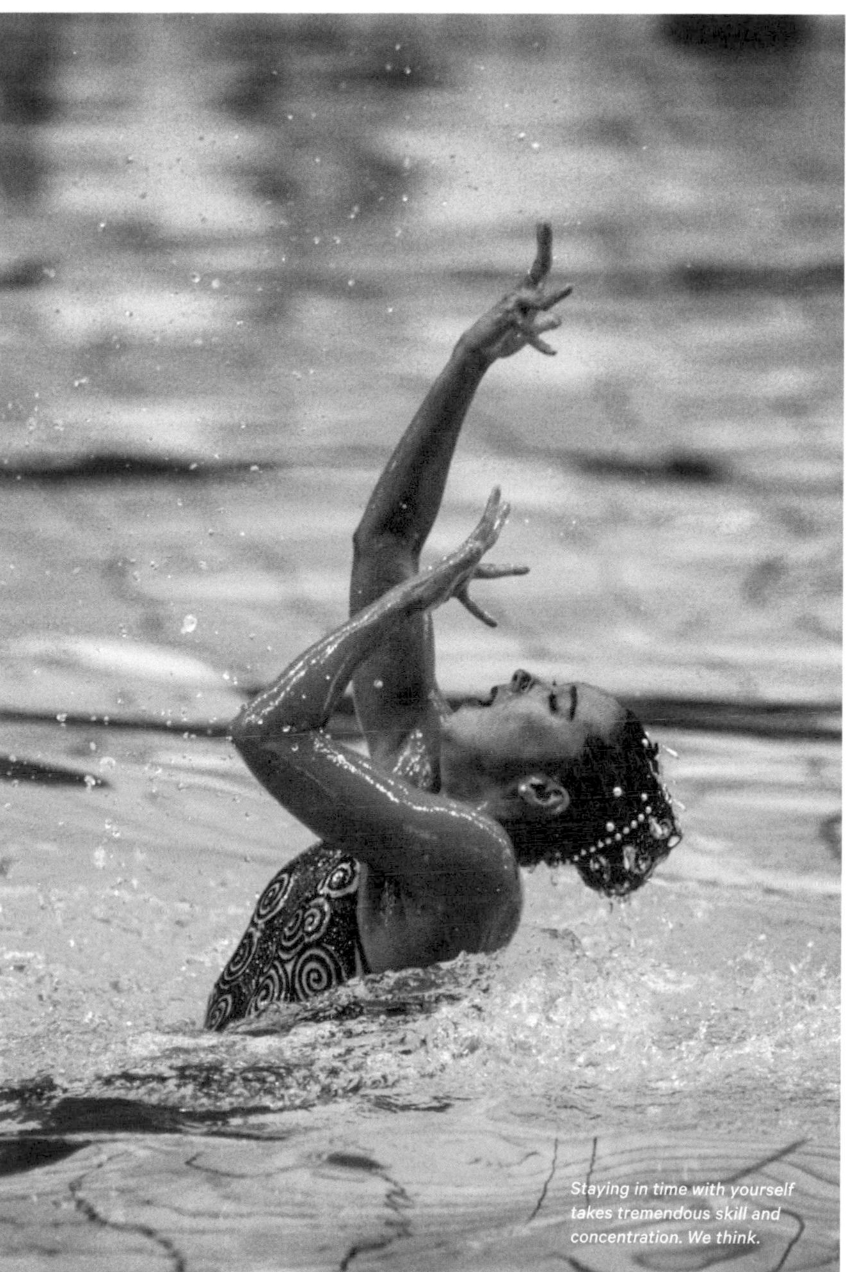

Staying in time with yourself takes tremendous skill and concentration. We think.

Tug-of-War

The Ultimate Rope Burn

For a brief, wonderful moment in 2015, fans of tug-of-war had hope. That beloved, rope-burn-inducing favorite from playgrounds and backyards everywhere almost made the Olympics. Again.

But before we explore the current campaign to bring tug-of-war back to the Olympics, let's recall the sport's rich history in the early days of the Games. Held in every Olympics from 1900 to 1920, tug-of-war's rules were simple: Five per side, the first group to pull the other over a line six feet from the starting point won. If it went past five minutes and no team had been pulled over, the team that had made the most progress won.

The first tug held in 1900 was a bit of a free-for-all. The winning team was a combined Danish-Swedish squad. The United States fielded a team, but withdrew because too many of its members were on the hammer throw squad, which took place at the same time. (It was worth it: The Americans swept that event.)

> **British police officers seemed to love the sport.**

Like any competitive schoolyard battle, Olympic tug-of-war was not without controversy. In 1908 in London, the Americans accused a British team made up of Liverpool police of wearing illegal boots. The Americans protested that the boots were weighted and had more traction, but the complaint went nowhere, and the United States withdrew from the event. One columnist wrote, "The American team was handed a real sour lemon . . . what was our surprise to find the English team wearing shoes as big as North River ferry boats, with steel-topped heels and steel cleats in the front of the soles, while spikes an inch long stuck out of the soles." Even so, fancy footwear couldn't save the Liverpudlians, who later lost the gold medal match to a squad of London police.

The 1920 event, which the Brits won again, was the last Olympic tug. It's not clear exactly why the IOC discontinued the sport, but one reason might have been the increased use of those controversial weighted boots.

Enthusiasm is growing ever stronger for tug-of-war to be reintroduced to the Olympics. In 2015, the IOC listed 26 sports that had applied for inclusion in the 2020 Games, ranging from baseball to ultimate Frisbee, sumo wrestling, snooker, and ballroom dancing. You'd better believe one of those sports was tug-of-war. This sparked immediate interest in the blogosphere and potential teams were drawn up. (One had the United States fielding Draymond Green, Katie Ledecky, and Hope Solo.)

In the end, the IOC went with five new sports for the 2020 Summer Olympics in Tokyo: baseball/softball, karate, skateboard, sports climbing, and surfing. "Most people who have witnessed a high-class tug of war competition can appreciate that it aspires to the Olympic traditions of strength, skill and stamina as well as a lot of technique," wrote England Tug of War Association Secretary Mick Copper. "Unfortunately, tug of war wasn't included, but the sport will keep aiming for this goal."

Sadly, for the 2024 Games in Paris, tug-of-war didn't make the cut either. That doesn't preclude it from 2028 and beyond, though. If tug-of-war is indeed the ultimate test of strength and endurance, all those wanting to include the sport in future Games should hold on tight.

The Danish-Swedish mixed team out-tugs France in the first-ever tug-of-war in 1900.

Skijoring

Hold onto Your Horses!

There's an alternate Olympic history in which one of the most popular sports is skijoring.

A demonstration event at the 1928 Winter Games in St. Moritz, skijoring is a Norwegian sport in which an object—a horse, a dog, or more recently, a snowmobile—drags a person on skis. Think water skiing on snow.

At the 1928 Games, however, the sport didn't live up to its enormous potential. Skiers were just dragged by horses on a boring oval track. The Swiss had the upper hand, apparently, and swept the medals. But look at

What looks harder, being pulled by the horse or staying on the saddle?

THE FLYING TOMATO

If there's any Olympian who should be considered a pioneer in modern times, it's Shaun White. He's in many ways responsible for making snowboarding must-see TV during the Games. Developed in the 1960s, the sport debuted at the 1998 Olympics in Nagano. But White, making his first Olympic appearance in 2006, quickly became a superstar. With his shock of long red hair—hence "The Flying Tomato" nickname—White became a household name after winning gold in Turin. He won gold again in 2010 and finished fourth in 2014. (Despite missing out on a medal, he was ranked as the most talked about athlete on Facebook during the Sochi games.)

After crashing and requiring 62 stitches in his face while training for the 2018 Games, White won his third gold medal—the only snowboarder to do so. It was also the 100th gold medal for the United States in winter Olympic history. As eyeballs tuned into White, snowboarding expanded. In 1998, there was just the giant slalom and halfpipe. By 2018, snowboard cross, slopestyle, and big air had been added to the program.

the sport today and you can imagine what incredible Olympic excitement it missed out on. There are jumps! Obstacles! Wipeouts! It could have been an early Olympic version of snowboard cross, only mixed with high-speed animals. Let the ratings bonanza ensue!

But alas, Pierre de Coubertin's apparent infatuation with the sport wasn't enough to make it stick, and skijoring was brushed to the margins of Olympic history, never to make another appearance. While skijoring lives on as a recreation sport in winter climes around the world, it doesn't have quite the name recognition that it could. Perhaps if the 1928 version weren't so vanilla, history might've turned out quite a bit differently.

Ski Ballet

Pleats and Snow Pants

It sounds like a sport that was dreamed up after consuming copious amounts of wine and marijuana. But ski ballet—yes, that's what it's called—was absolutely a thing, and it even laid down the roots for some of the freestyle skiing events you see in the Olympics these days.

Okay, let's first acknowledge the obvious: It looks ridiculous. "Nowadays the kids do chuckle when they see it—because it is humorous, right?" said Steve Hambling, a Canadian ballet skier. (Note: Don't call them "ski ballerinas.") "They'll laugh at it—we all had poofy hair and the one-piece suits and all that shit, right?"

A demonstration sport at the 1988 and 1992 Games, ski ballet is sort of like figure skating on snow. Athletes had 90 seconds, set to music, to do whatever they wanted. (They soared! They twisted! They did handstands on their poles! They boogied!) Though the sport never went mainstream—indeed, formal competition stopped in 2000—when you watch events like slopestyle and moguls, you're seeing ski ballet's influence. Today, skiing events feature big air, flips, and crazy moves. The freedom to experiment inspired free stylers to continue to push the boundaries.

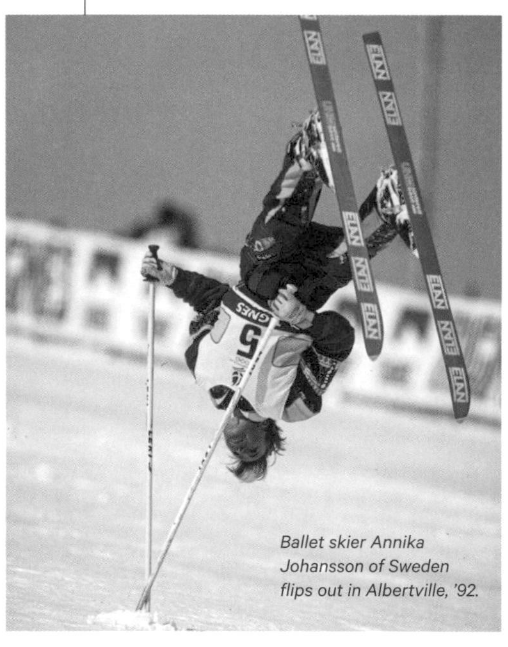

Ballet skier Annika Johansson of Sweden flips out in Albertville, '92.

And don't let anyone ever tell you that ski ballet is no honest way to earn a living. Suzy Chaffee, one of the breakout stars of ski ballet, starred in a 1978 ChapStick commercial with the tagline, "Hi! I'm Suzy ChapStick!" and would go on to earn some $100,000 per year in endorsements. Who says ski ballet can't pay?

Art

Picasso for the Gold!

"There is only one difference," Olympic founder Pierre de Coubertin said, "between our Olympiads and plain sporting championships. And it is precisely the contests of art as they existed in the Olympiads of Ancient Greece, where sport exhibitions walked in equality with artistic exhibitions."

Um, come again?

That's right, in every Games from 1912 to 1948, the Olympics featured art competitions, known collectively as the "Pentathlon of the Muses." Medals were awarded in five categories: Painting, sculpture, music, architecture, and literature. You name it, it was there. The events were popular, too—at the 1932 Summer Games, some 400,000 people visited the Los Angeles Museum of History, Science and Art to view the entries in competition. (There, they saw John Russell Pope, who designed the Jefferson Memorial, take silver for his design of the Payne Gymnasium, later constructed at Yale.)

Coubertin wanted, as he said, to "reunite in the bonds of legitimate wedlock a long-divorced couple—muscle and mind." The works were judged on how well they related to the idea of sports, and in particular, the Olympic ideal. The IOC even brought in big-time judges like Igor Stravinsky, who reviewed music submissions at the 1924 Games in Paris.

The "Pentathlon of the Muses" was a popular fixture at the Olympics until 1948.

Some of the athletes—that is, the ones doing the actual sports—moonlighted in the art competitions, too. Walter Winans won gold in both shooting and sculpture; Hungarian swimmer Alfred Hajos won two golds in swimming in 1896 and a silver in town planning in 1924. (There were also medals for lyric and speculative works, epic and dramatic works, watercolors, and statues.)

Even Coubertin got in on the action, winning a gold for his rather flowery poem "Ode to Sport!" in the literature category in Stockholm in 1912. Written under the pseudonyms George Hohrod and Martin Eschbach, it

Down goes Frazier! American artist Mahonri Young won gold in 1932 with his sculpture The Knockdown.

went over quite well: "It emanates as directly as is possible from the idea of sport," the judges wrote. "It praises sport in a form that to the ear is very literary and very sporting." (Hmm . . . sounds almost like sucking up to the boss.)

Formal competition ended in 1948 when the IOC ruled that art contestants were professionals and therefore violated amateurism rules. But the idea of art at the Olympics does still exist. The cultural program at each Games showcases various art forms, and former Olympians sometimes contribute. The melding of muscle and mind continues on.

6

FORGOTTEN HEROES

On the Olympic stage, seemingly tiny moments always seem to stand out. It's the competitor who battled through injury to reach the medal stand. It's the athlete who went out of their way to help an ailing foe. It's the dissident who fought back against grueling political circumstances to make it to the Games.

Winners are heroes, of course, and there are plenty of those to go around, but you don't need to wear gold around your neck to be heroic. You have to do something beyond the ordinary to get that label. Indeed, heroes abound at every Olympics. They come from countries big and small, compete in sports popular and lesser known. They forge the stories played on repeat on television, and yes, the stories that fall by the wayside. We must remember some of the heroes history brushed aside—and remind the world that their deeds do, in fact, last forever.

LAWRENCE LEMIEUX
The Gentlemanly Olympian

CANADA | SAILING | 1955–

LOS ANGELES 1984 • SEOUL 1988

Fair play is an Olympic tenet. Indeed, each Games one athlete is chosen as a representative of all competitors and recites the Olympic Oath, promising to play by the rules and "respect the Fundamental Principles of Olympism." Lawrence Lemieux played by those principles to a *T*.

At the 1988 Games in Seoul, Lemieux, an accomplished Canadian sailor, was racing in the one-man Finn class event off the coast of Busan, a city near Seoul. (There are numerous classes in Olympic sailing—Finn refers to a single-person cat-rigged dinghy.) Lemieux was sharing his course with two other races that September day: the men's and women's two-person 470 class. With winds blowing at some 25 knots, the currents were strong and the waves had become exceptionally steep. Joseph Chan and Siew Shaw Her, competing for Singapore in the men's 470, were struggling in the unexpectedly rough conditions. Midway through their race, the Singaporeans' boat capsized, throwing them into the dangerous water.

Lemieux saved two other sailors from drowning. Not a bad day's work.

Lemieux was holding second place in his race and in good position to secure a spot in the later medal round. But halfway through his heat, Lemieux spotted the crew from Singapore bobbing in the water. "The first rule of sailing is, if you see somebody in trouble, you help him," he told reporters after the race.

Lemieux noticed that one of the Singaporeans had made it back to their dinghy's hull, but another was floating away in open water. "The boat was drifting faster than he could swim," Lemieux said in 2012. "Who was going to see a little head bobbing in the water? He'd have been lost at sea."

Lemieux abandoned course and maneuvered to the drifting sailor, pulling him into his boat. The Canadian waited for a patrol boat to take the crew back to shore. Meanwhile, Lemieux's heat was still going on. Once the crew was safe, he rejoined the race, finishing in 22nd place. The International Yacht Racing Union, which governed the race, recognized Lemieux's heroics and reinstated him at the position he held before going off course.

Lemieux would go on to finish in 11th place in the final standings. But he didn't walk away empty-handed. At the medal ceremony, he was awarded the prestigious Pierre de Coubertin medal. Originated in 1964 and named after the founder of the International Olympic Committee, the award honors those who exhibit true sportsmanship in Olympic events. It has been given to only 13 athletes, eight sporting officials, and two artists.

Now a sailing coach living in Alberta, Lemieux surely would've loved a medal of a different color. But this one, at least, has put him in elite company with some of the noblest athletes in the annals of Olympic history.

Sailing has been an Olympic mainstay since its debut in 1900.

SHUN FUJIMOTO
Playing Through Pain

JAPAN | GYMNASTICS | 1 MEDAL | 1950–

MONTREAL 1976

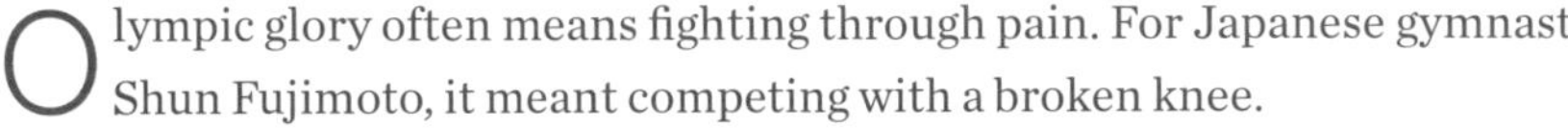

Olympic glory often means fighting through pain. For Japanese gymnast Shun Fujimoto, it meant competing with a broken knee.

Entering the 1976 Games in Montreal, the Japanese were the four-time defending champs in the team all-around and the favorite for a fifth. On the final day of competition, however, they found themselves down by a half point to the Soviets. Fujimoto was perhaps the least famous athlete on the team composed of well-known veteran gymnasts like 12-time medalist Sawao Kato and seven-time world champion Eizo Kenmotsu. The 26-year-old had injured his right knee during the tumbling portion, but he chose not to tell anyone, fearing he'd unnerve his teammates and his coaches would bench him for the remaining events.

> **The unshakable gymnast stuck the landing before collapsing into excruciating agony.**

Fujimoto was able to compete on the pommel horse because that apparatus applied minimal pressure to his knee. But the injury came to a head on the rings. For his dismount, he was set to do a double somersault, rising eight feet in the air before landing hard.

Fighting back the excruciating pain, Fujimoto stuck the landing, raising his hands in the air before falling to the ground in agony. The jump exacerbated the injury terribly: He dislocated his kneecap, and tore ligaments in his leg. Despite the damage, he scored a fantastic—and personal best—9.7. That score proved consequential, as the Japanese won gold by just four-tenths of a point over the Soviets.

After the rings, Fujimoto couldn't continue to compete in the remaining routines. He retired from competition after the Games, becoming a gymnastics coach and professor in Japan. Asked in subsequent years if he would do the rings again, he answered simply, "No, I would not."

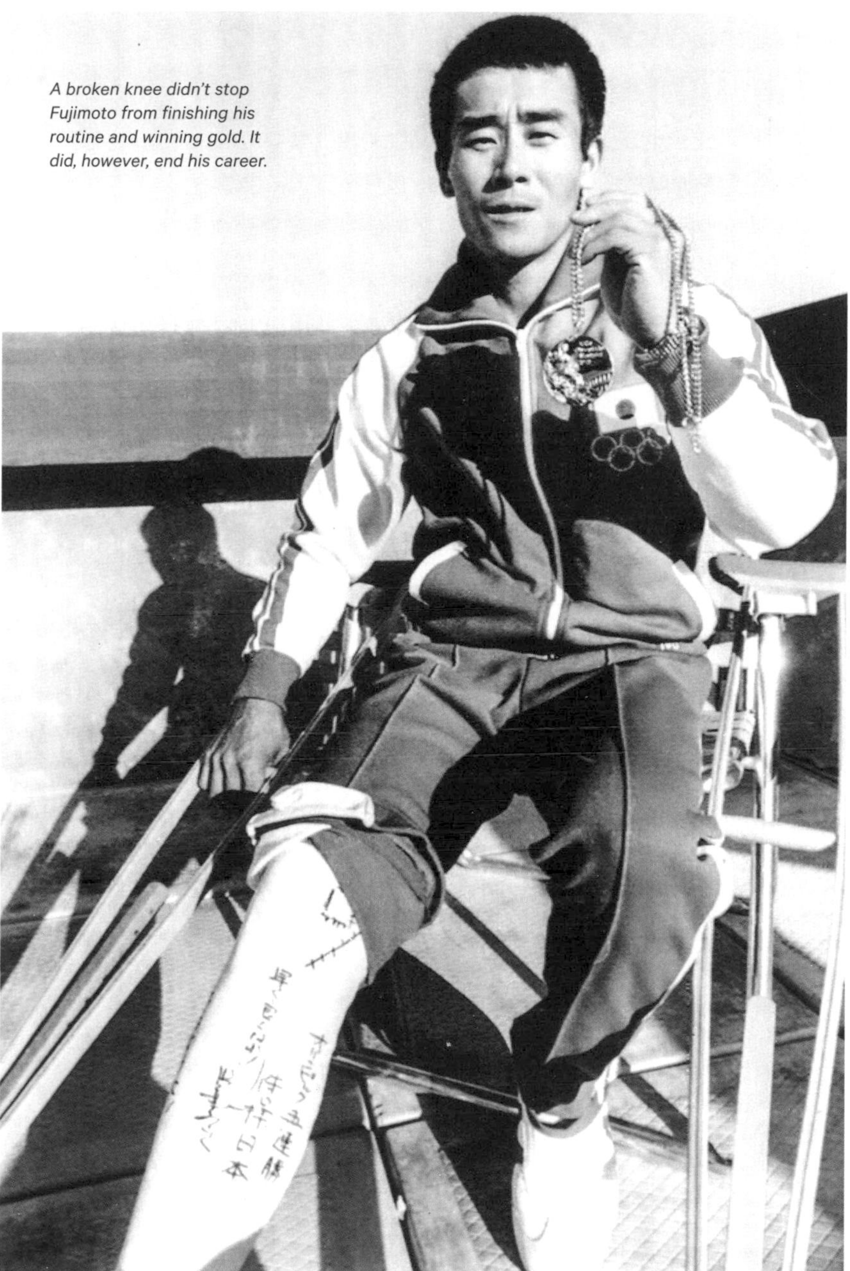

A broken knee didn't stop Fujimoto from finishing his routine and winning gold. It did, however, end his career.

VERA CASLAVSKA
The Defiant One

CZECHOSLOVAKIA | GYMNASTICS | 11 MEDALS | 1942–2016

ROME 1960 • TOKYO 1964 • MEXICO CITY 1968

Three months before the 1968 Summer Olympics, Vera Caslavska went into hiding. The Czechoslovakian gymnast, one of the most accomplished athletes of her time, had just signed "The Two Thousand Words," a manifesto written by reformist Czech intellectuals during the Prague Spring that advocated for more political freedoms. The document's provocative call to action was polarizing and kicked off a series of actions that led to the Soviet Union invading Prague that August.

Caslavska was a high-profile star at the time. She had won three gold medals at the 1964 Olympics in Tokyo, including a win over Soviet legend Larisa Latynina in the all-around. She led the Czechs to back-to-back silver medals in the team event and had won the 1966 all-around at the world championships in Dortmund, Germany. In 1968, with Prague under siege and her visible status as a dissenter, she decided to decamp to the mountains of Moravia, a rural region in the south of the country.

Now in hiding, she trained by lifting sacks of potatoes and other MacGyver-esque measures. "While the Soviet's gymnasts were already in Mexico City, adjusting to the altitude and the climate, I was hanging from trees, practicing my floor exercise in the meadow in front of the cottage and building calluses on my hands by shoveling coal," she recalled in 1990.

For Caslavska, facing off against the Soviets in Mexico City was of twofold importance. Not only was Latynina her number-one rival, but Caslavska was, in some ways, also representing her country's battle against their Soviet oppressors. She was determined to "sweat blood to defeat the invaders' representatives."

At the Games, Caslavska shone despite her improvised training regimen. She won four gold medals, including the all-around. In the floor exercise, she shared the gold with a Soviet competitor after a retroactive uptick in scoring created a tie. She also won silver on the balance beam when another Soviet gymnast earned a potentially questionable score to beat her out for the gold.

As the Soviet anthem blared during the medal ceremony for the floor exercise, Caslavska turned her head to the right and then down, an explicit rebuke of the country terrorizing her own. Though the protest earned her international recognition, it was met with furor at home. She faced persecution by the Czech government and was denied the right to travel, making it impossible to compete in any important gymnastics events. It would be six years before she was allowed to work as a coach. "After ascending the summit of Olympus," she once said, "the journey downward did not exactly follow the well-trodden path. It consisted of rocks, gorges, and a bottomless pit."

In 1989, the Velvet Revolution ended Communist rule. Caslavska was appointed as an adviser to President Václav Havel and later served as the chairwoman of the Czech Olympic Committee. She finished her career with 11 medals, seven of them gold. She is one of only two female gymnasts, along with Latynina, to win the all-around in back-to-back Olympics. She also won the Pierre de Coubertin Fair Play Prize in 1989. As extraordinary as she was as a gymnast, it was her stance against Soviet oppression—and her willingness to suffer the consequences—that became her lasting legacy.

Caslavska beat back political repression to become one of gymnastics' biggest international stars.

BILLY MILLS
The Out-of-Nowhere Winner

USA | TRACK AND FIELD | 1 MEDAL | 1938–

TOKYO 1964

A few years before he became an Olympic hero, Billy Mills looked out of a hotel window and thought about jumping. Fortunately, he didn't. Instead, he became a gold medalist—and a force for good for thousands of people in his community.

Born and raised on the Pine Ridge Indian Reservation in South Dakota, Mills was orphaned at age 12. He soon took up running and found solace in the sport. "It opened my senses," he told the *Financial Times* in 2012. "I could look off in the field, running, and see the flowers. It was like sacredness." He eventually earned a scholarship to the University of Kansas, where he was a three-time All-American.

While in the Marines, Mills began training for the 10,000 meters in the 1964 Summer Olympics in Tokyo. He was not the favorite—he wasn't even a blip on the radar. Mills had never won a major race, but he finished second in the US trials. In Tokyo, his times in the heats were more than a minute slower than the favorite and world record holder, Ron Clarke of Australia. Clarke's world record was 28:15.6—Mills had never run under 29 minutes.

Even during the finals, Mills looked out of his depth. At least four times he dropped out of the lead pack, falling behind by as many as 15 yards. But each time he found a way to climb back. With just a couple of laps to go, Mills and two other runners were out in front. In the final lap, Clarke pushed past Mills, who was then bumped by Mohamed Gammoudi of Tunisia. Mills stumbled to the middle lane, which turned out to be a big break. "Out there I found harder ground, better traction, and I was able to pick up immediately," he told *Sports Illustrated* after the race. With about 20 yards left, Mills passed Gammoudi and Clarke, and finished in front by three yards.

Mills's performance was one for the ages. He had run 45 seconds faster than his own personal best. It was the fourth-fastest time in a 10,000 ever

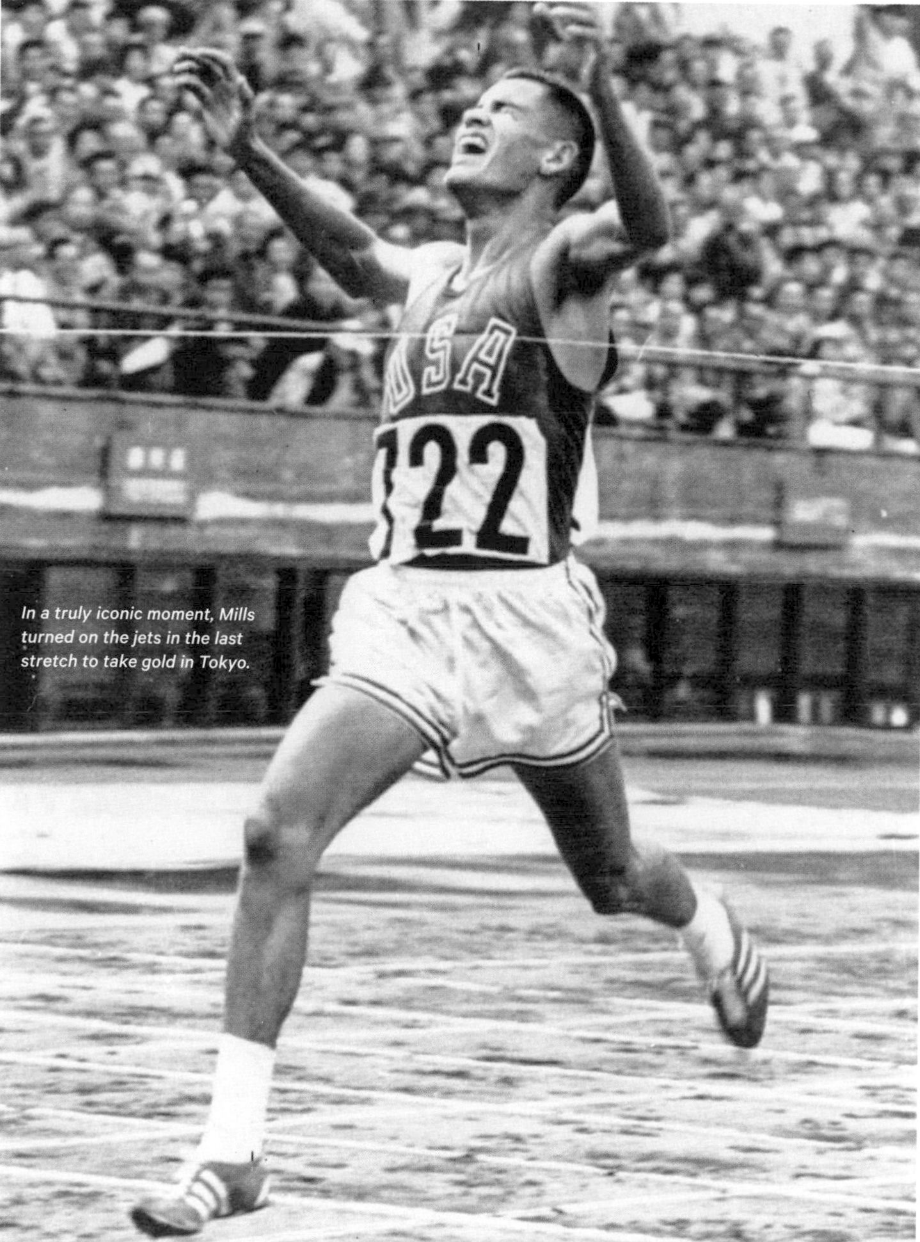

In a truly iconic moment, Mills turned on the jets in the last stretch to take gold in Tokyo.

IN THE BROADCAST BOOTH

It's a simple supply-and-demand problem. There are dozens of sports in the Olympics, many of them not broadcasted regularly. You need experts to break down the unfamiliar action for the viewer. What do you do? Bring in former Olympians, of course. Some, like three-time swimming medalist Rowdy Gaines or Trinidadian sprinter Ato Bolden, have found a niche, extending their fame to become a regular part of the Olympic diet.

Others have struggled mightily. Take Bode Miller, one of the most decorated skiers in American history, who made his broadcasting debut in 2018. He began his rough stint in Pyeongchang by suggesting that an Austrian skier might have struggled because she was a newlywed. (He apologized later.) Miller also punctuated his analysis with such monotone insights as "That was a solid run."

recorded, and the fastest in Olympic history. Mills became the first, and is still the only, American to win the race. Afterward an awestruck Olympic official came up to him and asked, "Who are you? Who are you?" In the race's final moments on the television broadcast, NBC color commentator Dick Bank screamed with delight, "Look at Mills! Look at Mills!" (Bank's obvious glee for the American got him fired immediately after the race.) Even Mills couldn't grasp the accomplishment. "I'm flabbergasted," he said. "I can hardly believe it."

At the AAU championships in 1965, Mills beat his own American record in the 10,000 and set both a national mark in the three-mile run and a world record in the six-mile run. Despite that burst of brilliance, he never won another Olympic medal. Instead, he devoted much of his time to giving back and helping Native youth. His story became the 1983 movie *Running Brave,* and he wrote a book, *Lessons of a Lakota*. He currently raises money for various nonprofit groups and is the spokesperson for Running Strong, a well-known organization that benefits Native Americans.

In 2012, Mills was awarded the Presidential Medal of Freedom. As Barack Obama placed the medal around Mills's neck, the president took a look at the then-74-year-old and remarked, "You still look fast."

AGNES KELETI
Alive and Thriving

HUNGARY | GYMNASTICS | 10 MEDALS | 1921–

HELSINKI 1952 • MELBOURNE 1956

In 1937, Agnes Keleti was a 16-year-old national champion in gymnastics and a leading medal contender for the 1940 Summer Olympics. International stardom, it would seem, was next on the horizon. But the course of world events intervened. Those Games, originally scheduled for Tokyo, were canceled amidst the outbreak of World War II. Keleti would have to wait.

The intervening years marked a time of terrifying uncertainty. Keleti, who is Jewish, was kicked out of her gymnastics club in Budapest in 1941. As with so many other Jews throughout Europe, she and her family were forced into hiding. Having heard a rumor that Jews married to Gentiles were not taken to concentration camps, she married Hungarian gymnast Istvan Sarkany in 1944. (While there was some truth to that rumor initially, many intermarried Jews were killed in concentration camps. Keleti and Sarkany divorced in 1950.)

Keleti took additional measures to ensure she survived the war. She purchased forged papers from a Christian girl, assuming the name Yuhasz Piroshka, and worked in a munitions factory. She was also a maid for a Nazi-sponsored Hungarian deputy commander. During the massively destructive Siege of Budapest, Keleti woke up in the mornings, collected the bodies of the dead, and placed them in a mass grave. "Is it possible to forget such a thing?" she once asked the Israeli newspaper *Haaretz*. Her mother and sister were two of the thousands of Hungarian Jews saved by Swedish diplomat Raoul Wallenberg, and Keleti supported them by smuggling food to their safe house. Her father, however, died at Auschwitz.

> **"Sport extends life, that's for certain . . . One must not stop."**

When the war ended in 1945, Keleti was 24 and immediately went back to training for the Olympics. In 1946, she won the Hungarian championship.

In 1947, she won the Central European Gymnastics Championships. To supplement her income, she worked as a furrier and played the cello professionally, which was a childhood dream. She was poised to compete at the 1948 Olympics in London but had to miss the Games after an ankle injury. She watched on the sidelines, devastated and in crutches, as the Hungarians finished with a silver in the team event.

Finally, after 12 years of unimaginable anguish and seemingly endless waiting, Keleti made her Olympic debut. She was 31, competing against gymnasts half her age. But that didn't stop her. At the 1952 Games in Helsinki, she won four medals, including gold in the floor exercise. Four years later, at the 1956 Games in Melbourne, she would win six medals, including four golds, becoming the oldest-ever female gymnastics champion.

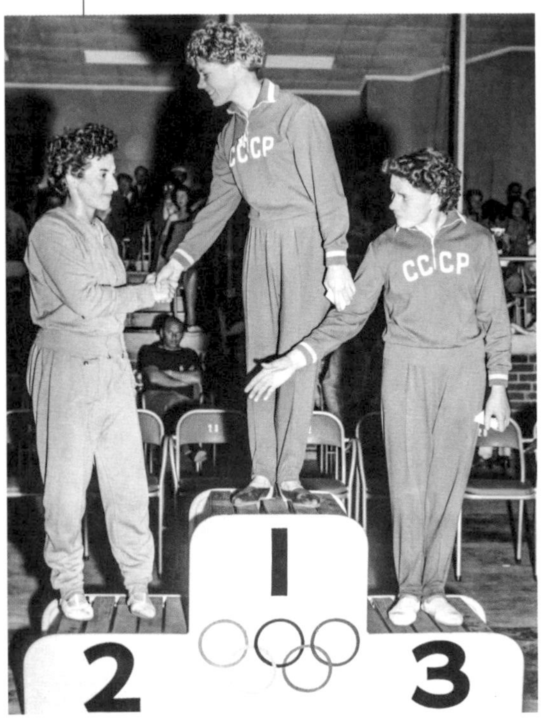

Soviet athletes congratulate Keleti (left), who won six medals in 1956.

Uncertainty and instability defined Keleti's early life, from surviving under Nazi occupation to competing at an older age. That wouldn't end after winning 10 medals in two Games. In 1956, just a month before the Olympics, Soviet forces entered Hungary and began a brutal occupation, violently quelling a burgeoning revolution. The Hungarian Olympic delegation had decamped to the mountains, and upon arriving at the Olympic Village in Melbourne, they tore down the Soviet flag and replaced it with that of Free Hungary.

Though many returned to their home country, more than half the Hungarian team members defected. Some came to the

EASTERN BLOC ATHLETICS AFTER THE SOVIET FALL

In the 1988 Olympics in Seoul, Bulgaria won 35 medals and Romania won 24. Four years later, Bulgaria won just 16 and Romania won 18. The reason for the sharp decline? The Soviet Union fell. As Eastern Bloc countries began to revolt and establish independence starting in 1989, funding dried up for national sports programs. Only East Germany, which reunified with West Germany in 1990, was spared.

Bulgaria and Romania were hit the worst. Coaches lost jobs, and travel for competition was all but prohibited. Both countries used to be athletic powers—now they barely register on the Olympic stage. Although the dissolution of the Soviet Union liberated many people, it may have shackled the athletes.

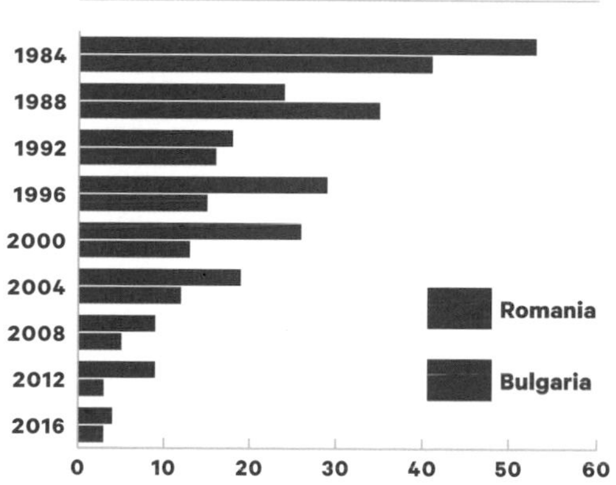

United States, and others, like Keleti, stayed in Australia. She lived in Sydney and worked in a factory. "I'd had enough of Communism," she said. After almost a year, she decided to move to Israel. She's resided there since 1957, where she introduced Israelis to the sport and served as the national team coach.

Approaching 100, Keleti became the oldest living Olympic champion in 2019. And despite being the most decorated Jewish female Olympian of all time—and owning the third-most medals for a female gymnast—Keleti remains focused on what truly matters. "Staying alive is more important than the medals," she once said.

PAAVO NURMI
A Most Mercurial Star

FINLAND | TRACK AND FIELD | 12 MEDALS | 1897–1973

ANTWERP 1920 • PARIS 1924 • AMSTERDAM 1928

Paavo Nurmi didn't look particularly imposing for a runner. He lacked Usain Bolt's long limbs or Michael Johnson's powerful legs. "What is there about this phlegmatic Finn that makes him the superior of every other athlete who has ever pulled on a spiked shoe?" *The Guardian* asked in 1925. "He is slight, fair-haired, sometimes moody, and always temperamental . . . there is nothing about him that suggests the superman the stopwatches have proved him to be."

There was nothing on the outside to suggest that the "Flying Finn" would become one of the most decorated Olympians of all time. But Nurmi's incredible career was forged by his hardscrabble upbringing. It was walking miles to school each day, and skiing the route in the winter. It was dropping out of school to work in a bakery after his father died and pushing carts of bread up the steep, frozen streets of Turku. While in the Finnish army, he would run through a 12.5-mile training march carrying a backpack filled with sand while others labored to even walk the course.

It was his mind, too, that changed running forever. In the early 1900s, most runners would sprint at the start of the race, conserve energy in the middle, and sprint again at the end. But Nurmi thought deeply about the mechanics and strategies of racing. He ran with a stopwatch, and kept an even pace throughout the race, a pioneering strategy that's standard today.

There was, of course, his mercurial disposition that signified a one-track mind. Despite being one of the most famous athletes of his time, Nurmi was averse to media. He didn't have many friends and was cold to his opponents. He was enigmatic, arrogant, mysterious, silent, intense. One newspaperman called him "a mechanical Frankenstein created to annihilate time."

Nurmi was also indifferent to his son, Matti, and felt, according to some reports, disappointed in the size of his progeny's feet. "Paavo even tried to arrange the boy's food so that Matti should be strengthened for athletics," his ex-wife once said. (Matti did run, albeit on a more local level, before becoming a successful businessman.)

Nurmi's aloof demeanor didn't prevent him from staggering success. In his Olympic debut at the 1920 Antwerp Games, he won three golds in the 10,000 meters and both the individual and team cross-country events. He also won silver in the 5,000 meters. In 1922, he set world records in the 2,000, 3,000, and 5,000 meters. A year later, he set the mile record, meaning he held—including the 10,000-meters mark—five world records at one time. In the 1924 Paris Games, Nurmi set an Olympic record in the 1,500 meter. Two hours later, he would win in the 5,000 meters by more than a meter.

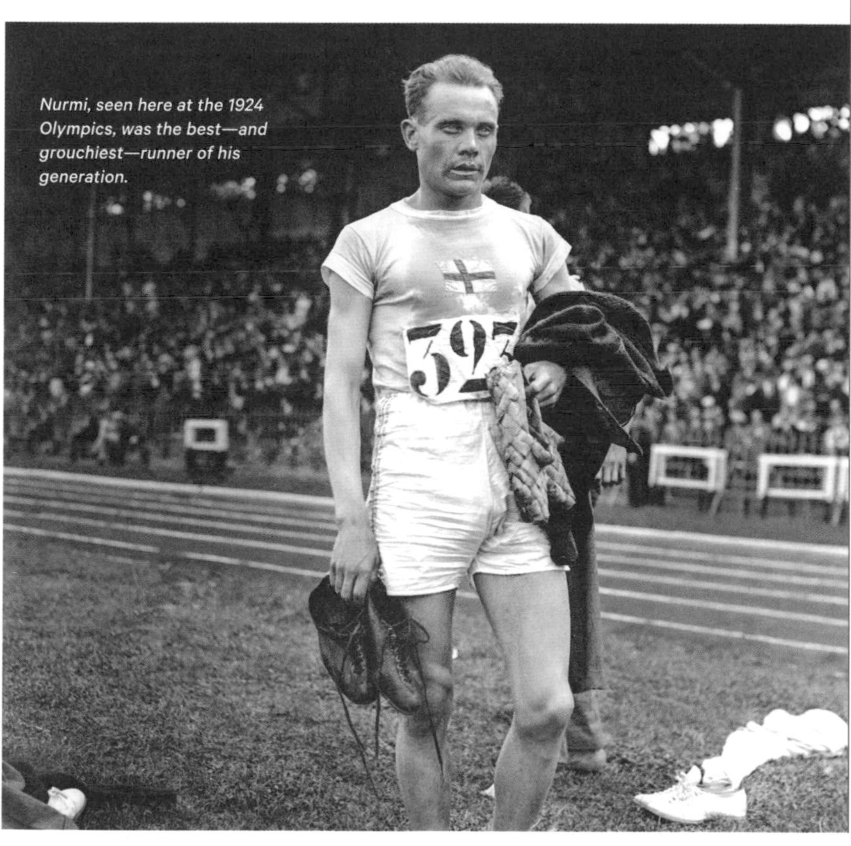

Nurmi, seen here at the 1924 Olympics, was the best—and grouchiest—runner of his generation.

All those long days pushing baked goods up the streets of Turku paid off in the 1924 cross-country event. The temperature at the Paris Games was 113 degrees; 23 of 38 competitors left the race. Eight exited on stretchers. One runner became delirious, running around in circles and walking off into the stands, where he eventually knocked himself unconscious. Nurmi, however, seemed unfazed, winning by a minute and a half. (After the spectacle of mass fainting, cross-country was banned from future Games forever.)

These two legendary Olympic performances in Paris made Nurmi an international star. He embarked on a publicity tour of the United States in 1925, competing in 55 events within a five-month period. He lost only once, bested by American star Alan Helffrich in a half-miler in Yankee Stadium. It was Nurmi's first loss in 121 races.

At the 1928 Games in Amsterdam, Nurmi won three more medals, including gold in the 10,000. Despite a sprained hip and foot, he won silver in both the 5,000-meter and the 3,000-meter steeplechase, an event he had participated in only twice before. Four years later, Nurmi decided on a whim to run the marathon at the 1932 Games in Los Angeles and turned into one of the favorites. However, the International Association of Athletics Federations (IAAF)—the governing body for track and field—had suspended Nurmi after an investigation into his amateur status.

Despite protests in Finland and the Finnish Athletic Federation finding no evidence of wrongdoing, the IAAF found him guilty of accepting between $250 and $500 per race in Germany in 1931—no small sum in those days. His suspension became indefinite, and Nurmi turned his one-track mind to business. He opened a clothing store, built apartments in Helsinki, and eventually became one of the country's richest people.

The man who broke 22 world records has been a source of inspiration for artists all over. A Finnish opera was composed about his life; at the 1928 Games, a Polish writer won gold in the literature competition for a poem that included a verse on Nurmi. Despite being a Finnish hero and an Olympic icon, he remained thorny till his death. Asked if he ran to put Finland on the map, Nurmi had a typically arrogant answer: "I ran for myself, not for Finland. At the Olympics, Paavo Nurmi mattered more than ever."

JOHNNY WEISSMULLER
From Olympic Pool to Silver Screen

USA | SWIMMING | 6 MEDALS | 1904–1984

PARIS 1924 • AMSTERDAM 1928

His yell is iconic. Starting low in the chest register, it moved up and down the octave scale, piercing through the jungle and onto the big screen, now embedded in popular culture forever. That the sound itself wasn't actually his—we can thank the combined voices of a baritone, a tenor, and a hog caller from Arkansas—doesn't really matter. The Tarzan call catapulted Johnny Weissmuller from Olympic hero to Hollywood legend.

Weissmuller's long tenure as Tarzan was possible only because of his tremendous success in the pool. Born in Romania, he fudged his records to list his birthplace as Windber, Pennsylvania, to satisfy the US Olympic citizenship requirement. (Some evidence also suggests he may have assumed his brother's identity.) As a boy in Chicago, Weissmuller took to swimming on doctor's orders to bulk up a sickly body after contracting polio. By the age of 16 he had won his first US national swimming title—one of 52 golds at national competitions—and by age 18 he had broken the world record in the 100 meters.

Weissmuller transitioned seamlessly to Hollywood, finding fame as Tarzan.

Weissmuller starred at the 1924 Summer Olympics in Paris, winning three gold medals in swimming and a bronze in water polo. He would win two more gold medals in 1928 at the Amsterdam Games. By the end of his swimming career, he boasted six medals and had set 67 world records. He had never lost a race. The Associated Press in 1950 named him the best swimmer of the half century. Winning was so routine that he looked forward to the backstroke simply for the view. "I got bored," he once said, "so I swam on my back where I could spend more time looking around." Weissmuller's coach, Bill Bachrach, promised him a dinner as a reward if he broke a record.

Weissmuller's Olympic exploits made him famous. He performed at exhibitions and endorsed bathing suits and other products. Then a chance encounter took his fame to another level when screenwriter Cyril Hume spotted him in the pool of the Hollywood Athletic Club. Hume took one look at Weissmuller and told him to test for the titular role in *Tarzan the Ape Man*. "They asked could I pick up a girl and walk away with her and I said yes," Weissmuller remembered. "I had the part."

He played Tarzan in 12 movies, earning an estimated $2 million. Though Weissmuller was, self-admittedly, not much of a thespian—"The public forgives my acting because they know I was an athlete," he once said—the film put him at the forefront of pop culture for decades to come. (Look for him

THE ANCIENT POLITICS OF SWITCHING SIDES

Astylos of Croton won six "victory wreaths" (ah, the good old days before medals) in various running distances in the fourth century BC. He ran in two Olympics for Croton, a city in present-day Calabria. In his other appearances, however, he ran for Syracuse in Sicily. Big mistake. In response, Crotonians broke down Astylos's statue in the city and turned his house into a jail. A similar fate awaited Sotades of Crete, who accepted a bribe to compete for Ephesus. He was banished by his hometown.

Sometimes the Olympics was a good source of positive PR—in fact, the Games traditionally marked a formal truce between any warring city-states. (There was a moratorium on armies invading Olympia, and all legal disputes—including executions—were also placed on hold.) But other times the Olympics were used as a political weapon to punish any athletes deemed traitorous. At least that doesn't happen when athletes switch countries nowadays!

on the cover of the Beatles' *Sgt. Pepper's Lonely Hearts Club Band.*) He was beseeched everywhere he went: "Tarzan, give us your elephant call!" He'd cup his hands over his mouth and scream at the top of his lungs: "AAAAAH-EEE-AAH!" Women approached him saying, "Me Jane, you Tarzan."

Weissmuller continued to act for many years, including starring in 16 *Jungle Jim* films. He remained in the public eye as a pitchman for pools, vitamins, and other health products. But for all his vitality on the screen and in the pool, the later years of his life were defined by illness. In 1979, while hospitalized after suffering a series of strokes, the hospital director noted that he frightened others by making his legendary Tarzan call at night. He died in 1984 at age 79.

Should Weissmuller be remembered most for his swimming? For swinging through trees and screaming at the top of his lungs? For hawking wares and profiting off his fame? Maybe all of the above. To Weissmuller, though, the answer was simple: "I owe everything to swimming," he once said. "It not only made my name, it saved my name. Without swimming, I'd be a nobody."

Weissmuller (center) beat out Sweden's Arne Borg (right) in the 400-meter freestyle in 1924.

NEROLI FAIRHALL
From Injury to Triumph

NEW ZEALAND | ARCHERY/TRACK AND FIELD | 1944–2006

HEIDELBERG 1972 (P) • ARNHEM 1980 (P) • LOS ANGELES 1984 (O) • SEOUL 1988 (P) • SYDNEY 2000 (P)

Riding her motorcycle in the hills outside Christchurch, New Zealand, Neroli Fairhall took a turn too hard and crashed. The 25-year-old was paralyzed from the waist down and lay helpless for 21 hours before being discovered. Fairhall, who was active and athletic before the accident, immediately took to para-sports. She tried shot put and discus and competed in the Paralympic Games in 1972 in track and field. Fairhall soon switched to archery, but struggled mightily at first. She began to succeed by building up her strength with swimming workouts four times a week at a pool in Christchurch.

By 1980, 11 years after the accident, Fairhall would be selected for the New Zealand Olympic archery team for the Moscow Summer Games. But New Zealand, along with 64 other countries, boycotted the Olympics in response to the Soviet invasion of Afghanistan. She would, however, participate in the Paralympic Games later that year in the Netherlands, where she won gold and set a world record.

Fairhall made the team again in 1984, when she became the first-ever paraplegic to compete in an Olympic Games. That she was able to recover from a paralyzing injury to participate

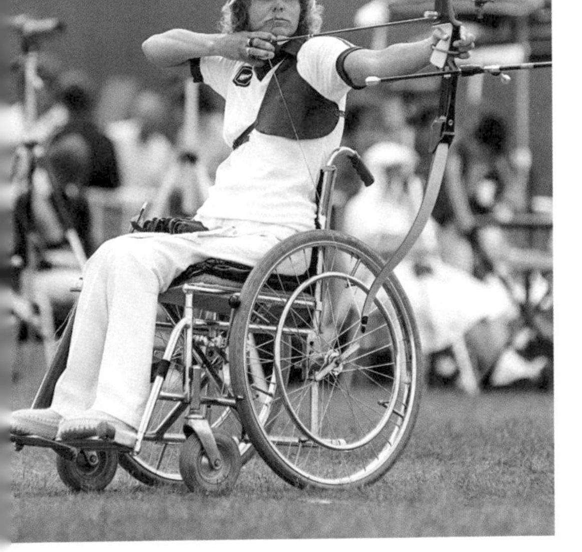

LEFT: *Fairhall became the first paraplegic to compete at the Olympics in 1984.*

A BRIEF HISTORY OF THE PARALYMPICS

The Paralympics are a nearly identical version of the Olympics. They are hosted in the same city, using the same venues. There are opening and closing ceremonies; medals are awarded and national anthems are played. The only difference, of course, is that the events are exclusively for athletes with disabilities. At the 2016 Summer Paralympics in Rio, 4,342 athletes competed in 528 events across 22 sports.

The forerunner of the Paralympics started in 1948 at Stoke Mandeville Hospital in Aylesbury, England, a town about 50 miles northwest of London. It was at the behest of Dr. Ludwig Guttman, who was hoping to rehabilitate war veterans with spinal cord injuries. Sixteen competitors participated in archery. Four years later, athletes from the Netherlands came to compete in the Stoke Mandeville Games. In 1960, the first Paralympic Games were held, with 400 athletes from 23 countries. By 1976, athletes with disabilities other than spinal cord injuries were included, and a movement was fully born.

in the world's biggest event—in a span of just 11 years—is absolutely astonishing, and a true testament to both her tremendous resolve and overall athletic ability. Fairhall's wheelchair, though, caused a buzz. Some rivals thought she had an advantage by sitting down, to which she replied, "I don't know. I've never shot standing up."

Hounded by media, Fairhall finished in 35th place. She would continue to compete, participating in the 1988 and 2000 Paralympics, before retiring and working as a coach. She died in 2006 at the age of 61. She was a true trailblazer who showed the world that a disability doesn't have to keep you down.

NATALIE DU TOIT
Just Keep Swimming

SOUTH AFRICA | SWIMMING | 15 PARALYMPIC MEDALS | 1984–

ATHENS 2004 (P) • BEIJING 2008 (P) • LONDON 2012 (P)

"I've lost my leg! I've lost my leg!" Natalie du Toit cried after a car hit her while she was riding her scooter. The 17-year-old's left leg was barely attached. It would be amputated at the knee a week later.

Du Toit could've thought that was the end of her promising swimming career. At age 14, she had represented South Africa at the Commonwealth Games, a competition for former and current territories of Great Britain. But even though that car accident took du Toit's leg, it did not take her spirit. In her hospital bed, she kept trying to pull herself up, because she knew she had to train. "I never ever wanted to give up swimming," she said. "It was something I would carry on with."

Du Toit started swimming again just five months after the accident. She learned to compensate for her disability by relying on her left arm to act like her left leg; unlike nondisabled swimmers, she is dependent primarily on arm strength. A year later, she won two races for disabled swimmers at the Commonwealth Games, where she also qualified for the 800-meter freestyle final for able-bodied athletes and earned the award for most outstanding athlete. And despite her right leg generally cramping in long races, she chose to participate in the 6.2-mile-long open water race. Clearly, du Toit has never shied away from an intense competitive challenge. "In the water, I'm just like everybody else," she said.

"In the water, I'm just like everybody else."

After winning five gold medals at the 2004 Paralympics, du Toit qualified for the 10 km open water race in Beijing, making her the first female amputee swimmer ever to qualify for the able-bodied Olympics. She was South Africa's flag bearer, and she would finish in 16th place. Du Toit stayed in China for the Paralympics, where she again won five gold medals.

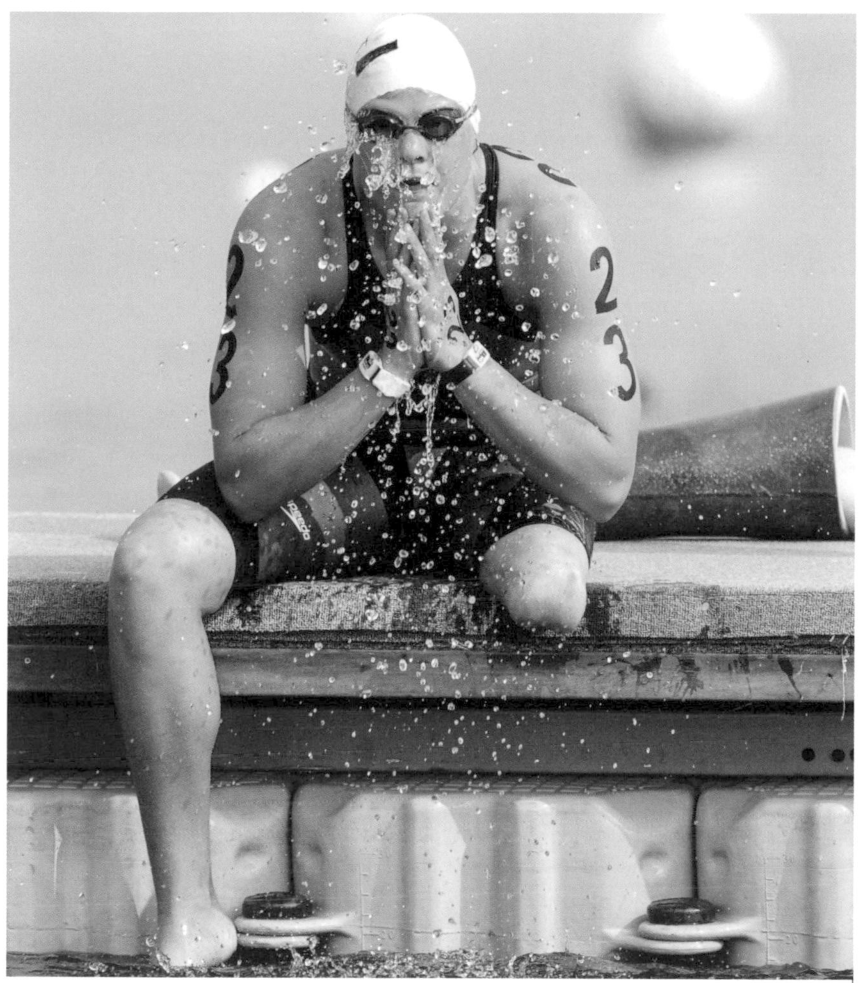

A gifted swimmer before her accident, Du Toit learned to rely on her upper body strength.

Du Toit may have ended up as a gold-medal-winning swimmer had the accident not happened. She may have become South Africa's Olympic golden girl. For du Toit, however, the accident was a blessing in disguise. "I have never ever thought of what I would have done or what I would have been," she once said. "I know that my life after my accident has changed and I always say that mostly it has changed for the better."

TRISCHA ZORN
The Ultimate

USA | SWIMMING | 55 PARALYMPIC MEDALS | 1964–

ARNHEM 1980 (P) • NEW YORK 1984 (P) • SEOUL 1988 (P) • BARCELONA 1992 (P) • ATLANTA 1996 (P) • SYDNEY 2000 (P) • ATHENS 2004 (P)

The Paralympics are every bit the spectacle that the Olympics are. The athletes are just as talented. They sacrifice just as much. The races are just as close. The drama is just as real. And it's well worth remembering this bombshell statistic: The most-decorated swimmer of all time is not Michael Phelps. Not even close. Yeah, Phelps's 28 medals are impressive—so are those 23 golds. But the real medal leader blows Phelps out of the water.

Trischa Zorn, an American swimmer, has a record 55 medals. A whopping 41 of those are gold. She competed in seven Paralympic Games and was unbeaten in every individual race from 1980 to 1992, collecting 25 straight golds in the process. And she did it all with severely limited sight.

Born without the part of the iris that sees color, Zorn's eyes flutter in and out of control very rapidly. As a result, her vision is compromised and she's sensitive to bright lights. She can see only the rough outlines of objects no farther than 20 feet away. Zorn was able to avoid the walls and lane lines because she could make out the black lines at the pool's bottom, which guide her. On backstroke, she counted the flags above her to mark her strokes.

The only thing, really, that her impairment has stopped her from doing is driving a car—she seems to have done everything else. Zorn started swimming seriously at age 10 in Mission Viejo, California. She earned scholarship offers from numerous colleges and chose the University of Nebraska, accepting the first full athletic scholarship ever awarded to a visually impaired person. At Nebraska, she earned All-America honors four times in backstroke and was named to the Big Eight All-Academic Team for three years. She then taught special education for 10 years in Indianapolis and now works as an attorney for the Department of Veterans Affairs. Oh yeah, and she runs half marathons, rides horseback, and water-skis.

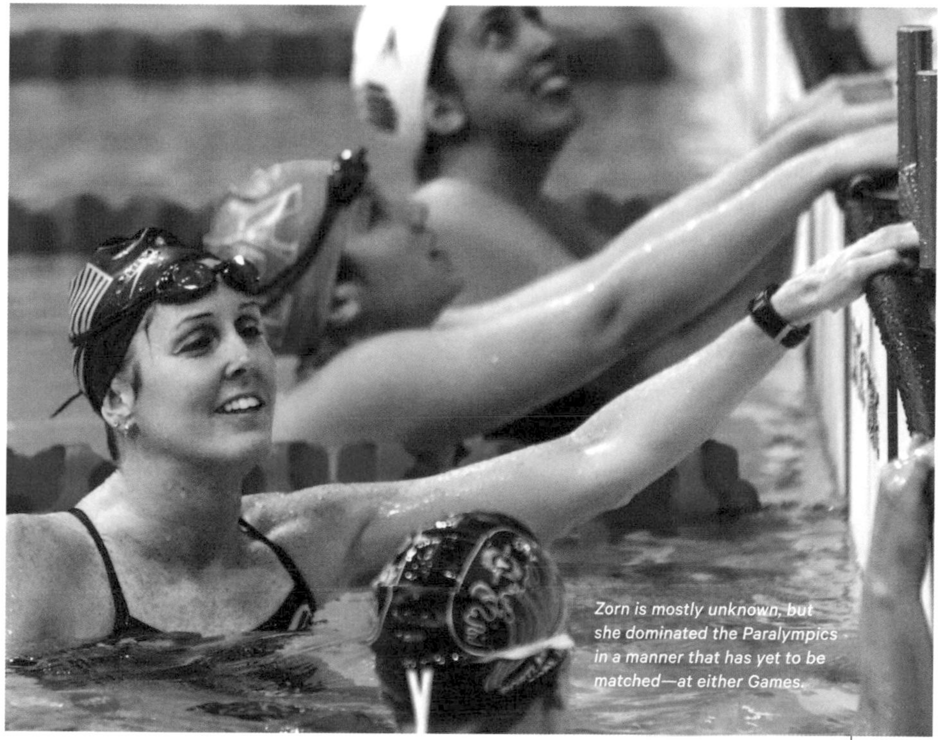
Zorn is mostly unknown, but she dominated the Paralympics in a manner that has yet to be matched—at either Games.

Of course, all those are great accomplishments worth celebrating in their own right. But what she did in the pool reflects a level of dominance simply never seen before in sports history. At her first Paralympics in 1980 in Arnhem, Netherlands, she won seven gold medals. She was just 16. (Phelps, it should be noted, won his record eight gold medals in a single Olympics, in his third Games at age 23.)

At the 1984 Paralympics in New York, Zorn won 10 gold medals. Four years later, in Seoul, she won a whopping 12 golds. "Everybody asked if it got boring going to the awards stand," she said. "But it never got old for me." Indeed, every successive Paralympics were just another show of unmatched greatness for Zorn. Barcelona: 12 medals. Atlanta: eight medals. Sydney: five medals. After those 2000 Games in Sydney, she held eight world records in her category.

Zorn came out of retirement to finish her Paralympic career in Athens in 2004. She earned a bronze at age 40. That medal, she said, was for her mom, who had passed away earlier that year and had never missed a Paralympics. "That was the most significant medal I won," she said. Zorn was chosen as the United States flag bearer for the closing ceremonies.

The end of Zorn's career was marked with little fanfare. That she finished her career with the most medals just didn't seem to register. That says something, of course, about how we see the Paralympics. Or, more accurately, how we too often don't see them at all. Even though they immediately follow the Olympics, many of us tend to simply tune out. But those who missed Trischa Zorn and her unparalleled dominance should hope that they don't miss the next one. Zorn sure won't: "Records are meant to be broken," she said.

Zorn's medal record, though, won't be broken for a while, if ever. Which means that we have plenty of time now to celebrate Zorn and marvel at her utter brilliance.

MOST PARALYMPIC MEDALS

NAME	COUNTRY	EVENT	MEDAL COUNT
Trischa Zorn	USA	Swimming	**55**
Heinz Frei	Switzerland	Track and field/cycling/ cross-country skiing	**34**
Jonas Jacobsson	Sweden	Shooting	**30**
Zipora Rubin-Rosenbaum	Israel	Track and field/basketball/ table tennis	**30**
Ragnhild Myklebust	Norway	Biathlon/cross-country skiing/ice sledge racing	**27**
Roberto Mason	Italy	Track and field/fencing	**26**
Beatrice Hess	France	Swimming	**25**
Sarah Storey	Great Britain	Swimming/Cycling	**25**
Claudia Hengst	Germany	Swimming	**25**
Daniel Dias	Brazil	Swimming	**24**

FU MINGXIA
The Prodigy

CHINA | DIVING | 5 MEDALS | 1978–

BARCELONA 1992 • ATLANTA 1996 • SYDNEY 2000

4 1 0

If there is such a thing as a prodigy, it would be confirmed by the presence of Fu Mingxia. A four-foot two-inch, 77-pound dynamo from Wuhan, China, Mingxia enjoyed a meteoric rise in diving that was unprecedented for any diver, much less a preteen.

Following her older sister's lead, Mingxia gave gymnastics a try at a local club. The coaches recognized her superior body control and talent, and decided she would be a better fit for diving. She was just seven years old and couldn't swim, but a prodigy was born. Minxia left home at age nine—a common practice in China for young athletes who show promise—traveling some 600 miles away and seeing her parents only twice a year. Following a long history of Chinese athletes who train in spartan conditions with few distractions, she practiced seven hours a day, six days a week, stopping only for massages and the occasional television show. She performed her dives outside in all types of weather. "If you can dive in the midst of a rainstorm," she once said, "then you can dive here even better."

Mingxia was a four-foot two-inch, 77-pound dynamo.

It's hard to explain her early success with hard work alone, however. How do you account for such dominance when most are kids still waiting for puberty? In 1990, at age 11, Mingxia won her first international competition. A year later, she won the world championship in Perth, Australia. Her win led the diving governing body to create a rule requiring competitors to be at least 14 in the year of a given meet. That worked out just fine for Mingxia—she turned 14 less than a month after the Barcelona Games in 1992.

It was clear by the time Barcelona came around that she was the best diver in the world. She won gold in the 10-meter platform, becoming the youngest female platform Olympic diving champion of all time. She

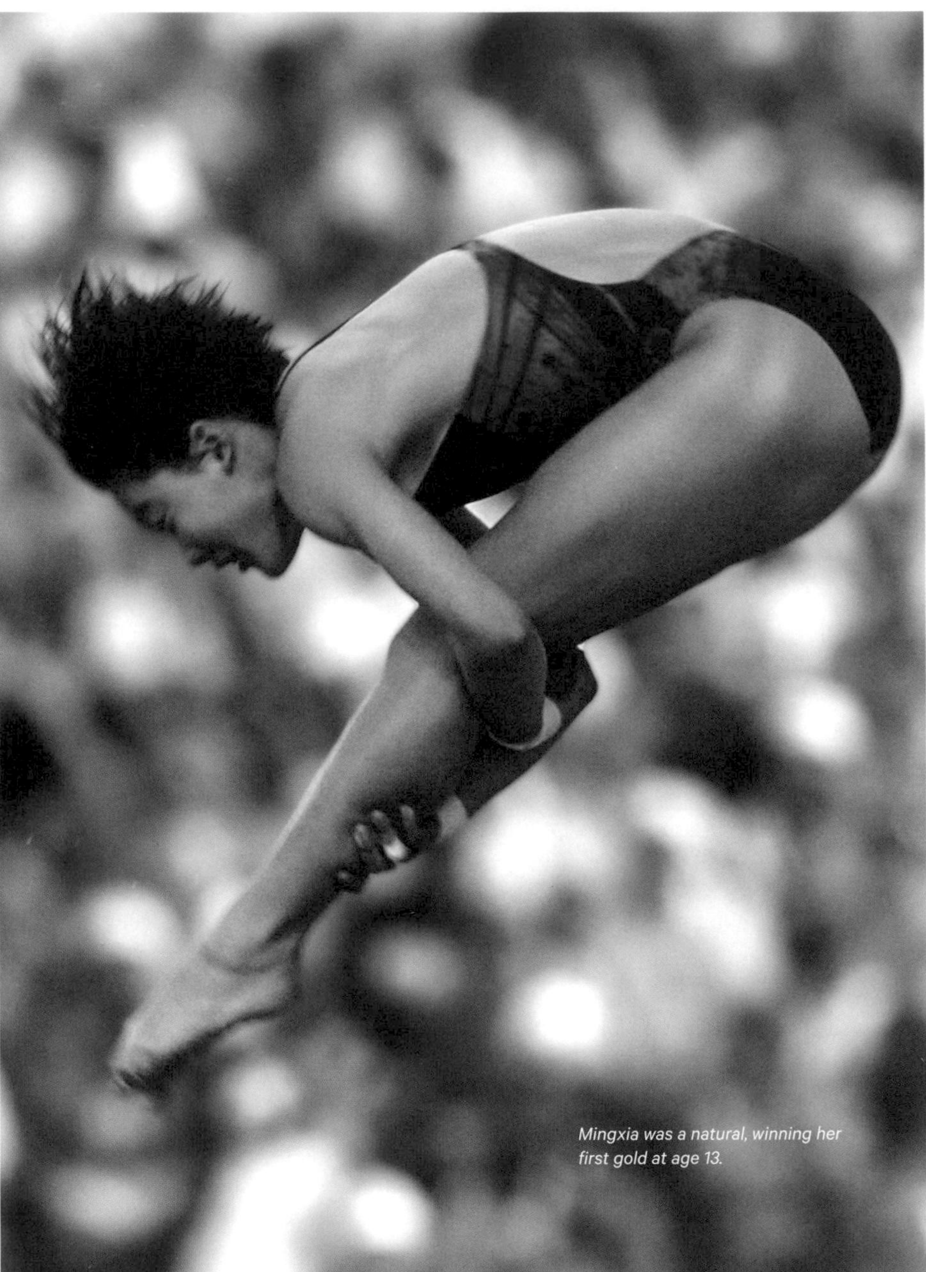

Mingxia was a natural, winning her first gold at age 13.

OLYMPIC MASCOTS

Since the 1968 Winter Games in Grenoble, France, the Olympic cities have chosen a mascot. The first one, Schuss, was a little stick-figure-type man, with a round red head and the Olympic rings as a tuft of hair. Typically, the mascots try to hew close to something representative of the host city. The 1972 Games in Munich featured Waldi, a Dachshund, which is a popular dog breed in Germany. The Montreal Games had Amik the Beaver, one of the national symbols of Canada. Others are a bit more abstract. In Atlanta, Izzy was, well, something. The first digital mascot, it could morph into different forms. (Its original name was Whatizit.) *Time* magazine dubbed it "sperm in sneakers," which, you might suppose, is one of the forms it could take? Atlanta might want a do-over.

Misha the Bear from the 1980 Moscow Olympics

continued her winning streak four years later—and 30 pounds heavier—in Atlanta, taking the platform and springboard golds, the first female competitor in 36 years to do so at a single Games. Still just 17, she sat at press conferences with a stuffed animal Izzy, the Olympic mascot.

After years of relentless training that sometimes left her in tears, she took a two-year break, studying business management in China. In 1997, at age 19, she served as a delegate to the Communist Party Congress. But Mingxia couldn't stay away forever. She joined the collegiate team at Tsinghua University, and won the highboard and springboard titles at the 1999 World University Championships. Mingxia then qualified for the 2000 Games in Sydney, taking up three-meter synchronized diving, in which she won silver. She won yet another gold in the springboard, her fourth, and became one of three divers to win two golds each in two different disciplines.

After Sydney, Mingxia retired at 22—this time for good. No more harsh training sessions, no more tears. The problem with being a child prodigy is that, eventually, you will no longer be a child, just a phenomenal talent who has outgrown her sport. What can you ever do as an encore?

EVELYN ASHFORD
Collateral Damage

USA | TRACK AND FIELD | 5 MEDALS | 1957–

MONTREAL 1976 • LOS ANGELES 1984 • SEOUL 1988 • BARCELONA 1992

4 1 0

It was supposed to be the year of Evelyn Ashford in 1980. The sprinter had finished fifth in the 100 meter as a 19-year-old at the 1976 Games in Montreal and had beaten world record holders in the 100 and 200 at the 1979 World Cup of Track. She became the first woman to run the 100 meter in less than 11 seconds and the 200 in less than 22. The Moscow Olympics, it seemed, would represent her coming-out party.

"Evelyn had a chance to do more than Edwin Moses, more than [Renaldo] Nehemiah," said Pat Winslow Connolly, a former Olympian and Ashford's coach at UCLA. "She had a chance at two gold medals for sure, and two more in the relays if things went well."

But then the Soviet Union invaded Afghanistan in December 1979. The international diplomatic community decried the military action, and the United States, along with 64 other countries, boycotted the Games in response. Ashford's breakout moment was broken by geopolitics. "I guess the best way to describe it was I felt as if my soul was ripped out of me," she once said. Making matters worse, later in 1980, she pulled her right hamstring and was out for the rest of the season.

> **"I felt as if my soul was ripped out of me."**

Ashford thought about quitting forever, but fortunately she stuck with it. In her first meet in 1981, the Albuquerque Invitational, she landed at the airport with only an hour to spare before the gun went off. No matter—she broke a two-year-old world record in the 60-yard dash. Ashford then set a world record in the 100 meter in 1983, setting her up for another shot at Olympic glory.

Sure, it wasn't the metallurgic splash that she was hoping for in 1980, but Ashford's performance in 1984 was still quite impressive. Despite dealing with a hamstring strain, she set an Olympic record in the 100 for gold and collected a second gold in the 4 x 100 relay. It ended up being the year of Ashford after all—she finished 1984 ranked first in the 100. She was the flag bearer at the 1988 Games and won silver in the 100 meter and gold in the relay. She won her fourth gold medal in 1992, again in the relay.

Ashford finished her career with five medals, four of them gold. She is one of only six women to collect four golds in track and field. Had the opportunity to compete in 1980 not been snatched away from her, surely that number would've been higher. She could've retired as one of the icons of Olympic history. Instead, geopolitics took the best years of her career away, her athletic legacy a casualty of the Cold War.

Ashford had the medals to be a superstar, but was lost in the political shuffle of the Cold War.

HASSIBA BOULMERKA

For Her Country, For Herself

ALGERIA | TRACK AND FIELD | 1 MEDAL | 1968–

SEOUL 1988 • BARCELONA 1992 • ATLANTA 1996

When Hassiba Boulmerka returned home to Algeria after winning the gold in the 1,500 meters at the 1991 world championship, she was treated like a rock star. Before she landed at the airport, they brought in the army to control the adoring crowds. Women threw out candies and wheat seeds, like they do at weddings. She was given the Medal of Merit, one of the country's highest honors, and President Chadli Bendjedid kissed her on the forehead. Politicians came up to her and said, "You did what we haven't been able to do for years. You brought us together."

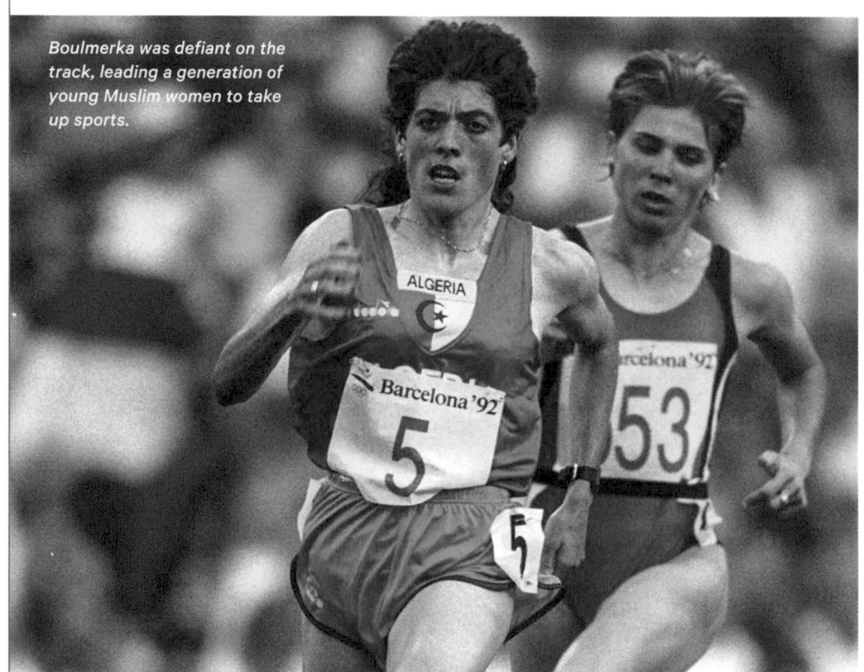

Boulmerka was defiant on the track, leading a generation of young Muslim women to take up sports.

That high praise was misleading, however, because powerful factors were at work against her back home. Things were changing in Algeria. Tensions rose as Islamist militants fought back against the secular government. In 1992, a civil war broke out, leading to more than 250,000 deaths. Conservative imams encouraged their followers to denounce Boulmerka. She was "un-Muslim," they said, upset that she had ditched the leggings and a headscarf she had worn previously during races.

Boulmerka soon received death threats. There were rumors of an assassination plot. All across Algeria, vandals sprayed graffiti labeling her a traitor. As the Islamist militias began to gain power in the country, Boulmerka's status as un-Muslim made life impossible. When she ran in Algeria, men would throw stones or spit at her. The post office refused to mail out her letters. She was forced to move to Berlin to keep training for the upcoming Olympics in Atlanta.

At 24, Boulmerka was one of the best runners in the world. But she was split in two. How could she account for being a stylish, talkative star athlete while also her own country's villain, barred from racing in Algeria and forced to carry a gun with her at all times? Even so, she was the "it girl" of international sports. She was seen as an easy quote by hungry journalists, waiting for her to denounce fundamentalism. As Algeria continued to descend into chaos, she became the go-to interview. "There was intense pressure from the media, trying to mix me up," she said. "I'm just one Algerian woman, trying to withstand the pressure for all the Algerian people. I'm tired of the questions. I'm on my knees."

But Boulmerka kept talking. She spoke of a more liberal Islamic faith, inspiring some 8,000 Algerian girls to enroll in athletics, where they proudly wore shorts. All she wanted was for women both in Algeria and all over the world to run. Her love for her country never faded. She has since returned to Algeria and has found success in business. After she won at the 1992 Olympics in Barcelona in the 1,500, marking Algerian's first-ever gold medal, she screamed to the world, "Algerie! Algerie!" and pumped her fist, pointing at her uniform. "It was a symbol of victory, of defiance," she said. "It was to say: 'I did it! I won! And now, if you kill me, it'll be too late. I've made history!'"

BIRGIT FISCHER
The Longevity Queen

GERMANY | KAYAK | 12 MEDALS | 1962–

MOSCOW 1980 • SEOUL 1988 • BARCELONA 1992 • ATLANTA 1996 • SYDNEY 2000 • ATHENS 2004

At 42 years old, Birgit Fischer would've been more than justified in retiring from competition to enjoy the fruits of her Olympic labor. Fate had other plans for her.

Over a career spanning nearly a quarter century, Fischer established herself as the greatest kayaker of all time. By that point she had amassed 10 medals, seven of them gold. Only the great Soviet gymnast Larisa Latynina won more medals among women. And Fischer almost surely would have won more in 1984, if not for East Germany's boycott of the Los Angeles Games. She had a remarkable 38 world championship medals as well, 28 of which were gold.

After winning her sixth and seventh gold medals at the Sydney Games in 2000, Fischer thought she was done. Hungarians were the rising power in the sport, having won the last three world championships between 2001 and 2003. Besides, Fischer had other obligations and interests to occupy her post-athletics life. She raised two children and took a shot at politics, running unsuccessfully for European Parliament.

Fischer is both the youngest and oldest kayaker to win a gold medal. It's safe to call her the greatest too.

But when Fischer participated in a TV documentary about her, everything changed. The filmmakers needed some footage of the all-time great paddling a kayak and she agreed. And then things clicked. "It felt good," she said. "Suddenly, the curiosity was there again and I asked myself: What can I still achieve? How fast can I get fit again?"

The answer, it turned out, was *very* fast. Her decades of experience would prove invaluable. In the K-4 (which refers to four racers in a single boat) 500-meter race at the 2004 Games in Athens, the Hungarians got out quick, whereas the German team lagged toward the back. Slowly, they had managed to move into second place, still .3 seconds behind the Hungarians. It was then that the old veteran took over.

"Birgit Fischer!" the German commentators screamed. "It is incredible how she is forcing herself forward here." With her strength propelling them, the Germans edged in front of the Hungarians, finishing just a slight .2 seconds ahead of the favorites for the gold. (She also added a silver in the K-2 500 for good measure.) And it made for some incredible record setting as well: She became both the oldest *and* youngest kayaking gold medalist ever, having first won in 1980 in Moscow.

Suffice it to say that coming out of retirement was the wise choice for Fischer. She ended her exceptional Olympic career with eight gold medals, good for eighth-most all-time, and third-most among all women.

Fischer (at right, with teammate Katrin Wagner in 2000) was just as good coming out of retirement as she was at the beginning of her career.

EUGENIO MONTI
The Ultimate Sportsman

ITALY | BOBSLED | 6 MEDALS | 1928–2003

CORTINA D'AMPEZZO 1956 • INNSBRUCK 1964 • GRENOBLE 1968

Eugenio Monti was hands down the best bobsledder in the world. He dominated his sport like no one else, winning three world championships in the four years leading up to the Olympics. The Italian known as "The Flying Redhead" had been bobsledding for only a few years, but he'd become completely obsessed and learned every in and out. He'd consistently walk up and down the track, looking for tiny cuts in the ice, lingering for so long that the public address announcer had to beg him to get off.

Monti, the ultimate mensch, makes a turn at the 1956 Winter Games in Cortina.

The clear favorite for the 1964 Winter Games in Innsbruck, Austria, Monti had only a gold medal missing from his otherwise sterling résumé. He had previously won silvers in both the 2-man and 4-man events in 1956, and he probably would've medaled in 1960 in Squaw Valley had bobsled not been canceled to save costs.

After setting a course record in his second run of the two-man with teammate Sergio Siorpaes, Monti was in an excellent position to win. But then Antony Nash and Robin Dixon of Great Britain—the only competitors with a fighting chance—discovered that their bobsled's axle bolt had fallen off. What do you do? Do you mind your own business? Do you keep going, knowing your victory is assured?

Monti did something else entirely: He stripped a spare bolt off his sled and gave it to them. The Brits had their best run and went into first place. Monti and his teammate finished third and won bronze. "Nash didn't win the gold medal because I gave him a bolt," Monti said. "He won because he was the fastest." That may be technically true, but Nash would not have been able to run the fastest route if it hadn't been for Monti's incredible act of sportsmanship.

So let's say you're the best bobsledder in the world and you lost after lending a bolt to a competitor. What do you do if the situation arises again? If you're Monti, you do the exact same thing. Later on at that very same Innsbruck Games, the Canadian sled set an Olympic record in its first run of the four-man event, but the sled was ruined. Monti lent his mechanics to fix the sled and the Canadians won gold. Monti settled for another bronze. He was awarded the Pierre de Coubertin medal for fair play after the Games, one of the highest honors for an Olympian.

Surely Monti was frustrated by his inability to win the highest prize he coveted most. By the 1968 Games in Grenoble, he was 40 years old and had nearly called it quits. "Now I can stop," he said. "At 40 it is too old for the bob."

Luckily for Monti, neither he nor his competitors made any technical snafus. He went on to win gold in both the two-man and four-man. The Olympian who epitomized sportsmanship finally had what he wanted. It was time to go. "I can now retire peacefully," he said. "I'm a satisfied man."

DOING THE RIGHT THING

At the 1932 Summer Olympics in Los Angeles, British fencer Judy Guinness was about to win a gold in the individual foil. But she had a secret. She knew that her opponent, Ellen Preis of Austria, had not been given two points for successful touches. But that scoring error would cost Guinness the lead. What would *you* do? Guinness told the judges and took home a silver medal. Silver and a clean conscience is better, one would think, than a secret-laden gold.

KAROLY TAKACS
True Grit

HUNGARY | SHOOTING | 2 MEDALS | 1910–1976

LONDON 1948 • HELSINKI 1952 • MELBOURNE 1956

Karoly Takacs, a world-class shooter, might have won a medal for Hungary at the 1936 Summer Olympics in Berlin had the military allowed non-commissioned officers like him to compete. But he got his medal anyway in 1948—this time with the other hand.

In 1938, during training, a defective army grenade exploded on his right arm and it was soon amputated. Having lost his shooting arm, Takacs despaired for a while, and spent a month in the hospital. But in secret, he taught himself how to shoot left-handed. Ten years after the accident, he surprised the world by winning gold at the 1948 Games in London in the 25-meter rapid fire. Four years later, he repeated the gold in Helsinki. He would compete again in 1956 in Melbourne, but finished in eighth place.

Takacs became just the third known physically disabled athlete to compete in the able-bodied Olympics. (The first was Takacs' fellow countryman Oliver Halassy, a swimmer with an amputated leg who won three medals in three Olympics from 1928 to 1936.) After retiring, he worked as a coach and finished his service in the military.

The tough-as-nails Takacs takes aim during the 1948 Olympics in London.

TOM COURTNEY
Mind over Matter

USA | TRACK AND FIELD | 2 MEDALS | 1933–

MELBOURNE 1956

You know that pain you get when you run? That all-consuming, fire-in-the-chest, how-am-I-going to-even-finish-this pain? Every runner has experienced it. And surely most weekend warrior runners have gawked at their screens during the Olympics, regarded the distance runners in disbelief, and thought, *How do they make it look so easy?*

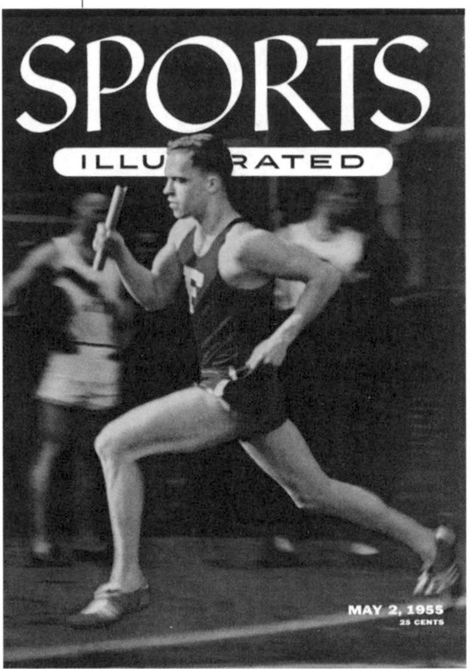

Courtney barely made it across the finish line, but he at least looked good on a 1955 cover of Sports Illustrated.

The secret: They don't. Take Tom Courtney, who was one of the favorites in the 800-meter run at the 1956 Summer Games in Melbourne. An NCAA champion in the 880 yards while at Fordham University, Courtney won the AAU championship in the 400 in 1956 and set an American record in the 800 at the Olympic trials. But for some reason, the finals of the 800 in Melbourne were his greatest pain.

It was a mad dash to the finish. The sheer agony was evident on Courtney's face. The cold, windy weather surely didn't help. But out of the depths of that anguish came his final, heroic push. Courtney caught up to England's Derek Johnson in the final 40 meters and lunged for the win, setting an Olympic record of 1:47.7, just one-tenth of a second before Johnson.

After tumbling over the finish line, Courtney was so exhausted that he lay speechless and didn't move for an hour. "It was a new kind of agony for me," he said. "My head was exploding, my stomach ripping and even the tips of my fingers ached. The only thing I could think was, 'If I live, I will never run again.'"

Fortunately for Courtney, he would live to run again, competing in the 4 x 400 relay and winning a second hard-earned gold. That race, at least, was a little more tolerable.

MARLON SHIRLEY
From the Streets to the Stars

USA | TRACK AND FIELD | 5 PARALYMPIC MEDALS | 1978–

SYDNEY 2000 (P) • ATHENS 2004 (P) • BEIJING 2008 (P)

Playing in a storage room at the Blue Angel Motel in Las Vegas—the one with the 16-foot-tall statue of a blond-haired, blue-eyed descendant from heaven on top—four-year-old Marlon Lebolo had the life of a vagrant. He'd cajole leftovers from the manager at Carl's Jr. and sometimes sleep under the freeway. His mother, Lindy, was in the throes of a heroin addiction. When he needed money, young Marlon would cut the back pocket of his mom's jeans while she was passed out and fish out the cash.

The situation was dire, and Lindy's sister told the police where to find them. Marlon was picked up on the street at age five. He bounced around orphanages before settling in 1984 at the Children's Home in Boulder City, Nevada, about 25 miles from Las Vegas. It was there, while chasing the caretaker on a lawn mower, that he slipped and his foot got caught.

"It was disgusting," he recalled. Though he had received stitches, Marlon didn't realize that his foot was mostly gone. That night he jumped out of his bed and re-ruptured it, leading to an amputation.

Marlon moved between many different foster homes, and even returned to the Children's Home. But he never felt down for himself. "What distinguished Marlon? Not once did I see him use his foot to get something, to get pity," said John Sproule, the social work supervisor at the facility. "He just got on with life."

He found a lifeline from the Shirley family in Thatcher, Utah, a small farming town near the Idaho border. Marlene Shirley, a devout Mormon, wanted a fourth child, and a picture of Marlon convinced her to adopt him. But the transition to a permanent home in Utah wasn't exactly easy. He stole money from a teacher and appeared in juvenile court a few times. His frustration with his adoptive mother was often palpable. Making matters worse, in high school, a football injury led to another amputation, this time of the rest of his lower left leg.

After yet another big fight with Marlene, he decided to take a chance, enrolling in the Simplot Games, a high-level amateur track and field competition in Pocatello, Idaho. His hope was a college scholarship. The result? Shirley high-jumped six feet and six inches—a para-athlete world record.

It was from there that he began to tick off the accomplishments: Only leg amputee to break 11 seconds in the 100 meters; a gold medal in the 100 and a silver in the high jump in Sydney; another gold four years later in Athens; sponsorships from Visa, McDonald's, and Home Depot; a shoe deal from Reebok. He became the world's most recognized

LEFT: *Shirley overcame injury and family strife to become one of the world's most famous Paralympians.*

Paralympian and, after three Olympics, a five-time medalist over three running disciplines.

It was in 2008, though, that Shirley faced even more adversity. He battled with knee issues, multiple operations, and staph infections throughout the year. He was hoping to become the first person to win three-straight 100-meter dashes in the Paralympics. It wouldn't be his knee that failed him—it was his Achilles tendon, which tore in the middle of the race. Well accustomed to challenges, Shirley battled tremendous pain and finished the race to a loud cheer from the stands.

The kid who wandered around the streets of Las Vegas went from destitution to being draped in gold medals. He travels the world now as a corporate spokesman, spreading his story and his message. It all worked out for him. And he wouldn't change anything—not even his foot getting caught in a lawn mower. "One of the best things that happened to me," he said.

KEEP ON GOING

Maybe a broken leg can be a good thing? Okay, maybe not, but it ended up working for Manteo Mitchell. The American sprinter was running the first leg (no pun intended) in the second heat of the 4 x 400 relay in London in 2012 when, as he recalls, "I felt it break. I felt like somebody literally just snapped my leg in half." Mitchell had broken his left fibula. But there were still 200 meters to go. So what did he do? Mitchell defied every instinct to "just lie down." Instead, he powered through.

Mitchell's perseverance helped give the United States one of the top qualifying times, and they would go on to win silver. Mitchell got a shout-out from Barack Obama too. "Now, this has to be one of my favorite stories of the whole Olympics," said the president during a ceremony honoring American Olympians and Paralympians after the Games. "Unbelievable."

DON SCHOLLANDER
The Reluctant Star

USA | SWIMMING | 6 MEDALS | 1946–

TOKYO 1964 • MEXICO CITY 1968

If he had had his way—and had genetics been on his side—Don Schollander would've played football. It was his favorite sport, and it still is. Hailing from a family of football players, he expected to follow in their footsteps, but there was one little problem: He was too short.

So Schollander, who enjoyed swimming with his friends on Lake Oswego in Oregon, where he grew up, tried out for the swim team and found instant success. He won the 100 freestyle and butterfly to win a state championship in his freshman year of high school. "I still had mixed emotions, because I loved football," he said. "But I was more convinced I was making the right decision."

That was in 1960. The next four years proved just how good a decision that was. By the time Schollander turned 18—and had grown to five feet eleven—in 1964, he had set 37 American and 22 world records. At the 1964 Olympics in Tokyo, he won four

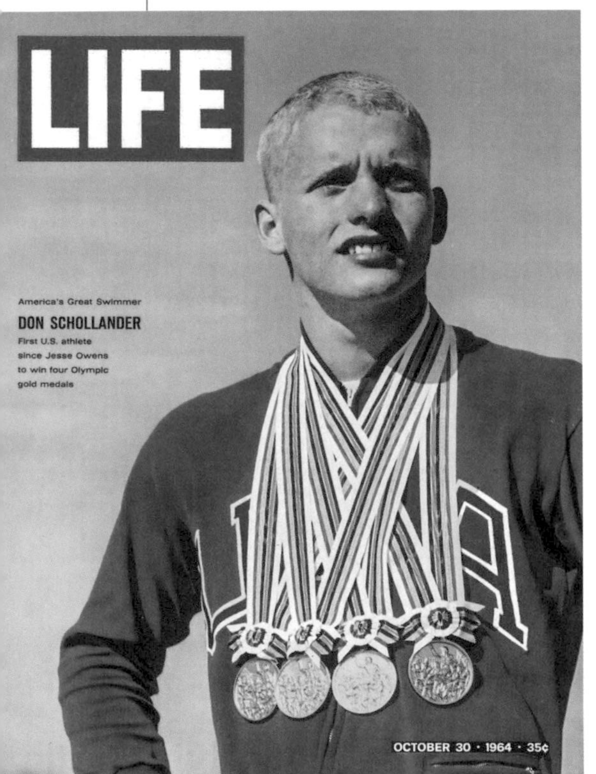

LIFE
America's Great Swimmer
DON SCHOLLANDER
First U.S. athlete since Jesse Owens to win four Olympic gold medals
OCTOBER 30 · 1964 · 35¢

LEFT: *Though he graced magazine covers, Schollander was press-shy and critical of the Olympics themselves.*

gold medals, becoming the first American since Jesse Owens to win four golds in a single Games. He was named both the World's Best Athlete and Athlete of the Year by the Associated Press that year, winning over NFL Most Valuable Player Johnny Unitas. But to hear Schollander tell the story, he still probably wished he was on a football field in Oregon, far away from the Olympic limelight.

"It's nice to be recognized for your accomplishments, but some people like to give speeches," Schollander told *Sports Illustrated* in 1968. "I'm not one of them. I'm a private person."

The constant attention got so invasive that, before the 1968 Games, Schollander had to be talked out of resigning from the US team as a form of protest against what he saw as the Olympic movement straying from its original ideals of amateurism. While he would end up with two more medals in Mexico City, including another gold, he did publish a version of that resignation speech in his 1971 book *Deep Water*, which shines a light on the hidden personal and political toll of the Olympics.

A true believer in Olympic amateurism, Schollander would've traded his four gold medals in swimming for a chance to play on the gridiron.

The five-time gold medalist, who was deeply ambivalent about swimming, never even called himself a swimmer. Indeed, after the 1968 Games, he retired from the sport at age 22. Although Schollander can never get away from his superb Olympic performances, he's certainly tried. In the 1980s, a friend begged him out of retirement to try to set a national record for masters swimmers in the relay. They succeeded, "but I didn't enjoy it," he said. "I told my friend afterward, 'I hope we set the record, because you have just seen the last race I am ever going to swim.'" Have you ever heard of a less enthusiastic champion?

So maybe Schollander wasn't the biggest fan of his chosen sport. But even he would have to admit it: Winning six medals isn't the worst thing in the world.

WYOMIA TYUS
A Winner Ignored

USA | TRACK AND FIELD | 4 MEDALS | 1945–

TOKYO 1964 • MEXICO CITY 1968

3 1 0

Wyomia Tyus got overshadowed at the 1968 Games in Mexico City. The fact that she became the first person, man or woman, in Olympic history to win the 100-meter dash in consecutive Games wasn't the massive deal it should have been at the time. And few people seemed to notice that she followed that up with another gold, in the 4 x 100 relay.

Also unnoticed was the fact that Tyus wore black shorts instead of the standard white as a show of support for the Olympic Project for Human Rights, a group that spoke out against racial segregation. Her act of protest didn't grab headlines like teammates John Carlos and Tommie Smith, who had raised their fists in a Black Power salute on the medal stand. Also ignored was the fact that she had dedicated her relay gold medal to them. Tyus believes that that powerful statement was never printed anywhere "because I was a woman," she said. "Who cared?"

That didn't stop her from conducting the protest in the first place. "You're doing it for yourself," she said 40 years later. "You're doing it because this is what you believed in."

Tyus, who grew up on a dairy farm in Georgia, spent most of the 1960s mired in a deep depression. In the span of a year, her family lost everything in a house fire, and then her father died of an illness. Despite her win at the 1964 Olympics in the 100 meters, she did not receive the hero's welcome afforded to

LEFT: *The three-time gold medalist shows off her wares in 1968.*

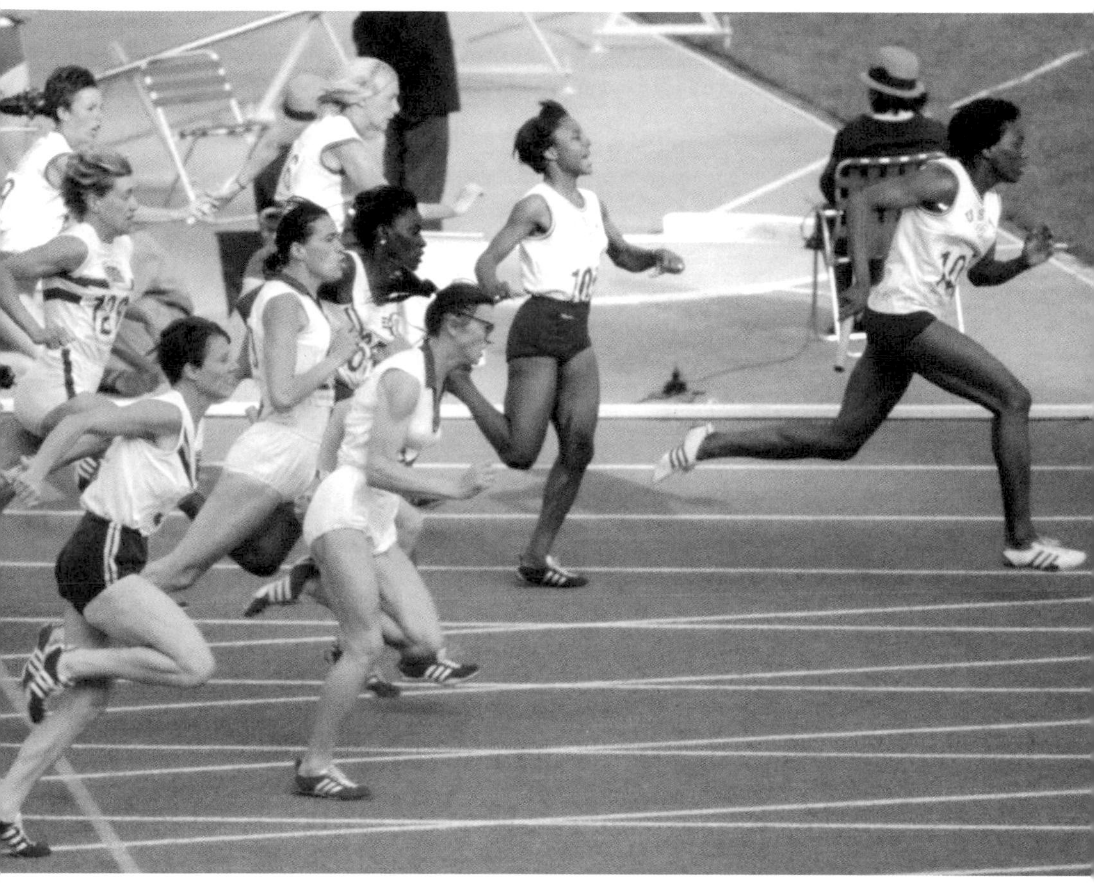

Tyus repeated her gold in the 100, but her historic win was practically forgotten when her track teammates made a powerful protest of their own.

most gold medalists upon returning home to Atlanta. "They only gave us the parade in the black neighborhood," she said.

The world did eventually catch up to her. Tyus was inducted into the National Track and Field Hall of Fame in 1980. Four years later, she was one of 11 athletes to carry the Olympic flag at the Los Angeles Games, and in 1985, she was inducted into the US Olympic Hall of Fame. In 2018, Tyus released a memoir, *Tigerbelle*, which received rave reviews from critics. Maybe this time, her accomplishments won't go unnoticed.

RAY EWRY
The Frog Man Cometh

USA | TRACK AND FIELD | 8 MEDALS | 1873–1937

PARIS 1900 • ST. LOUIS 1904 • LONDON 1908

8 0 0

Had Ray Ewry been born today, he might be the biggest star in Olympic history. He checks all the boxes. The first is the incredible underdog backstory: Orphaned at age five in Lafayette, Indiana, he found out two years later that he had contracted polio and would never walk again. That's what the doctors said, at least. Ewry refused to accept that cruel fate, teaching himself to stand and, later, to jump.

He grew into a six-foot-three-inch athletic marvel. Ewry attended Purdue, led the school to its first ever track title, and set world records in the standing high jump, standing long jump, and standing triple jump. (Now discontinued, these events are the same as their modern versions, except that there was no running start.) He played football and earned undergraduate and graduate degrees in mechanical engineering.

On one Paris day in 1900, Ewry won three Olympic gold medals. His standing high jump of five feet, five inches was four inches higher than anyone else in the field. It would've won a silver medal in the traditional high jump, which came with a running start, four years later. The French, enamored with Ewry, called him *L'homme Grenouille,* or the Frog Man.

At the 1904 Games in St. Louis, he repeated his triple-medal feat. Ewry likely would've won another trio in London in 1908, but the standing triple jump was eliminated. That was fine—he still took home the other two.

Take a moment to marvel at the records that would have made Ewry an absolute megastar, had the still-fledgling 1900 Olympics received even a fraction of the attention that the Games enjoy nowadays. His record eight gold medals in individual events stood for more than 100 years until Michael Phelps broke it in 2008. His record of three straight golds in one event stayed for 60 years, broken by Al Oerter's four in the discus. His record of three gold medals in two events remained for 104 years. He still holds the record for most Olympic golds without losing. (Ewry was eight for eight in events he participated in.) Including his two gold medals from the 1906 Intercalated Games, he has the second-most golds of all time. And not only that: Ewry would still blow today's athletes out of the water. His farthest standing long jump was 11 feet, 4⅞ inches. (The world record for the standard *running* long jump, set in 2015, is 12 feet, 3 inches.)

So how did Ewry's home country receive this athletic superhero? By not noticing. He moved to New York and worked for four decades for the Board of Water Supply, building dams and reservoirs. He did, however, get some recognition eventually, albeit nine decades too late: In 1990, the US Postal Service issued a special commemorative stamp in his honor.

Ewry, one of the best athletes in Olympic history, takes gold in the high jump in 1908.

TENLEY ALBRIGHT
Queen of the Ice

USA | FIGURE SKATING | 2 MEDALS | 1935–

OSLO 1952 • CORTINA D'AMPEZZO 1956

The American obsession with Olympic figure skating started, in some ways, with Tenley Albright. Her medal was the first of four American golds by female skaters over the next five Olympics, and it kickstarted a streak of American dominance in the sport: In every Games from 1956 to 2010, the United States had at least one medal in ladies figure skating.

Tenley began skating as a girl as a form of therapy. Diagnosed with polio at age 10, and unable to move her legs, back, or neck for months, she was released from the hospital in 1946 and won her first skating title just four months later. At age 16, she won a silver at the 1952 Olympics in Oslo.

In 1956, despite tripping on the ice two weeks before the Cortina d'Ampezzo Games and creating a huge gash on her right ankle, she became the first female American skater to win gold. Although Albright lacked the show-stopping jumping ability we see nowadays, she captured the crowd's imagination with her elegance and style. "I thought it was in my head, but I suddenly realized that the audience was humming the music," she once said of her routine to the barcarolle from *The Tales of Hoffmann*. "It was such an amazing feeling of connection."

Rather than continue to compete, Albright decided to pursue a career in medicine. She was one of only five women in a class of 135 students at Harvard Medical School in 1957. She became a surgeon and is currently the director of MIT Collaborative Initiatives, which works to solve societal issues. With such a distinguished résumé in medicine, it's easy to forget that *other* big accomplishment. But there is a through-line between careers. From a young age, Albright was intrigued by what the human body could accomplish. "I'd like to encourage people in athletics," she once told Harvard's newspaper. "Whatever you're doing now will apply to whatever you're doing in the future." Nobody is a truer example than Tenley Albright.

Albright was the first in a long line of American figure skaters who captured the public's attention and admiration.

SUSAN WILLIAMS
Brains and Brawn

USA | TRIATHLON | 1 MEDAL | 1969–

ATHENS 2004

Growing up as a navy brat, Susan Williams had two lofty goals: to become an astronaut and compete in the Olympics. She got close to the first, and more than completed the second.

Williams was a collegiate swimmer at Alabama who set the junior national record in the 200-yard butterfly as a 15-year-old. She graduated from the university with a degree in aerospace engineering and followed it up with a master's at Colorado. "She'd talk all the time about wanting to go into space," her mother, Donna Bartholomew, told the *Washington Post*. "We believed her."

Williams got a job at Lockheed Martin and helped create a Titan-4 launch vehicle for rockets. Still, she found herself wishing she was running outside instead of stuck in an office. She took up triathlon—an Olympic event since 2000—at age 24, originally as a way to stay in shape. Within 16 months, she placed third in the USA Triathlon National Championships. The Olympics, it turns out, was the dream that would be more easily realized.

Williams missed qualifying for the 2000 Games by a sizable 13 seconds. It may have been a good thing: The day before the race, she found out she was six weeks pregnant and would've been quite far along by the time the Olympics rolled around. (She named her daughter Sydney.) After quitting her job for good in 2003, Williams earned the final spot on the US triathlon team for the Athens Games. Despite crashing in the race, she made up enough ground to finish in third and earn bronze. She became the first American to win a triathlon medal.

Williams achieved her Olympic dream, and looking back, it was all for the better that her other goal of launching into space didn't come true. "It's just as well that never happened," she said. "I get claustrophobic."

NAIM SULEYMANOGLU
Pocket Change Agent

TURKEY | WEIGHT LIFTING | 3 MEDALS | 1967–2017

SEOUL 1988 • BARCELONA 1992 • ATLANTA 1996 • SYDNEY 2000

3 0 0

Before a competition, Naim Suleymanoglu's former coach made a prediction: On his first lift, he would win. On his second lift, he would set a world record. On his third lift, well, there would be no need for a third lift.

So dominant was Naim Suleymanoglu in weight lifting that it would be more surprising if he *didn't* rewrite the history books. He won nearly every possible event, set nearly every record. At 14, he conquered the world 19-and-under title. At the 1988 Summer Olympics in Seoul, he set the world record in the clean and jerk (in which a competitor lifts a barbell across his

Small, but mighty: Suleymanoglu was a top lifter, and helped his family escape repression in Bulgaria.

shoulders, then above his head) by lifting 190 kg (about 420 pounds). That lift was 3.15 times his body weight, still the highest-ever ratio. He broke his own world record six times that day. In 1992, he again won gold, and in 1996, he became the first lifter in history to win three gold medals, trading world record lifts with Valerios Leonidis of Greece.

For all his accomplishments as the greatest of all-time, the four-foot-ten-inch, 132-pound Suleymanoglu, whom they called Pocket Hercules, had a stirring backstory that matched his work with barbells. Born in Bulgaria, he was a member of the heavily persecuted Turkish ethnic minority. Growing up, he attended a sport-specific school under the harsh direction of coach Ivan Abadjiev, known as the Butcher. Abadjiev helped produce 12 Olympic champions in his time as the head of Bulgarian weight lifting. The other kids mocked Suleymanoglu for the way his legs bowed out wide—they stood a full brick length apart. But by age 12, he was a regional champion. Four years later, however, his dreams were put on hold.

"Pocket Hercules" was both a hero to ethnic Turks and an Olympic force to be reckoned with.

As a response to the boycott of the 1980 Moscow Games, Bulgaria, along with 13 other countries, refused to attend the 1984 Games in Los Angeles. Though only 16 years old, Suleymanoglu would've been the favorite in his weight class. Also that year, the Bulgarian government amplified their persecution of ethnic Turks, ordering them to adopt Christian names. They closed schools and mosques, and removed all tombstones with Turkish names. Bulgarian Turks were on the verge of being eradicated.

Suleymanoglu thought of defecting, but he was unsure if he could succeed outside of Abadjiev's rigid training structure. He began to make up his mind when a Bulgarian newspaper published a fabricated quote attributed to him, saying, "Bulgar blood runs through my veins. I want to lift weights for Bulgaria with my true Bulgarian name." Suleymanoglu, proud of his Turkish heritage, was horrified.

His phone tapped, his every move observed by two government agents, he rebelled after Abadjiev increased his eight-hour workout—already double the length of any other country—to nine hours. Suleymanoglu, along with four other teammates, wrote a letter stating they would all leave if the training time increased. Abadjiev responded, "You think you cannot be replaced, but you can. It is the system that made you." That was the final straw. While competing in Australia, he slipped into the bathroom at a team dinner, stepped into a car belonging to a Turk who lived in Melbourne, and put his Bulgarian life behind him.

Once Suleymanoglu arrived in Ankara, the Turkish people treated him like a star. Photographers followed him day and night. The prime minister said he thought of him as a son. He received $34,000 worth of gold coins and owned 10 apartments. His family, who had remained in Bulgaria after he defected, would eventually join him in Turkey. Soon after, some 320,000 Bulgarians Turks emigrated to Turkey in 1989 alone.

"Bulgaria was a closed box," he said. "I escaped it."

Suleymanoglu would attempt to compete in the 2000 Games, but the weight lifter, who reportedly smoked up to 55 cigarettes a day, failed on his three lifts. "Bye-bye, it's over," he told reporters. Suleymanoglu would also attempt a run at politics, though he was unsuccessful in three bids for office. A heavy drinker, he suffered liver failure from cirrhosis and received a transplant. He suffered a brain hemorrhage just a month later and died at age 50 in 2017.

Suleymanoglu lifting impossibly large weights in the clean and jerk.

The Turkish people adored him. "God save you, Naim!" they cried as he returned from Seoul in 1988. He realized, early after his defection, that he belonged not to himself but to Turkey, the nation that wanted him after he was forced out of the country where he was born. "These are not my gold medals," he said. "These are the Turkish people's medals. I owe all of my success to you!"

LOUIS ZAMPERINI
The War Hero

USA | TRACK AND FIELD | 1917–2014

BERLIN 1936

Louis Zamperini earned his place in American lore after crash-landing in the Pacific and surviving the brutal Naoetsu POW camp outside Tokyo during World War II. But first, the war hero was an Olympian.

The long-distance runner set the national high school record in the mile at Los Angeles Memorial Coliseum in 1934, a record that stood for 29 years. Four years later, he set a national collegiate mile record. He qualified for the Olympics at age 19, and at the 1936 Summer Games in Berlin, he finished in eighth place in the 5,000-meter race. He made a strong effort in the final lap, which reportedly caught the attention of Adolf Hitler, who was in attendance. Zamperini said that after the race, Hitler shook his hand and remarked, "Ah, you're the boy with the fast finish."

In the war, however, Zamperini's plane malfunctioned, causing him to crash into the ocean. He survived on rainwater and fish before his capture by the Japanese and transfer to Naoetsu, where he languished for two years. After his release and return home, he became popular on the lecture circuit, and many years later he was the subject of the bestselling biography *Unbroken* and its 2014 film adaptation directed by Angelina Jolie. Zamperini returned to the Olympics—and Japan—in 1998, when he ran a leg in the torch relay in Nagano, not far from the POW camp where he had persevered.

LEFT: *Zamperini was a good runner, but he's better known for his time as a POW in World War II.*

RESULTS AND STATS

ALL EVENTS

Summer

Archery
Artistic Swimming
Athletics
Badminton
Basketball
Beach Volleyball
Boxing
Canoe Slalom
Canoe Sprint
Cycling BMX
Cycling Mountain Bike
Cycling Road
Cycling Track
Diving
Equestrian Dressage
Equestrian Eventing
Equestrian Jumping
Fencing
Football (Soccer)
Golf
Gymnastics Artistic
Gymnastics Rhythmic
Handball
Hockey (Field Hockey)
Judo
Marathon Swimming
Modern Pentathlon
Rowing
Rugby
Sailing
Shooting
Swimming
Table Tennis
Taekwondo
Tennis
Trampoline
Triathlon
Volleyball
Water Polo
Weightlifting
Wrestling Freestyle
Wrestling Greco-Roman

Winter

Alpine Skiing
Biathlon
Bobsleigh
Cross-Country Skiing
Curling
Figure Skating
Freestyle Skiing
Ice Hockey
Luge
Nordic Combined
Short Track Speed Skating
Skeleton
Ski Jumping
Snowboard
Speed Skating

SUMMER GAMES LOCATIONS

Athens, 1896
Paris, 1900
St. Louis, 1904
London, 1908
Stockholm, 1912

(No Berlin Olympics in 1916, canceled because of World War I.)

Antwerp, 1920
Paris, 1924
Amsterdam, 1928
Los Angeles, 1932
Berlin, 1936

(No Tokyo Olympics, later Helsinki, in 1940 and no London Olympics in 1944 because of World War II.)

London, 1948
Helsinki, 1952
Melbourne-Stockholm, 1956
Rome, 1960
Tokyo, 1964
Mexico City, 1968
Munich, 1972
Montreal, 1976
Moscow, 1980
Los Angeles, 1984
Seoul, 1988
Barcelona, 1992
Atlanta, 1996
Sydney, 2000
Athens, 2004
Beijing, 2008
London, 2012
Rio de Janeiro, 2016
Tokyo, 2020
Paris, 2024
Los Angeles, 2028

WINTER GAMES LOCATIONS

Chamonix, 1924
St. Moritz, 1928
Lake Placid, 1932
Garmisch-Partenkirchen, 1936

(No Sapporo Games in 1940 and no Cortina d'Ampezzo Games in 1944 because of World War II.)

St. Moritz, 1948
Oslo, 1952
Cortina d'Ampezzo, 1956
Squaw Valley, 1960
Innsbruck, 1964
Grenoble, 1968
Sapporo, 1972
Innsbruck, 1976
Lake Placid, 1980
Sarajevo, 1984
Calgary, 1988
Albertville, 1992
Lillehammer, 1994
Nagano, 1998
Salt Lake City, 2002
Turin, 2006
Vancouver, 2010
Sochi, 2014
Pyeongchang, 2018
Beijing, 2022

MOST MEDALS, INDIVIDUAL

Michael Phelps, USA, Swimming, 28

Larisa Latynina, Soviet Union, Gymnastics, 18

Marit Bjorgen, Norway, Cross-Country Skiing, 15

Nikolai Andrianov, Soviet Union, Gymnastics, 15

Ole Elnar Bjoerndalen, Norway, Cross-Country Skiing, 13

Edoardo Mangiarotti, Italy, Fencing, 13

Boris Shakhlin, Soviet Union, Gymnastics, 13

Takashi Ono, Japan, Gymnastics, 13

Birgit Fischer, Germany, Kayaking, 12

Paavo Nurmi, Finland, Track and Field, 12

Bjorn Daehlie, Norway, Cross-Country Skiing, 12

Sawao Kato, Japan, Gymnastics, 12

Jenny Thompson, USA, Swimming, 12

Ryan Lochte, USA, Swimming, 12

Dara Torres, USA, Swimming, 12

Natalie Coughlin, USA, Swimming, 12

Alexei Nemov, Russia, Gymnastics, 12

MOST MEDALS BY COUNTRY, SUMMER

USA, 2,522

Soviet Union, 1,010

Great Britain, 851

France, 716

Germany, 615

Italy, 577

China, 546

Australia, 497

Sweden, 494

Hungary, 491

MOST MEDALS BY COUNTRY, WINTER

Norway, 368

USA, 305

Germany, 240

Austria, 232

Canada, 199

Soviet Union, 194

Finland, 167

Sweden, 158

Switzerland, 153

Netherlands, 130

MOST OLYMPIC APPEARANCES WITHOUT A MEDAL BY COUNTRY

Monaco, 30

San Marino, 24

Andorra, 23

Bolivia, 20

Malta, 18

Myanmar, 17

Nepal, 17

Bosnia and Herzegovina, 14

Madagascar, 14

Mali, 13

MOST PARALYMPIC MEDALS

Trischa Zorn, USA, Swimming, 55

Heinz Frei, Switzerland, Track and Field/Cycling/Cross-Country, 34

Jonas Jacobsson, Sweden, Shooting, 30

Zipora Rubin-Rosenbaum, Israel, Track and Field/Swimming/Basketball/Table Tennis, 30

Ragnhild Myklebust, Norway, Biathlon/Cross-Country/Ice Sledge Racing, 27

Roberto Marson, Italy, Track and Field/Fencing, 26

Beatrice Hess, France, Swimming, 25

Sarah Storey, Great Britain, Swimming/Cycling, 25

Claudia Hengst, Germany, Swimming, 25

Daniel Dias, Brazil, Swimming, 24

US FLAG BEARERS

1906: Matthew Halpin, Team Manager

1908: Ralph Rose, Athletics/Tug-of-War

1912: George Bonhag, Athletics

1920, 1924: Pat McDonald, Athletics

1924: Taffy Abel, Hockey

1928: Bud Houser, Athletics

1928: Godfrey Dewey, President of Lake Placid Organizing Committee

1932: Morgan Taylor, Athletics

1932: Billy Fiske, Bobsled

1936: Al Jochim, Gymnastics

1936: Rolf Monsen, Cross-Country Skiing

1948: Ralph Craig, Athletics

1948: Jack Heaton, Skeleton

1956: Norman Armitage, Fencing

1956: James Bickford, Bobsled

1960: Rafer Johnson, Athletics

1960: Don McDermott, Speed Skating

1964: Parry O'Brien, Athletics

1964: Bill Disney, Speed Skating

1968: Janice Romary, Fencing

1968: Terry McDermott, Speed Skating

1972: Olga Fikotova, Athletics

1972: Dianne Holum, Speed Skating

1976: Gary Hall, Swimming

1976: Cindy Nelson, Alpine Skiing

1980: Scott Hamilton, Figure Skating

1984: Ed Burke, Athletics

1984: Frank Masley, Luge

1988: Evelyn Ashford, Athletics

1988: Lyle Nelson, Biathlon

1992: Francie Larrieu Smith, Athletics

1992: Bill Koch, Cross-Country Skiing

1994: Cammy Myler, Luge

1996: Bruce Baumgartner, Wrestling

1998: Eric Flaim, Speed Skating

2000: Cliff Meidl, Canoeing

2002: Amy Peterson, Speed Skating

2004: Dawn Staley, Basketball

2006: Chris Witty, Speed Skating

2008: Lopez Lomong, Athletics

2010: Mark Grimmette, Luge

2012: Mariel Zagunis, Fencing

2014: Todd Lodwick, Nordic Combined

2016: Michael Phelps, Swimming

2018: Erin Hamlin, Luge

GYMNASTICS ALL-AROUND GOLD MEDALISTS, MEN

1900: Gustave Sandras, France
1904: Julius Lenhart, Austria
1908: Alberto Braglia, Italy
1912: Alberto Braglia, Italy
1920: Giorgio Zampori, Italy
1924: Leon Stukelj, Yugoslavia
1928: Georges Miez, Switzerland
1932: Romeo Neri, Italy
1936: Alfred Schwarzmann, Germany
1948: Veikko Huhtanen, Finland
1952: Viktor Chukarin, Soviet Union
1956: Viktor Chukarin, Soviet Union
1960: Boris Shakhlin, Soviet Union
1964: Yukio Endo, Japan
1968: Sawao Kato, Japan
1972: Sawao Kato, Japan
1976: Nikolai Andrianov, Soviet Union
1980: Alexander Dityatin, Soviet Union
1984: Koji Gushiken, Japan
1988: Vladimir Artemov, Soviet Union
1992: Vitaly Scherbo, Unified Team
1996: Li Xiaoshuang, China
2000: Alexei Nemov, Russia
2004: Paul Hamm, United States
2008: Yang Wei, China
2012: Kohei Uchimura, Japan
2016: Kohei Uchimura, Japan

GYMNASTICS ALL-AROUND GOLD MEDALISTS, WOMEN

1952: Maria Gorokhovskaya, Soviet Union
1956: Larisa Latynina, Soviet Union
1960: Larisa Latynina, Soviet Union
1964: Vera Caslavska, Czechoslovakia
1968: Vera Caslavska, Czechoslovakia
1972: Ludmilla Tourischeva, Soviet Union
1976: Nadia Comaneci, Romania
1980: Yelena Davydova, Soviet Union
1984: Mary Lou Retton, USA
1988: Yelena Shushunova, Soviet Union
1992: Tatiana Gutusu, Unified Team
1996: Lilia Podkopayeva, Ukraine
2000: Simona Amanar, Romania
2004: Carly Patterson, USA
2008: Nastia Liukin, USA
2012: Gabby Douglas, USA
2016: Simone Biles, USA

100-METER FREESTYLE SWIMMING, MEN

1896: Alfred Hajos, Hungary
(not contested in 1900)
1904: Zoltán Halmay, Hungary
1908: Charles Daniels, United States
1912: Duke Kahanamoku, United States
1920: Duke Kahanamoku, United States
1924: Johnny Weissmuller, United States
1928: Johnny Weissmuller, United States
1932: Yasuji Miyazaki, Japan
1936: Ferenc Csik, Hungary
1948: Wally Ris, United States
1952: Clarke Scholes, United States
1956: Jon Henricks, Australia
1960: John Devitt, Australia
1964: Don Schollander, United States
1968: Michael Wenden, Australia
1972: Mark Spitz, United States
1976: Jim Montgomery, United States
1980: Jorg Woithe, East Germany
1984: Rowdy Gaines, United States
1988: Matt Biondi, United States
1992: Alexander Popov, Unified Team
1996: Alexander Popov, Russia
2000: Pieter van den Hoogenband, Netherlands
2004: Pieter van den Hoogenband, Netherlands
2008: Alain Bernard, France
2012: Nathan Adrian, United States
2016: Kyle Chalmers, Australia

100-METER FREESTYLE SWIMMING, WOMEN

1912: Fanny Durack, Australia
1920: Ethelda Bleibtrey, United States
1924: Ethel Lackie, United States
1928: Albina Osipowich, United States
1932: Helene Madison, United States
1936: Rie Mastenbroek, Netherlands
1948: Greta Andersen, Denmark
1952: Katalin Szoke, Hungary
1956: Dawn Fraser, Australia
1960: Dawn Fraser, Australia
1964: Dawn Fraser, Australia
1968: Jan Henne, United States
1972: Sandy Neilson, United States
1976: Kornelia Ender, East Germany
1980: Barbara Krause, East Germany
1984: Nancy Hogshead, United States; Carrie Steinseifer, United States (tie)
1988: Kristin Otto, East Germany
1992: Zhuang Yong, China
1996: Le Jingyi, China
2000: Inge de Brujin, Netherlands
2004: Jodie Henry, Australia
2008: Britta Steffen, Germany
2012: Ranomi Kromowidjojo, Netherlands
2016: Simone Manuel, United States; Penny Oleksiak, Canada (tie)

100-METER DASH, MEN

1896: Thomas Burke, USA
1900: Frank Jarvis, USA
1904: Archie Hahn, USA
1908: Reggie Walker, USA
1912: Ralph Craig, USA
1920: Charley Paddock, USA
1924: Harold Abrahams, Great Britain
1928: Percy Williams, Canada
1932: Eddie Tolan, USA
1936: Jesse Owens, USA
1948: Harrison Dillard, USA
1952: Lindy Remigino, USA
1956: Bobby Morrow, USA
1960: Armin Hary, Germany
1964: Bob Hayes, USA
1968: Jim Hines, USA
1972: Valeriy Borzov, Soviet Union
1976: Hasely Crawford, Trinidad and Tobago
1980: Allan Wells, Great Britain
1984: Carl Lewis, USA
1988: Carl Lewis, USA
1992: Linford Christie, Great Britain
1996: Donovan Bailey, Canada
2000: Maurice Greene, USA
2004: Justin Gatlin, USA
2008: Usain Bolt, Jamaica
2012: Usain Bolt, Jamaica
2016: Usain Bolt, Jamaica

100-METER DASH, WOMEN

1928: Betty Robinson, USA
1932: Stanisława Walasiewicz, Poland
1936: Helen Stephens, USA
1948: Fanny Blankers-Koen, Netherlands
1952: Marjorie Jackson, Australia
1956: Betty Cuthbert, Australia
1960: Wilma Rudolph, USA
1964: Wyoma Tyus, USA
1968: Wyoma Tyus, USA
1972: Renate Stecher, East Germany
1976: Annegret Richter, West Germany
1980: Lyudmila Kondratyeva, Soviet Union
1984: Evelyn Ashford, USA
1988: Florence Griffith-Joyner, USA
1992: Gail Devers, USA
1996: Gail Devers, USA
2000: Marion Jones, USA (vacated)
2004: Yulia Nestsiarenka, Belarus
2008: Shelly-Ann Fraser-Pryce, Jamaica
2012: Shelly-Ann Fraser-Pryce, Jamaica
2016: Elaine Thompson, Jamaica

FIGURE SKATING GOLD MEDALISTS, MEN

1908: Ulrich Salchow, Sweden
1920: Gillis Grafstrom, Sweden
1924: Gillis Grafstrom, Sweden
1928: Gillis Grafstrom, Sweden
1932: Karl Schafer, Austria
1936: Karl Schafer, Austria
1948: Dick Button, USA
1952: Dick Button, USA
1956: Hayes Jenkins, USA
1960: David Jenkins, USA
1964: Manfred Schnelldorfer, Germany
1968: Wolfgang Schwarz, Austria
1972: Ondrej Nepela, Czechoslovakia
1976: John Curry, Great Britain
1980: Robin Cousins, Great Britain
1984: Scott Hamilton, USA
1988: Brian Boitano, USA
1992: Viktor Petrenko, Unified Team
1994: Alexei Urmanov, Russia
1998: Ilia Kulik, Russia
2002: Alexei Yagudin, Russia
2006: Evgeni Plushenko
2010: Evan Lysacek, USA
2014: Yuzuru Hanyu, Japan
2018: Yuzuru Hanyu, Japan

FIGURE SKATING GOLD MEDALISTS, WOMEN

1908: Madge Syers, Great Britain
1920: Magda Julin, Sweden
1924: Herma Szabo, Austria
1928: Sonja Henie, Norway
1932: Sonja Henie, Norway
1936: Sonja Henie, Norway
1948: Barbara Ann Scott, Canada
1952: Jeannette Altwegg, Great Britain
1956: Tenley Albright, USA
1960: Carol Heiss, USA
1964: Sjoukje Dijkstra, Netherlands
1968: Peggy Fleming, USA
1972: Beatrix Schuba, Austria
1976: Dorothy Hamill, USA
1980: Anett Potzsch, East Germany
1984: Katarina Witt, East Germany
1988: Katarina Witt, East Germany
1992: Kristi Yamaguchi, USA
1994: Oksana Baiul, Ukraine
1998: Tara Lipinski, USA
2002: Sarah Hughes, USA
2006: Shizuka Arakawa, Japan
2010: Yuna Kim, South Korea
2014: Adelina Sotnikova, Russia
2018: Alina Zagitova, Olympic Athletes from Russia

MARATHON WINNERS, MEN

1896: Spyridon Louis, Greece
1900: Michel Theato, France
1904: Thomas Hicks, USA
1908: Johnny Hayes, USA
1912: Ken McArthur, South Africa
1920: Hannes Kolehmainen, Finland
1924: Albin Stenroos, Finland
1928: Boughera El Ouafi, France
1932: Juan Carlos Zabala, Argentina
1936: Sohn Kee-chung, Japan
1948: Delfo Cabrera, Argentina
1952: Emil Zatopek, Czechoslovakia
1956: Alain Mimoun, France
1960: Abebe Bikila, Ethiopia
1964: Abebe Bikila, Ethiopia
1968: Mamo Wolde, Ethiopia
1972: Frank Shorter, USA
1976: Waldemar Cierpinski, East Germany
1980: Waldemar Cierpinski, East Germany
1984: Carlos Lopes, Portugal
1988: Gelindo Bordin, Italy
1992: Hwang Young-cho, South Korea
1996: Josia Thugwane, South Africa
2000: Gezahegne Abera, Ethiopia
2004: Stefano Baldini, Italy
2008: Samuel Wanjiru, Kenya
2012: Stephen Kiprotich, Uganda
2016: Eliud Kipchoge, Kenya

MARATHON WINNERS, WOMEN

1984: Joan Benoit, USA
1988: Rosa Mota, Portugal
1992: Valentina Yegorova, Unified Team
1996: Fatuma Roba, Ethiopia
2000: Naoko Takahashi, Japan
2004: Mizuki Noguchi, Japan
2008: Constantina Tomescu, Romania
2012: Tiki Gelana, Ethiopia
2016: Jemima Sumgong, Kenya

DOWNHILL SKIING, MEN

1948: Henri Oreiller, France
1952: Zeno Colo, Italy
1956: Toni Sailer, Austria
1960: Jean Vuarnet, France
1964: Egon Zimmermann, Austria
1968: Jean-Claude Killy, France
1972: Bernhard Russi, Switzerland
1976: Franz Klammer, Austria
1980: Leonhard Stock, Austria
1984: Bill Johnson, United States
1988: Pirmin Zurbriggen, Switzerland
1992: Patrick Ortlieb, Austria
1994: Tommy Moe, United States
1998: Jean-Luc Cretier
2002: Fritz Strobl, Austria
2006: Antoine Deneriaz, France
2010: Didier Defago, Switzerland
2014: Matthias Mayer, Austria
2018: Aksel Lund Svindal, Norway

DOWNHILL SKIING, WOMEN

1948: Hedy Schlunegger, Switzerland
1952: Trude Jochum-Beiser, Austria
1956: Madeleine Berthod, Switzerland
1960: Heidi Biebl, United Team of Germany
1964: Christl Haas, Austria
1968: Olga Pall, Austria
1972: Marie-Theres Nadig
1976: Rosi Mittermaier, West Germany
1980: Annemarie Moser-Proll, Austria
1984: Michela Figini, Switzerland
1988: Marina Kiehl, West Germany
1992: Kerrin Lee-Gartner, Canada
1994: Katja Seizinger, Germany
1998: Katja Seizinger, Germany
2002: Carole Montillet, France
2006: Michaela Dorfmeister, Austria
2010: Lindsey Vonn, United States
2014: Dominique Gisin, Switzerland; Tina Mase, Slovenia (tie)
2018: Sofia Goggia, Italy

SNOWBOARD HALFPIPE, MEN

1998: Gian Simmen, Switzerland
2002: Ross Powers, United States
2006: Shaun White, United States
2010: Shaun White, United States
2014: Iouri Podladtchikov, Switzerland
2018: Shaun White, United States

SNOWBOARD HALFPIPE, WOMEN

1998: Nicola Thost, Germany
2002: Kelly Clark, United States
2006: Hannah Teter, United States
2010: Torah Bright, Australia
2014: Kaitlyn Farrington, United States
2018: Chloe Kim, United States

TENNIS SINGLES, MEN

1896: John Pius Boland, Great Britain
1900: Laurence Doherty, Great Britain
1904: Beals Wright, United States
1908: Josiah Ritchie, Great Britain
1912: Charles Winslow, South Africa
1920: Louis Raymond, South Africa
1924: Vincent Richards, United States
(not contested from 1928-1984)
1988: Miloslav Mecir, Czechoslovakia
1992: Marc Rosset, Switzerland
1996: Andre Agassi, United States
2002: Yevgeny Kafelnikov, Russia
2004: Nicolas Massu, Chile
2008: Rafael Nadal, Spain
2012: Andy Murray, Great Britain
2016: Andy Murray, Great Britain

TENNIS SINGLES, WOMEN

1900: Charlotte Cooper, Great Britain
(not contested 1904)
1908: Dorothea Lambert Chambers, Great Britain
1912: Marguerite Broquedis, France
1920: Suzanne Lenglen, France
1924: Helen Wills, United States
(not contested from 1928–1984)
1988: Steffi Graf, West Germany
1992: Jennifer Capriati, United States
1996: Lindsay Davenport, United States
2000: Venus Williams, United States
2004: Justine Henin-Hardenne, Belgium
2008: Elena Dementieva, Russia
2012: Serena Williams, United States
2016: Monica Puig, Puerto Rico

MOST MEDALS BY HOST NATION, SUMMER

United States, 1904, 239
Soviet Union, 1980, 195
United States, 1984, 174
Great Britain, 1908, 146
France, 1900, 131
United States, 1932, 103
United States, 1996, 101
China, 2008, 100
Germany, 1936, 89
Sweden, 1912, 65

MOST MEDALS BY HOST NATION, WINTER

United States, 2002, 34
Russia, 2014, 29
Norway, 1994, 26
Canada, 2010, 26
South Korea, 2018, 17
Norway, 1952, 16
United States, 1932, 12
Austria, 1964, 12
United States, 1980, 12
Italy, 2006, 11

PIERRE DE COUBERTIN MEDAL

Luz Long, Germany, long jumper, 1964 (awarded posthumously)

Eugenio Monti, Italy, bobsledder, 1964

Franz Jonas, Austria, President of Austria, 1969

Karl Heinz Klee, Austria, ski official, 1977

Lawrence Lemieux, Canada, sailor, 1988

Justin Harley McDonald, Australia, bobsledder, 1994

Raymond Gafner, Switzerland, ice hockey referee, 1999

Emil Zatopek, Czechoslovakia, long-distance runner, 2000 (awarded posthumously)

Spencer Eccles, United States, Olympic organizer, 2002

Tana Umaga, New Zealand, rugby player, 2003

Martin Franken, Netherlands, Olympic organizer, 2006

Vanderlei Cordeiro de Lima, Brazil, marathon runner, 2004

Elena Novikova-Belova, Belarus, fencer, 2007

Shaul Ladany, Israel, race walker, 2007

Petar Cupac, Ivan Bulaja, Pavle Kostov, Croatia, sailors, 2008

Ronald Harvey, Australia, sports administrator, 2009

Eric Monnin, France, Olympic educator, 2012

Bob Nadin, Canada, ice hockey referee, 2012

Richard Garneau, Canada, journalist, 2014 (awarded posthumously)

Manfred Bergman, Israel, philatelist, 2008

Michael Hwang, Singapore, lawyer, 2014

Eduard von Falz-Fein, Liechtenstein, Olympic organizer, 2017

Lu Junjie, China, artist, 2018

Han Meilin, China, artist, 2018

INTERNATIONAL OLYMPIC COMMITTEE PRESIDENTS

Demetrius Vikelas, 1894–1896

Pierre de Coubertin, 1896–1925

Henri de Baillet-Latour, 1925–1942

Sigfrid Edstrom, 1942–1952

Avery Brundage, 1952–1972

Lord Killanin, 1972–1980

Juan Antonio Samaranch, 1980–2001

Jacques Rogge, 2001–2013

Thomas Bach, 2013–present

1936, Berlin: Fritz Schilgen, Track and Field

1948, London: John Mark, Track and Field

1952, Oslo: Eigil Nansen, grandson of polar explorer Fridtjof Nansen

1952, Helsinki: Paavo Nurmi, Hannes Kolehmainen, Track and Field

1956, Cortina d'Ampezzo: Guido Caroli, Speed Skating

1956, Melbourne: Ron Clarke, Track and Field (At the Equestrian event in Stockholm, Hans Wikne, an equestrian rider, lit it.)

1960, Squaw Valley: Ken Henry, Speed Skating

1960, Rome: Giancarlo Peris, Track and Field

1964, Innsbruck: Josef Rieder, Alpine Skiing

1964, Tokyo: Yoshinori Sakai, Track and Field

1968, Grenoble: Alain Calmat, Figure Skating

1968, Mexico City: Enriqueta Basilio, Track and Field

1972, Sapporo: Hideki Takada, non-athlete

1972, Munich: Gunther Zahn, Track and Field

1976, Innsbruck: Christl Haas, Alpine Skiing; Josef Feismantl, Luge

1976, Montreal: Sandra Henderson, Gymnastics; Stephane Prefontaine, Track and Field

1980, Lake Placid: Charles Gugino, doctor

1980, Moscow: Sergei Belov, Basketball

1984, Sarajevo: Sandra Dubravcic, Figure Skating

1984, Los Angeles: Rafer Johnson, Track and Field

1988, Calgary: Robyn Perry, aspiring figure skater

1988, Seoul: Chung Sun-man, teacher; Sohn Mi-chung, dancer; Kim Won-tak, Track and Field

1992, Albertville: Michel Plantini, Football; Francois-Cyrille Grange, aspiring alpine skier

1992, Barcelona: Antonio Rebollo, Archery

1994, Lillehammer: Haakon, Crown Prince of Norway

1996, Atlanta: Muhammad Ali, Boxing

1998, Nagano: Midori Ito, Figure Skating

2000, Sydney: Cathy Freeman, Track and Field

2002, Salt Lake City: 1980 US Hockey team

2004, Athens: Nikolaos Kaklamanakis, Sailing

2006, Turin: Stefania Belmondo, Cross-Country Skiing

2008, Beijing: Li Ning, Gymnastics

2010, Vancouver: Steve Nash, Basketball; Nancy Greene, Alpine Skiing; Wayne Gretzky, Ice Hockey; Catriona Le May Doan, Speed Skating

2012, London: Desiree Henry, Katie Kirk, Aidan Reynolds, Adelle Tracey, teenage track and field athletes; Callum Airlie, teenager sailor; Cameron MacRitchie, teenager rower; Jordan Duckitt, non-athlete

2014, Sochi: Irina Rodnina, Figure Skating; Vladislav Tretiak, Hockey

2016, Rio: Vanderlei Cordeiro de Lima, Athletics

2018, Pyeongchang: Yuna Kim, Figure Skating

Ian Millar, Canada, Equestrian, 1972, 1976, 1984–2012

Hubert Raudaschl, Austria, Sailing, 1964–1996

Afansijs Kuzmins, Soviet Union/Latvia, Shooting, 1976–1980, 1988–2012

Oksana Chusovitina, Unified Team, Uzbekistan, Germany, Gymnastics, 1992–2020

Piero d'Inzeo, Italy, Equestrian, 1948–1976

Raimondo d'Inzeo, Italy, Equestrian, 1948–1976

Durward Knowles, Great Britain/Bahamas, Sailing, 1948–1972, 1988

Paul Elvstrom, Denmark, Sailing, 1948–1960, 1968–1972, 1984–1988

Rajmond Debevec, Yugoslavia/Slovenia, Shooting, 1984–2012

Josefa Idem Guerrini, West Germany/Italy, Canoeing, 1984–2012

Lesley Thompson, Canada, Rowing, 1984–2000, 2008–2016

Francisco Boza, Peru, Shooting, 1980–2004, 2016

Nino Salukvadze, Soviet Union/Unified Team/Georgia, Shooting, 1988–2016

Noriaki Kasai, Japan, Ski Jumping, 1992–2018

ACKNOWLEDGMENTS

As far back as I can remember, I've always wanted to write a book. I would share the list of ideas that I've kept since I was a kid, but I fear I'd embarrass myself now that I've joined the ranks of published authors. But that process of taking an idea, developing it, nurturing it, and seeing it through to its final product has long been thrilling to me. That's why writing this book has been so fulfilling and wonderfully amazing. It's been everything I could've imagined.

I want to thank the team at Workman Publishing for making *Total Olympics* possible. In particular, I want to thank my talented editor, Danny Cooper. Danny has walked me through this entire process and is an incredibly skilled and thoughtful editor who has made this book infinitely better. He has embraced all the wacky storylines in this book, the offbeat events and ideas I've explored with incredible detail, and helped them all come to life.

I also want to thank production editor Hillary Leary for her diligent eye and hard work and thanks to the publicity and marketing team at Workman—Rebecca Carlisle, Chloe Puton, and Cindy Lee in particular—for making this book shine.

I am beyond lucky to have the incredible support and encouragement of my family and friends. They have been there for everything I've done and this endeavor has been no different. I would mention them all by name, but it would end up filling half the book.

I do, however, want to mention the following: Thank you to Matt Elkin for being my eyes and to Chelsea Elkin for being there always—I'm so excited for Charlotte's first Olympics.

Thank you to Scott Curkin for being a sounding board of reason. Thank you to my friends—Alec Levin, Alex Estis, Jason Schunkewitz, Josh Weiss, Doug Wiedman, and Max Suitovsky—for being my biggest cheerleaders. Thank you to Gloria, Henry, and Jordan Aaron for welcoming me and being such dedicated fans.

Thank you to my parents, Steve and Sandi Fuchs, for being my guiding light, my compass, and my inspiration. Thank you for permitting me to dream big and helping to make my dreams come true.

And most of all, thank you to my wife, Ashley, whom I remain in awe of every day, whose kindness and example make me a better person, and whose encouragement, support, and love make me feel invincible.

PHOTO CREDITS

Alamy: Ajax News & Feature Service p. 245; Album pp. 7, 22 (above); Allstar Picture Library p. 274; Alto Vintage Images p. 176; Archive Pics p. xi. (left); Archive PL pp. xi. (right), 288; Asar Studios p. 9; Azoor Photo p. 96; Chronicle pp. 32, 219 (right); PCN Photography p. 109; dpa picture alliance pp. 17, 28, 37; Everett Collection Historical pp. 4 (above), 210; Historic Collection pp. 35, 60, 170, 194, 217 (full), 233 (1/2); Historic Images p. 278; History and Art Collection, pp. 133 (below), 172, 180, 193, 222; INTERFOTO pp. xii., 4 (right), 216; ITAR-TASS News Agency pp. 41, 48, 53; Keystone Press p. 130; Lanmas p. ix.; Lebrecht Music & Arts p. 1; PA Images pp. 50, 62, 119 (full), 125 (1/2), 127, 183, 186, 221, 226, 257, 261, 281; PCN Photography pp. 58, 103, 109, 195, 239; PJF Military Collection p. 136; Science History Images p. 20; Sueddeutsche Zeitung Photo pp. 31, 105, 107, 243 (Full), 291 (1/2); The Advertising Archives pp. 113, 129, 205; The History Collection p. 77; The Picture Art Collection pp. 99, 151, 174, 209; The Print Collector p. 123; TP p. 263; Nick Turner p. 22 (right); UPI p. 94; Ivan Vdovin p. 149; Viktoriia Novokhatska p. 46; World History Archive pp. 87, 206; Xinhua p. 5; YAY Media AS p. 271; Zoonar GmbH p. 213 (btm left and btm right); ZUMA Press p. 68. **AP/ Wide World Photos:** ASSOCIATED PRESS p. 121. **Can Stock Photo:** createfirst p. xiv.; ggraphstudio (cover spot); scusi (cover spot); sportpoint (cover spot); weter777 (cover spot). **Getty Images:** ABC Photo Archives p. 89; ABC Photo Archives/Walt Disney Television p. 111; Al Bello/Getty Images Sport pp. 42, 91; Daniel Berehulak/Getty Images Sport p. 66; Andrew D. Bernstein/National Basketball Association p. 83; Bettmann pp. 3, 12, 39, 64, 78, 88, 90, 117, 142, 145, 152, 164, 181, 191, 254, 293; Lutz Bongarts pp. 169, 277; Lou Capozzola/Sports Illustrated Classic p. 18; Central Press p. 71; Central Press/Hulton Archive p. 201; Ed Clark/The LIFE Picture Collection pp. 159 (Full), 188 (Full); Co Rentmeester/The LIFE Picture Collection p. 29; THOMAS COEX/AFP p. 115; DEA/C. SAPPA/De Agostini p. 148; John Dominis p. 11; John Dominis/The LIFE Premium Collection p. 286; Tony Duffy/Getty Images Sport pp. 101, 163; DON EMMERT/AFP p. 131; Fototeca Storica Nazionale/Hulton Archive p. 146; GAROFALO Jack/Paris Match Archive p. 138; Herbert Gehr/The LIFE Images Collection p. 242; Chris Cole/Getty Images Sport p. 240; HABANS Patrice/Paris Match Archive p. 27; Hulton Deutsch/Corbis Historical p. 219 (above); Inpho Photography/Getty Images Sport p. 126; MICHAEL KAPPELER/DDP p. 265; Mark Kauffman/Sports Illustrated Classic p. 282; Mark Kauffman/The LIFE Picture Collection p. 184; Heinz Kluetmeier/Sports Illustrated Classic p. 65; Kyodo News p. 165; Robert Laberge/Getty Images Sport p. 97; Ed Lacey/Popperfoto p. 289; Feng Li/Getty Images Sport p. 285; Bob Martin/Hulton Archive p. 80; Leo Mason/Popperfoto pp. 75, 212, 295; OLIVIER MORIN/AFP p. 93; NCAA Photos p. 56; Marvin E. Newman/Sports Illustrated Classic p. 73; KAZUHIRO NOGI/AFP p. 161; Terry O'Neill/Iconic Images p. 55; George Pickow/Hulton Archive p. 230; David Pollack/Corbis Historical p. 120; Popperfoto pp. 133 (right), 215, 225, 229, 237, 297; Steve Powell/Getty Images Sport p. 273; Vyacheslav Prokofyev/TASS p. 223; Michael Regan/Getty Images Sport p. 140; Bob Riha Jr/Archive Photos p. 298; George Rinhart/Corbis Historical p. 198; Michael Rougier/The LIFE Picture Collection p. 197; Tom Shaw/Getty Images Sport p. 284; SI Cover/Sports Illustrated Classic p. 44; STAFF p. 15; STF/AFP p. 155; The AGE/Fairfax Media p. 203; The Asahi Shimbun p. 235; Bob Thomas/Bob Thomas Sports Photography pp. 227, 262; Topical Press Agency/Getty Images Sport Classic p. 224; Topical Press Agency/Hulton Archive pp. 98, 179; ullstein bild Dtl. p. 238; Universal History Archive/Universal Images Group p. 150. **NewsCom:** Album/Oronoz p. 143; Everett Collection/Newscom p. 45; Kyodo p. 249; Lennart M/Nsson/ZUMA Press pp. 102, 157; M.G.M./Album p. 259; World History Archive/Newscom p. 135. **Shutterstock.com:** AP pp. 247, 251; Katsumi Kasahara/AP p. 267; Michel Lipchitz/AP p. 167; Denis Oaquin/AP p. 270. **Wikimedia Commons:** United States Army p. 137.

INDEX

Note: Page references in *italics* indicate photographs or images.